"This is a consummate toolbox for directors. From navigating financing to the set to festival circuits, Pete Chatmon inspires, teaches, helping everyone. Filmmakers of tomorrow, read this book."

—DAVE WATSON, Editor, *Movies Matter*

"If you are the type of person who admires successful people and find yourself asking 'How did they do it?' then this book is for you. Chatmon's book is both educational and inspirational. Follow along in his failures and victories in filmmaking and be better prepared to start . . . or continue your own journey toward a triumphant career in making movies."

—FORRIS DAY JR., Contributor to *Hitch 20*: Alfred Hitchcock Web-series, Cohost of *Get Real: Indie Filmmakers* podcast

"The master becomes the student again in this vulnerable examination of the hills and valleys of life as a filmmaker. It's not just a job. It's a way of life. Chatmon takes nothing for granted as he reexamines every aspect of the craft with some of the best in business, while looking back on a career spanning two decades. A must-read for anyone daring to leap into the void."

—THEO TRAVERS, Writer/Executive Producer, *Billions*

"I met Pete my freshman year at NYU (1996). Pete is one of the few people in life that I relate to as being as intense as me while still down to earth. Pete's passion for film making was immediately clear to me. His senior thesis, *3D*, was selected for the Sundance Film Festival, which led many to dub Pete as 'the next Spike Lee.' Well, things don't always go as planned. For me, I moved to Atlanta after graduation. So, it had to be sometime around 2001 or 2002 when I was visiting New York and met up with Pete for lunch. While discussing our individual futures, he said to me in a very intense Pete way, 'If I never make a film, it won't be because I stopped trying. It will be because I ran out of time.' And there you have it, that's Pete in a nutshell; unrelenting and dedicated to his craft."

—W. SEAN McPHILLIP, Esq.

"Never before have I read something that lays out, in such detail, the necessary steps one needs to take both personally and professionally to be successful. Whether you want to become a filmmaker or not, this book is an essential read for your own personal development."

—DORIAN CROSSMOND MISSICK, International Renaissance Man

"Those who have had the great pleasure of working with Pete know when he commits to something, it will happen. When he first said he was writing this book, I knew that if he could provide even just a glimpse into how he manages to identify, meet, and then exceed his goals in such a challenging industry, it would be an invaluable tool for so many. True to form, in *Transitions*, Pete has done more than that. He has provided an honest, accurate, and most importantly, encouraging roadmap to build the career and life you desire. Read this book, do the work, and you will be eternally grateful for the personal journey you embark on. Thank you, Pete, for sharing your story with the world."

—CANDICE SANCHEZ McFARLANE, Writer, Producer, Creative Director

"When Pete stepped on to our set, there was an immediate sense of a methodical zen, a humble peace in the journey of his artistry that was clearly a familiar ritual to him, as he crafted one of our most memorable episodes. In these pages are the de-mystifying stories I wish I had known as a young filmmaker, a blistering honesty about what modern storytelling truly requires of the artists entrusted with the weight of words. In what I hope to be a coming era that moves past the ego-driven directors who cartoonishly shout, who brood an insufferable performance of their own 'genius,' and who lead with a toxic authority, Pete is here in these pages, offering a welcome and needed antidote for the future of the storyteller kind."

—RAFAEL CASAL, Co-creator & Showrunner, *Blindspotting* on Starz

"*Transitions* is exactly the kind of resource I wish I'd had when I was first starting out, clumsily trying to navigate a career in the entertainment industry. Pete is as elegant with his pen as he is with his camera, and reading this book is like having an old friend and mentor take you out for coffee and give you the real on the beautiful craft and ugly business of filmmaking."

—ADAM COUNTEE, Television Writer/Producer, *Community*, *Silicon Valley*, *The Shrink Next Door*

"Pete Chatmon is one of the most generous directors I've ever had the pleasure of collaborating with. That holds true in the pages of this book. No matter what stage of your career you're at, this is an inspiring read. *Transitions* is the rare master class that not only teaches practical skills of filmmaking, but the even more important skills of honest self-reflection and keeping your ego in check. Pete is the mentor you (and I) have been looking for."

—MIKE BERLUCCHI, Director of Photography, *Our Flag Means Death*, *Mythic Quest*, *You're The Worst*

"It has been a joy to be a part of Pete's directing journey, starting with hiring him for his first episode of network television. The combination of personal anecdotes, invaluable tips, and practical worksheets make this book a must-read for any future director."

—SYDNEE RIMES, Vice President, Current Series, ABC Signature

"I worked with Pete Chatmon when he directed an episode of *Blindspotting*. Every day he was with us I left set feeling like I had received some gems. Some about directing, some about producing, some about being a human relating to other humans. By the end of the week he spent with us, my pockets were full of gems. After this book, my pockets are overflowing. It's an incredible joy and resource to have the meticulously organized thoughts of one of the hardest working, yet joy producing artists I've ever met. The book reads much in the same way it feels to talk to Pete about the craft. You will find yourself with a smile on your face and your head alternating between nodding in emphatic agreement and shaking in wonder of how something you always thought was so impossible has just been made obvious. If you want to learn about the business of making movies and TV shows, whatever your proximity to the business is, *Transitions* is a great book to pick up."

—DAVEED DIGGS, Co-creator & Showrunner, *Blindspotting* on Starz, Original Cast of *Hamilton* on Broadway

"I've known Pete for over a decade, during which his work ethic, discipline, preparation, and generosity have never waned. His innate wish to lighten the learning curve for others, is an endless source of inspiration. *Transitions* gets straight to the point on what it takes to succeed in any creative profession. For me, the transition from indie films to episodic television, and now studio features, was wholly self-taught. Stumbling along my determined route, it seemed as if my peers were granted access to a hidden manual. If you're searching for practical insight, Pete's book is the very manual I longed for — a treat of monumental value, awaits you."

—VICTORIA MAHONEY, Director, *Lovecraft Country*, *The Morning Show*, upcoming *The Old Guard II*, and 2nd Unit Director on *Star Wars: The Rise of Skywalker*

TRANSITIONS

A DIRECTOR'S JOURNEY & MOTIVATIONAL HANDBOOK

MICHAEL WIESE PRODUCTIONS

Michael Wiese Productions
12400 Ventura Blvd. #1111
Studio City, CA 91604
(818) 379-8799, (818) 986-3408 (FAX)
mw@mwp.com
www.mwp.com

Cover design by Johnny Ink. www.johnnyink.com
Copyediting by Sarah Beach

Manufactured in the United States of America

Library of Congress Cataloguing-in-Publication Data
Names: Chatmon, Pete, 1977- author.
Title: Transitions : a director's journey and motivational handbook / by
    Pete Chatmon.
Description: Studio City, CA : Michael Wiese Productions, [2022] | Summary:
    "Becoming a Director is not just about making a film, webseries,
    commercial, or music video. If that were the case, with today's access
    to equipment and free distribution, there'd be thousands more working
    professionals. Turning your passion into a profession requires the
    ability to make transitions, at the exact moment a pivot is needed, with
    creativity and precision. Chatmon's book helps Directors carve out a
    career with targeted anecdotes, worksheets, and other resources, all of
    which fall into three designated categories: How-To, Self-Help, and
    Inspiration"-- Provided by publisher.
Identifiers: LCCN 2021005466 | ISBN 9781615933310 (trade paperback)
Subjects: LCSH: Chatmon, Pete, 1977- | Television producers and
    directors--United States--Biography. | African American television
    producers and directors--Biography. | Television--Production and
    direction--Vocational guidance.
Classification: LCC PN1992.4.C494 A3 2022 | DDC 791.4502/33092 [B]--dc23
LC record available at https://lccn.loc.gov/2021005466

DEDICATION

To Kelly
The most important part of any journey is the person by your side.
With you . . . I know that nothing is impossible.

And, to our Little Lady
You didn't have a name at the time of this writing, but your mom and
I are here for you in every way imaginable. We're ready to love and
learn about the world anew through your eyes.

CONTENTS

Dedication iv

Acknowledgments xi

Foreword xiii

Introduction xvi

ACT I:
THE SET-UP
[1977–2005]

CHAPTER 1 2
CURIOSITY

■ THE EARLY YEARS. 2
How To Quit 5
Resources 11
Worksheet 1: *Finding My Voice* 11

CHAPTER 2 13
DISCIPLINE

■ NYU FILM SCHOOL 13
Self Help: *The Adjustment: Emotional Intelligence* 23
Resources 35
How to Budget 36
Worksheet 2: *The Six Building Blocks Of Your Craft*. 38

CHAPTER 3 40

FLEXIBILITY

■ THE REAL WORLD AKA THE SCHOOL OF HARD KNOCKS...... 40

How To Design A Short Film 42

Self Help: *The Adjustment: Attitude* 44

Resources 59

Worksheet 3: *Writing Your Bio and Origin Story*.................... 59

CHAPTER 4 60

HONESTY

■ WHO'S GOT $520,000? ANYONE? ANYONE? 60

How To Write What You Know 61

How To Raise Funds.. 66

How to Identify Investors.. 67

Resources 77

Worksheet 4: *What's The Worst That Could Happen?* 79

CHAPTER 5 81

SACRIFICE

■ *PREMIUM* — THE MAKING OF MY FIRST FEATURE FILM 81

How to Prepare for a Feature vs. a Short Film..................... 83

Resources 90

Worksheet 5: *Scheduling Your Day For Optimal Success* 92

● *THE DIRECTOR'S CUT: ACT I*...................................... 94

ACT II:
THE CONFRONTATION
[2006-2014]

CHAPTER 6 102

REPUTATION

■ BILLS TO PAY: 12 YEARS OF EMPLOYMENT AT NYU 102

How to Politic 103

Self Help: *The Adjustment: Allies* 109

Resources 114

Worksheet 6: *The Five Pillars Of Reputation* 114

CHAPTER 7 116

REPETITION

■ *PREMIUM* – THE ROAD TO DISTRIBUTION 116

Resources 120

CHAPTER 8 121

RESILIENCE

■ *761ST* AND TRIBECA ALL ACCESS 121

How To Design a Documentary Interview 124

Resources 134

CHAPTER 9 135

PIVOT

■ A PRODUCTION COMPANY, A PODCAST, AND
A MONTHLY EVENT 135

How to Identify the Market 137

Self Help: *The Adjustment: Angles* 145

Resources 152

Worksheet 7: *Three Questions To Ask Before Pivoting* 153

CHAPTER 10 154

EXPECTATION

■ *BLACKCARD*: THE PSYCHOLOGICAL PIVOT..................... 154

How To Put Your Money On Screen 156

Resources 160

● *THE DIRECTOR'S CUT: ACT II*..................................... 163

ACT III:
THE RESOLUTION
[2015–PRESENT]

CHAPTER 11 188

HUMILITY

■ TELEVISION DIRECTOR DEVELOPMENT PROGRAMS 188

How To Design Your Blocking and Coverage For Television 197

Resources 202

Worksheet 8: *What You Know Vs. What You Don't Know*.......... 203

CHAPTER 12 204

BRANDING

■ SECURING REPRESENTATION 204

Resources 206

CHAPTER 13 207

SERENDIPITY

■ THE ROAD TO MY FIRST EPISODE............................. 207

How To Design A Good Meeting 212

How To Keep Track Of Your Network 218

How To Manage Your Emotions On Set 226

Resources 233

CHAPTER 14 234
BALANCE

■ REFLECTIONS AND NEXT STEPS............................234
   Self Help: *The Adjustment: Arrival*...............................236
   Resources 239

● *THE DIRECTOR'S CUT: ACT III* 241

HOW I DID IT

■ DIRECTORS REFLECT ON THEIR JOURNEY
TO THE DIRECTOR'S CHAIR......................................247
   Matthew A. Cherry..248
   Romany Malco 252
   Seith Mann 255
   Rob McElhenney 260
   Molly McGlynn 264
   Keith Powell 269
   Millicent Shelton 274
   Michael Spiller..279
   Nzingha Stewart 283
   Anu Valia 286

About the Author...290

ACKNOWLEDGMENTS

I hear silence. I see an ocean of people. A clock. It's counting down from what must have been, maybe, thirty seconds? I'm wasting time.

I've never attended the ceremony, nor have I ever won an Emmy, but writing these acknowledgments feels like what I imagine my fellow Directors experience when recognizing the amazing people that have propelled them on their journey.

Authoring a book is no less collaborative an endeavor than directing a television show. I am indebted to many, but with that ticking clock, plus a desire to avoid that embarrassing orchestral musical interruption — I'd like to thank:

My family — Jackie (*my mom*), Jennifer and Tait (*my sisters*) — for never questioning my lofty goals and providing me with both food and shelter at times when the pursuit of my art, let's just say, challenged the reality of my pockets.

Kelly (*my wife*) for taking the baton from the family I was born into and putting some distance between me and my toughest competitor — the man in the mirror.

Stephen Marks, Bradley Glenn, and Andre Des Rochers (*my manager, first agent,* and *lawyer*) for working all the angles to not only build this episodic television directing career with me, but to land a publishing deal when everyone said it would be a "tough sell." Words I've been hearing since 1999, when I started producing my first feature film.

There are so many more to name.

People who ensured I'd never have to walk this journey alone. Creative comrades and friends like Candice Sanchez McFarlane, Dorian Missick, Joe Mettle, Sean McPhillip, Tristan Nash, Anthony Artis, Eric Van't Zelfden, Maurice Morgan, ELEW, Christina DeHaven-Call,

Idil Ibrahim, Troy Bigby, Tamara Bass, Stephen Rider, Theo Travers, Keith Powell, Dylan Verrechia, Giga Shane, Tahir Jetter, Hannelore Williams, Nicole Sylvester, Wayne McElroy, and Benjamin Ahr Harrison.

People who helped me understand the distinction between a Writer's medium and a Director's medium. Television Director Program executives like Brett King, Kelly Edwards, Janine Jones-Clark, Emerlynn Lampitoc, Tim O'Neill, DMA, Karen Horne, and Jeanne Mau.

I also have to thank Sydnee Rimes for being the first network executive to really champion me, as well as the generous Directors that graciously allowed me to observe them in action, including Charlie McDowell, Michael Watkins, Phill Lewis, Janice Cooke, Millicent Shelton, Ken Whittingham, Nzingha Stewart, and Linda Mendoza.

And, I can't forget the talented team that helped bring this book to life, including storyboard artist Bridget Shaw, my editor Sarah Beach, and the MWP team including Michael Wiese, Geraldine Overton-Wiese, Ken Lee and Bill Morosi.

I've clearly exceeded my time, but for those not named here, please know that you have already been thanked in person.

As for that clock, maybe one day I'll be able to tell everyone just how long you have to give that Emmy speech.

FOREWORD

BY KENYA BARRIS

Pete and I met in 2002 at a Fatburger in West Hollywood.

He was in Los Angeles taking meetings for what would later become his debut feature film, *Premium*, but this was long before we became the men we are today. On this day, we were just a couple of headstrong kids, talking shit and fantasizing about breaking down industry doors.

When I reflect on these moments, I can't help but think about how sacred collaboration is for an artist — especially in one's early years. We are only as good as the team we stand with. We are only as strong as the people we dream with....

We didn't realize we were manifesting our futures in that dirty burger joint, casting spells while speaking our desires and just like that — the universe made it all happen.

Today, I realize success isn't so much about the outcome, but instead about the road one travels. It has been quite a journey for Pete and me.

To be honest, it is difficult to know where to start.

Back then, we didn't have companies, employees, or representation. Our visions were nothing more than words on a page collecting dust while we waited for an opportunity.

We had no idea what the future had in store.

At the time, I had been an assistant on *Sister, Sister* and written for both *The Keenen Ivory Wayans Show* and *Soul Food*. Even with my foot in the door, the industry seemed like a tough nut to crack. Being Black didn't make things any better, but I was determined to make a way for myself.

I began dissecting the inner workings of Hollywood. I tried everything, no role was too small and I worked harder than everyone else. My ambitions were much more than finding a career — I wanted to create a space for not only myself but for my community. In my eyes, it was time for us to not just take a seat at the table but to build that table from scratch.

Hollywood is an incredibly unpredictable and volatile industry — you can go from the mailroom to the Oscars and back to the mailroom in 72 hours. Regardless of your work or work ethic, one of the unfortunate rules of entertainment is that "it's all about relationships." So, back in 2003, it was a no-brainer to partner with my childhood friend, Tyra Banks. We created *America's Next Top Model*, it premiered on UPN, expected to fail, but in the end, we proved everyone wrong. The series became a cultural phenomenon, it's almost 20 years after the fact, yet Tiffany and Tyra memes flood social media for a whole new generation to enjoy. That show was an astronomical step for me and it allowed me to gain valuable experience as a producer, while showcasing my ability to craft a story in what was an emerging genre of reality TV.

This Transition, much like the title to this book, is essential. Knowing how to adapt is necessary, you cannot be afraid to step out of your comfort zone because you never know how a new skill will aid you later on.

In 2005, I went on to write for *Girlfriends*, which happened to be the same year that Pete reached his goal, successfully raising $520,000 to direct *Premium*. Over the next few years, I wrote over 18 pilots which eventually led me to my breakout series *Black-ish* in 2014.

We all hear the success stories and know that some folks catch fire quickly in this industry, but my experience has shown that to keep the fire lit, talent alone isn't enough. You need passion, persistence, and a thick skin… shit, luck doesn't hurt, but in the end "there are no shortcuts."

Experience has to be lived and lessons need to be learned.

In 2017, I gave Pete his first shot at television with a Season 4 episode of *Black-ish*. He had been trying to Transition into TV for several years and having been aware of the journey, I knew what it felt like to stare into the abyss — hoping for a "yes." I had watched how hard Pete worked. It was his time to shine, and I knew he would be able to hop into the Director's chair with ease.

I may not know what the future holds for the industry or the artists that create the work, but I'm confident that Directors and creatives alike will find *Transitions* useful as they forge their path.

But, just remember, there are no shortcuts.

Kenya Barris

INTRODUCTION

"I've just gotta get my foot in the door. . . ."

How many times have you said that? Whether as a confidence booster, or with bitterness and contempt because of how long the journey to being paid for your directing skills is taking — we all know that nothing is given to us. We all know that getting our feet in the proverbial door requires that we "push ourselves" and "work the angles" . . . "running the marathon" . . . until "opportunity meets preparation" . . . and we can finally jam our Nikes into a sliver-sized opening, from which we'll "take the reins" . . . and, of course . . . "never look back."

But, what if your idea of what it takes to get your foot in the door is just plain wrong? Misguided? Incomplete?

What if your playbook is designed for the wrong sport entirely?

This book is about the journey of the Director, and how to succeed within a landscape that is constantly shifting. I've focused my lens on the **TRANSITIONS** that many Directors will be challenged with over the course of their career. I'll also share the principles I've learned about how to excel once you've ascended to each new rung on your Director's ladder.

I've made a variety of transitions over the course of my journey, going from:

- Short film Director to Director of a $520,000 independently financed feature film . . .
- Indie feature Director to NYU Film School Faculty . . .
- NYU Faculty to Creative Director of my own Digital Studio, while simultaneously directing my second feature film . . .
- Creative Director to Episodic Television Director . . .
- Episodic Television Director to Executive Producer and Pilot Director to Author to _____ . . .

Let's be clear: transitioning from one directorial space to the next does not leave the previous craft behind. I'm still writing feature films, still creating branded content and commercials through my Digital Studio, TheDirector, and still sharing my experiences through teaching. You're holding the by-product of that craft in your hands right now. And, while all of the above may seem like easily executed, logical next steps or lateral moves, trust me when I tell you that they were not. It took just as much focus and energy to transition between bullet points as it did to secure the prior accomplishment. I started at the proverbial bottom each and every time, but over the course of my journey, I began to realize that the principles of success, once identified, could be replicated. These principles were, in fact, the *only* reason I'd been able to transition from one directorial space to the next.

In 2014, after six unsuccessful years of unrealized efforts to break into episodic television directing, I asked myself a series of probing, existential questions:

- *What's not working?*
- *What if everything I'm doing is wrong?*
- *How can I pivot?*

I knew I had what it takes — I've always been pretty confident — but I clearly wasn't playing my cards right. Under closer analysis and with a lot of soul searching, I recognized that a lack of humility and gratitude had been crippling my progress. I had discounted the fact that each new directorial space was akin to graduating at the top of your senior class, only to become a freshman with zero connections or clout at your next educational institution. I'd developed an underlying bitterness as I transitioned from directorial space to directorial space, "climbing the ladder," all the while "finding it impossible" to segue into both episodic television directing and studio films. I'd done everything that I was told would make people "see" me. Appreciate my talents. Select me. But there I was, making event videos for clients, where I had to produce, shoot, cater, drive the van, edit, create graphics, and often more — just to deliver the job at the super low budgets we'd been given. Now, I'm not thumbing my nose at those jobs in any way, as I learned a great deal as a storyteller and implement those lessons on every episode of television that I continue to direct, but as far as the transition I was focused on making, I was unsatisfied and growing more bitter with every shoot.

So, what wasn't working?

My bitterness, though I hadn't considered it, was driven by unrealized expectations. In social and professional settings, I was giving off a very potent aura of "I shouldn't even have to go through all of this because I went to Sundance" or "made two feature films" or "won this many awards." Again, I was a senior in my mind, but a freshman in standing.

Who wants to work with that guy? Answering with brutal honesty, I knew I didn't. So, why would anyone else?

Was everything I was doing wrong?

No. Not everything. But, if I was going to break into this new space of episodic television directing, I was going to have to add something new and singularly unique to showcase my abilities. I realized I'd been trying to write, sell, and direct projects that the industry would love, but that's a moving target, and can be quite unsatisfying even if you're lucky enough to strike it.

I decided to make a short film, but with the mentality of my eleventh grade self. The teenager with a head full of dreadlocks that picked up a Super 8mm film camera and made whatever he was most passionate about. The wide-eyed, future Director who examined each finished product with pride, unconcerned with the impact it would have on anyone else. He was fulfilled because he was working to master his craft and find his voice.

I knew that guy was still in there somewhere.

How to pivot?

I would position this short film, *BlackCard*, as my new conversation piece. My new calling card. I decided that it could no longer matter that I'd gone to Sundance with my NYU thesis, made two feature films, and won a competition at Tribeca Film Festival. Those milestones were thirteen, nine, and six years in the past, respectively. They didn't reap the rewards I had expected, and that . . . would . . . have . . . to . . . be . . . alright. I was present with a new project and as excited as I'd ever been because I LOVE TELLING STORIES.

I would work to build a network of people in the industry who could educate me as to how episodic television works. I'd assume I knew nothing and I'd embrace the journey, illustrating my worth every day, with the expectation that no one knows what I'm capable of and I can show them with passion, patience, and a pleasure for politics. Because, frankly, working with people *is* politics and that was the biggest pivot I'd need to make, if I would be successful in directing multi-million dollar shows with crews of 100 or more people.

The results?

I'm happy to say that the actions triggered by my answers to the above questions have yielded results that have, if I'm being honest, surpassed my expectations. As I write this, I've directed both half hour single camera comedies and one-hour dramas. I'm attached to direct a pilot for a premium cable network, and I'm pitching my first episodic series to major production companies with my sights on selling to a network in the coming months. I am also outlining my next feature film as I finish this book.

Now, let's get back to you.

As you read this book, you'll notice that I've presented my experiences through three different lenses.

LENS 1: How-To

You can't create your own sauce until you know the ingredients. Whether it's the early stages of finding your path, or the intricacies of creating shot lists, I'll answer questions like:

- *How do I find my voice?*

- *How do I raise money?*
- *How do I sell myself and design a good meeting?*

LENS 2: Self-Help

Some folks master the *how-to,* while perfecting the age-old craft of letting their emotions eliminate any possibility of success. They say you can't learn to control the horse until you can control yourself, and your career is no different.

From my experience, Emotional Intelligence (EQ) is the biggest factor (or obstacle) in ever being able to showcase your skills. To that end, you'll find a recurring section throughout the book, entitled "The Adjustment," where I'll take a timeout to dissect a crucial decision that changed the trajectory of my career. For all of you Directors, the adjustment is no different than the notes you'd give to an actor to get a better performance in take two. Why not apply our storytelling skills to our most important narrative — our very own Hero's Journey?

LENS 3: Inspiration

Lastly, I know that I'm just one guy, on one journey, and some additional voices just might help this resonate with more impact. In the "How I Did It" section of the book, I've invited some talented folks that inspire me to share their paths to directorial success with you.

I hope this book will serve as a catalyst for the next steps of your journey. It's never too late to reflect, to ask questions, or to pivot.

I also hope you'll share the roadmap of your success with your creative community. As far as I'm concerned, artists reaching their goals translates into a better world for us all.

Lastly, I invite you to hit me up on social media so I can bear witness to the beauty of your transitions.

Let's get to work!

Pete Chatmon
Los Angeles, California
@petechatmon [Instagram & Twitter]

ACT I:
THE SET-UP
[1977–2005]

CHAPTER 1

THE EARLY YEARS

Ah, yes. The obligatory first chapter. Where does one begin? As with any story, I'm working to focus my narrative on plot points that propel the journey forward. Nuggets that will pay off in the later acts. With that in mind, let's start with my parent's decision to move from Brooklyn, New York to South Orange, New Jersey. Having both been the first in their families to reach new rungs on America's corporate ladder, they had a special appreciation for the value of education. My mother worked in banking and my father was an entrepreneur in the shadows of Wall Street. So, while ironically, we may have moved out of the borough of the filmmaker that would first inspire me years later, Mr. Spike Lee, it would be in the enclave of South Orange and our sister town of Maplewood where I'd be exposed to the arts and find what would become my voice.

Throughout this book, I'll be providing "keywords" to serve as guiding principles to keep in mind as you move through your creative journey.

▶ CHAPTER 1'S KEYWORD is: CURIOSITY

We landed in New Jersey in 1983. I was five years old, my older sister, Jennifer, would soon be entering the third grade, and my parents were excited about an exceptional public school system with a short commute into Manhattan. Bingo! The town was somewhat diverse, which basically meant I'd soon discover what it felt like to be "other."

An April 20, 1986, *New York Times* article, "Racial Incidents Beset 2 Towns" went into great detail about cross burnings and other violent vandalism against the Black families in South Orange and Maplewood, many of whom were my friends.

As a young, middle-class Black kid, I was somewhat different from my Black classmates who lived on the other side of town. Yet together, all of us were different from the Black kids growing up just outside our city limits in East Orange, Newark, and the other neighboring cities. And, of course, all of these multidimensional Black kids were different from the white kids. Looking back, I believe it was my proximity to all of these different ways of life and cultures that would propel me into my professional career as a Director. Living and playing with folks from all walks of life substantially informed my ability to feel. Add to the fact that my summers were spent in the deep south of Birmingham, Alabama, and the mid-Atlantic swelter of Newport News, Virginia, and I guess it makes perfect sense why a show like *Black-ish* would be the first episode of TV I'd ever direct (more on that later.)

Luckily, my curiosity was well fed in my hometown and, fortunately, supported by my family. I am well aware that for some Directors, this support may not be there, making the path that much more challenging, and lonely. But, trust that a community of artists is waiting to assist you on your journey. And, while this is no consolation prize, the burden of having to make a way out of no way often yields the most honest and impactful work.

From the age of six or seven, I can remember being impacted by the arts. I didn't have the vocabulary for what I was witnessing or experiencing, but I knew the arts meant *something*. I felt what they *added* to people's lives. Whether it was hearing my mom sing Sam Cooke's "I'll Come Running Back To You" (in her very own special key) or my sister and I listening to Richard Pryor's *Bicentennial N*gger* concert record on vinyl (hoping we wouldn't get caught for breaking strict orders to *not* play it) — I knew there was something being transferred from creator to audience that I wanted to be a part of.

My first foray into the arts was creative writing. In the second grade, we had an assignment to make a book and I put together a construction paper gem about my love of cars. I focused on a trip to the Javits Center for the New York International Auto Show, complete with photos and musings about my seven-year-old life. It wasn't a bestseller, but it was something tangible. Just like those vinyl records that I could hold in my hand, this book was something I could pass on to family members and friends, and it gave me the chance to examine their response to what *I* created.

My second foray into the arts was in the fourth grade when I performed in *Willy Wonka and The Chocolate Factory*, blessing the audience with a solo rendition of "The Candy Man." I could carry a tune (still can, a li'l something), but I didn't see a future as the next Sam Cooke. Perhaps, I was learning the difference between being the focal point and creating behind the scenes. Without the lesson having been fully absorbed, however, that same year I picked up the alto saxophone and competed for first chair against the super talented Yolanda Singletary. I never elevated above second chair, but it was the first time I learned that one's limitations can be revealed by the talent of others. In the future, I'd learn that talent can lose to passion and persistence. But more on that later, too — I had to find my passion first.

After two years, I got tired of carrying that damn saxophone case, and decided to do something that, from time to time, you just have to do: I quit. My reasoning would be driven by more nuanced concerns in the future, but it's important to know when it's time to move on from something, take what you learned from that experience, and apply it when you find your true passion.

HOW TO QUIT

The idea or practice of "quitting" gets a bad rap, but that's okay. What I'm talking about is the fact that in order to move closer to your passions and desires, you're going to have to step away from *something*. Besides, being a jack-of-all-trades and master-of-none does not land you at the top of your craft.

While some in your circle (or maybe on social media) may think that you're quitting, trust your instincts and move on to new challenges when the time is right. Curiosity yields exploration. Just make sure you're not abandoning a pursuit because it's hard or challenging. See a task through to its completion, then make a decision as to whether or not you need it to move closer to your dreams.

My time at South Orange Middle school introduced me to the world of soccer. I played competitively on a local team, the Eagles, who were second fiddle to the Dynamos, coached by the legendary Gene Chyzowych (inducted into the National Soccer Coaches Association of America Hall of Fame in 2009). I performed well, learned that I had a super competitive spirit and did not like to lose, and for the first time, I saw what happens when one's talent is not recognized or taken advantage of. I remember being in a game that came down to a penalty kick, fully expecting that I would be called to bring home a victory for our team. My fundamentals were great, I had the strongest, most accurate leg, but the call went to one of the coach's favorites. Who missed the shot. Obviously, there was no guarantee that I would have made it, but I never forgot my first time experiencing politics within what should have been a meritocracy.

I quit soccer in the seventh grade, and dedicated myself to pick-up basketball at Baird Community Center. Basketball, to this day, remains my favorite sport, and while I disabused myself rather quickly of any NBA dreams, my first heroes and inspirations were found in Michael Jordan, Kareem Abdul-Jabbar, and most recently, Kobe Bryant. I saw how important incremental, repetitive efforts are key to success. The age-old adage "practice makes perfect" can lead to a championship, or an individual award, or whatever glory — especially if you adopt that "Mamba Mentality." To this day, I maintain a pretty rigid commitment to staying in shape, because peak performance is tethered to peak conditioning (yes, even directing is a physical job, particularly with the emotional dynamics of making the day).

My time at Columbia High School would bring girls to the forefront. It would also introduce me to the cultural realities of America in the 1990s. My major friendships coming out of South Orange Middle School were divided along racial lines. On the "Black side," I had the homies Trevor Graves and Joe Mettle (who would later partner with me in my first production company, as well as serve as the best man at my wedding). On the "white side" were my buddies Robbie Kramer and Mark Goldwert. Weekend hangs and sleepovers were split pretty evenly between the two groups, giving me a window into vastly different versions of America, but when we hit the hallways and the lunchroom on the first day of ninth grade, there was an unwritten acknowledgment that choices would have to be made as to whom you would hang out with. I chose my Black friends, and while that was never at the dismissal of my white friends, as we would all hit the keg parties come junior year, and remain cool with each other in the world of athletics, I wonder what we each missed out on in our personal development by choosing sides.

My next creative foray would be as a rapper. I loved creative writing back in the second grade, and here I was in my sophomore year, getting recognition for what I could do with words over a beat, or in an *a capella* after-school battle. I went by the name Grim Reaper, and while I did not rap about death or killing, I was making no small metaphor towards the fact that I was going to kill the competition with my verses. As the battles became a regular thing, two of my other good friends, Mo Ziyambe and Jayson Blaine, and I decided to form a group. We'd all seen *The Five Heartbeats* (1991), so we knew this was the next step. Obviously. Our name was Metro3, which I think Mo and I came up with, and we got so far as to have a recording deal on the table. We ended up passing, for reasons I don't quite remember and I'm sure worked out for the best, as music deals have been notoriously whack since time immemorial. But I would never stop writing verses. Even now, if I hear a dope beat and I'm driving solo through Los Angeles' notorious traffic, I'll let out a sloppy freestyle that has moments of shining mediocrity every couple of bars. Somebody call Drake and let him know.

My final creative foray in these early years, after a brief stint where I wanted to be an architect, was a Super 8mm filmmaking class taught by Mr. George Chase. To say I had finally found my passion would be an understatement. This class was an elective, mostly populated by students trying to find an extra forty-five minutes in the day to nap, but for me it was exactly what I'd been looking for. It was also where I'd first met Emily Konopinski, a freshman in the class and someone who would prove, like Joe Mettle, to be a crucial partner on my post-film school endeavors.

The first film project I made was met with a nugget of praise that inspired me to keep going. I was shooting at the South Orange train station, and my girlfriend at the time, Savena, was the star of the project. My story required that I get her character from the train platform down to the street. Thinking I could condense time (because who wants to watch a character walk down two flights of stairs and open multiple doors), I cut from a shot of her on the platform to a shot of the AT&T logo above the street level payphone, tilting down to her as she walked up to make a call. I don't know where I got that shot from, or how I knew it would "work," but Mr. Chase sure noticed, and commended me on understanding the language of film. I was hooked.

It was 1993, so Mr. Chase would show us laser discs of some of the most obscure films I'd ever seen. From Godfrey Reggios's *Koyanisqaatsi* (1982), to Billy Wilder's *Double Indemnity* (1944), to Stanley Kubrick's *2001* (1968), my eyes were being opened to a world I'd never known existed. But when we watched *Do the Right Thing* (1989), I was locked in. My fellow Brooklynite, up until the age of five when we moved to New Jersey, had made something that resonated with me like nothing before. It seems minor, but when Giancarlo Esposito's character "Buggin' Out" gets his Air Jordans scuffed by the Boston Celtics fan, triggering an argument, it was the first time I saw something and said "That is MY life." This little moment gave credibility, in a weird way, to the world in which I lived. It also told me that the life I lived was worthy of being put on the big screen — or a screen at all — that wasn't the criminal narrative that governed the 11 o'clock news.

While most of the other students were barely passing, I was making eight to ten projects per quarter. The requirement was one. I read every book that Mr. Chase had, watched every laser disc he had in that classroom, developed my own black-and-white film, and did whatever I could to absorb this art form I'd become so infatuated with. What's interesting, in hindsight, is that whatever I was searching for in the architecture class, was given life in this filmmaking elective. The math may have been a turnoff for me, but being the architect of a world

and the characters within it was what I wanted to do. Focusing my lens on people who don't often get the camera pointed in their direction was my calling.

It sounds pretentious, or maybe precocious, but at this moment, I made a very specific choice about what I would do with my life. I decided to quit one more thing. I said goodbye to music (as a professional goal) and focused all of my efforts on filmmaking. I felt that film would be the harder road, but as far as impact, and with no disrespect to music, my personal experience was that while music captured moods, films could change lives by inspiring new ways of thinking. I wanted to have my hands in that.

Armed with this new worldview, I dedicated my time to building the best possible portfolio for submission to New York University's Tisch School of the Arts. Mr. Chase was an NYU alumnus and every anecdote of his since I picked up that Super 8mm camera began with "When I was at NYU." When my research revealed that Spike Lee, Martin Scorsese, Oliver Stone, and other Directors were also alums, I became obsessed with the idea of joining their ranks.

I applied for early admission and was accepted into the Class of 1999. Now, it was time to call "Action!" on my own story.

▶ **CHAPTER 1 KEYWORD: CURIOSITY**

Curiosity will help you find your passion. Try everything. Explore and learn as you discover your vision, define your tastes, and identify your skills.

Once you find your professional footing, curiosity will also be necessary to continuously elevate your craft above your peers.

When you stop being curious, you stop being relevant.

RESOURCES

- *SELF HELP:*
Worksheet 1 — Finding My Voice (Page tbd)

- *INSPIRATION:*
Podcast:
Let's Shoot! with Pete Chatmon, Episode 07
Romany Malco on The Million Little Things He's Learned and
"Tijuana Jackson"
Available on Apple Podcasts, Spotify, and all Podcast Platforms

WORKSHEET 1:
FINDING MY VOICE

When we were young, we tried everything in search of an activity, art, hobby, or sport that excited us. Some of us were fortunate to find a craft early and remain dedicated to mastering it (think: Tiger Woods, Stephen Spielberg, or Mozart, to name a few). Others may have found their passion, but stepped away from it, in pursuit of something more "stable."

When speaking specifically to Directors, I've always encouraged them to ask three simple questions in pursuit of finding their voice. Honest answers are a must.

(1) What are your top five movies, television shows, and books of all time?
This is likely to reveal things about yourself that you might never have considered. You will discover common threads and themes that engage your soul.

Movies	Television Shows	Books
1.	1.	1.
2.	2.	2.
3.	3.	3.
4.	4.	4.
5.	5.	5.

If you're later in your career and have developed a body of work, take a look at the projects you're most proud of, and see what thematic elements repeatedly appear. When I did this exercise in 2014, I discovered that every story I'd told since 1999 was anchored by my protagonist's pursuit of the American Dream and what that pursuit looked like if you are Black. From romantic dramedy to documentary to short film — this theme was always present.

(2) If you could say anything in the world, what would it be?
Hopefully, your answer to #1 indicates the stories you'd most like to explore. Love and loss? Race and culture? Sports and adventure? As far as genre, have you found that you really love satire, but have been afraid to develop content in that space? Have you been working in drama, but really love horror? Be honest and see what is revealed.

(3) What is the path to directing the stories I most want to tell?
Even a skyscraper begins with the first shovel of dirt. Rather than picking up a camera, I'd advise you to slow down and, instead, watch everything you can that operates in the thematic worlds that excite you. See how the masters have done it. Identify what's been said well, ignored, or could be better said in your hands with your unique vision.

Once you've got a sense of history within your thematic lane, explore your theme(s) in as many genres as possible — at whatever budget level you can. You'll be on your way toward mastery, while developing a community of collaborators and a body of work that truly represents who you are.

DISCIPLINE

NYU FILM SCHOOL

August 1995. I stood on the sidewalk of Washington Square East and watched my mother's car disappear into the distance as she headed for the Holland Tunnel. I was officially a college freshman at New York University's Tisch School of the Arts, with $120 in my pocket to make it through the semester. I'd figure out how to stretch that later (as well as every production budget in my future). My first order of business was to shuttle my cart of belongings, aka my life, into Goddard Hall, meet my suitemates, and begin plotting my moves for the next four years.

> ▶ **Chapter 2's keyword is: DISCIPLINE**

Let's pause for a second and talk about the whole idea of film school. My point with this chapter is not necessarily to advocate for an NYU film school education, or the like. In actuality, I don't think you need it, and that's coming from someone that both attended and taught at the university. But that's *only* if you're willing to design a curriculum of your own to challenge yourself en route to mastering your craft.

If we agree that, like all arts, there is a value in treating the craft and business of filmmaking as something that can be taught, then skipping out on a formal education puts the onus on you to be the dean or department chair of your own future.

The other benefit of a school environment is the community you join and the community you build. Relationships are the secret sauce to success in the industry and all of mine began in film school. Straight up. As an example, during Orientation Week, one of the first people

I met in my dorm and in my classes was Reed Morano — long before becoming a director-cinematographer and the creative force behind Hulu's *The Handmaid's Tale* as well as director of episodic shows including *Billions,* and feature films including *The Rhythm Section* (2020). When the day comes that we're finally able to work together, this shared bond will be a part of the fabric of that journey. Today, I often have general meetings with producers, writers, and executives, and upon discovering our shared NYU experience, there's an immediate bond on which to build further rapport. Obviously, plenty of people go to film school and become accountants, never again picking up a camera after they graduate, while others drop out of NYU, go on to make their own films, and become household names, like Paul Thomas Anderson. Nevertheless, it's more about your curiosity and discipline (*keywords!*) to find a way that works for you.

My final sidebar on this topic is that to be an artist, you have to have something to say. You need to find your voice. I was young and dumb at eighteen years old when I entered college, but the new ideas that college would expose me to, coupled with the people and experiences that would challenge my perspective, put me on the fast track toward solidifying a specific point of view and way of seeing the world. It's this point of view that I continue to explore today, in every project that I direct.

Now, back to the story. 1995 was an entirely different world from today, and the best way to get your hands on equipment was through a film school program. Digital video cameras were not deemed acceptable for professional storytelling (that was still about a decade away) and no one had a cell phone, let alone a smartphone. Apple hadn't even begun its resurgence with the all-in-one iMac. Film equipment needed to be rented, and rentals required insurance, both of which demanded money. And, weirdly, while college tuition was exorbitant, requiring multiple loans, work study, and other combinations of financial aid, getting a check that could cover an entire semester (while putting you in debt) was easier than coming up with money to produce film after film outside of school. Lastly, film school offered a protective cocoon in which I could fail. Renting equipment weekends at a time to essentially "practice" would have increased my stress levels to heights I can't imagine.

As I sat on my extra-long twin bed, freshly made with my lone set of sheets, I studied the NYU course book and analyzed the path to graduation. NYU's liberal arts curriculum was designed to mix film school requirements with general education electives that would propel students toward developing a point of view. Within the program at Tisch

School of the Arts, I was excited to begin immersing myself in the journey of becoming what I like to call a "complete filmmaker." Over the course of my next four years, I saw that I'd be required to wear every hat at some point or another, moving through all key crew positions, and learning what it meant to create a film from top to bottom. I'd also learn how to collaborate with friends and "not-really-friends," as well as how to critique the work of my fellow classmates. I can't tell you how much I appreciate that now, as much of what I do as a Director is providing a result-oriented critique through emotional triggers that don't feel critical.

What follows is a comprehensive breakdown of what I learned during my undergraduate years, more than two decades ago. Again, film school may not be for everyone, but perhaps this will provide a sense of what you might design for yourself, as you step into your directorial path.

Freshman Year

Frame and Sequence: This class was a bit of a challenge because our first year in the program essentially put the idea of making a "film" on pause.

"Wait . . . what?"

I was amped, coming from high school with ten whole Super 8mm films under my belt, but here we were, spending the entire year, yes . . . both semesters, isolating the individual elements of storytelling. We were given multiple photographic assignments, to be captured with our manual cameras and manual light meters. When those first rolls of film were developed, you best believe that 90% of us discovered that we had no idea what we were doing, evidenced by either under or over-exposed negatives. But we were learning the principles of shutter speed, aperture, framing, and the like. Our final presentation was a three to five minute slideshow, incorporating everything we'd learned, to tell a story with twenty to twenty-five pictures, set to music. I captured a day in New York City with my girlfriend at the time, set to D'Angelo's ballad, "Lady." Essentially, each student was making their version of Chris Marker's, *La Jetée* (1962) — which was an inspiration for Terry Gilliam's *Twelve Monkeys* (1995). I walked away with a better understanding of what I could do with a film camera, and how manipulating the image, one frame at a time, is one of the go-to skills of a successful Director.

Sound Image: The other art we focused on in isolation was sound. The title of the class is a bit of an oxymoron, but the idea was to get students to appreciate that what we hear conjures up visual images, and knowing how to tell a story with sound is important to being a good Director. In this course, each student produced a radio drama, a la Orson Welles' *War of the Worlds* (1938). We were designing our own environments of sound, using different microphones, recording distances, the art of foley, as well as the direction of actors. We edited on reel-to-reel machines using ¼" tape and captured sound on location with the legendary Nagra recorder. Check out Brian DePalma's *Blowout* (1981) to get a sense of what we did in this class (you'll also see some early John Travolta that might surprise you). To be honest, I hated Sound Image, as it required a great deal of intricate, nuanced work, and I was itching to shoot all of those film ideas that were burning a hole in my notebook. The irony, however, is that today, sound design is one of my favorite parts of post-production. It's my final opportunity to protect and elevate my vision as a Director. In 2020, it was this course that gave me the confidence to transition my project "Wednesday Morning" from a short film to an audio podcast.

History and Criticism: These classes taught us about the films that have been made since the inception of the art form, starting with the likes of Georges Méliès and the Lumière brothers. We learned how the studio system grew, how the Hays Code (1934–1968) affected what could and could not be shown on screen, and how the Paramount Decrees (1948) broke up monopolies. Once the studios could no longer control the production, distribution, and exhibition arms of the business, the door was opened to independently financed films like Dennis Hopper's classic *Easy Rider* (1969). I was particularly enamored by our weekly forays into cinema from around the world. I learned about Ousmane Sembène and Senegalese cinema with his debut, *Black Girl* (1966), Italian Neorealist Cinema and Vittorio De Sica's *The Bicycle Thief* (1948), the French New Wave and Godard's *Breathless* (1960), and Spike Lee's indie classic *She's Gotta Have It* (1986). I ate all of this up, when I wasn't sleeping in the theatre (those school days were long, y'all). I was beginning to understand not only the importance of the practice of an art, but the theory.

General Education Classes: I took Geology (for my math requirement), Asian Art I (the hardest D+ I ever worked for, putting my financial aid at risk), and Fundamentals of Writing (where we learned the MLA rules for citations and other gems — rules I break all day, every day, in everything I write). I carried a full eighteen-credit course load, knocking out all of my assignments as soon as I received them, so I could travel back to New Jersey every weekend to pump gas at the Gulf Station owned by my girlfriend's father (more on that later, when we get to my first feature film and adhering to the rule "write what you know").

Sophomore Year

Sight & Sound Film: I returned to NYU in the fall of 1996, excited to pick up a camera and finally get back to the moving image. It had been almost a year and a half since I'd shot something. In this course, I graduated to black & white 16mm film from Super 8mm, the equivalent today of going from a consumer video camera to shooting in 8K. The class was taught by David K. Irving, chair of the undergraduate department at the time, and really one of the best teachers you could have at a moment when you needed guidance, challenge, and mentorship.

Like Frame and Sequence the year prior, each week our crews of four would be tasked with a different storytelling technique — parallel action, tracking shots, panning shots, montage, etc. — rotating Directors through each assignment. The typical rotation was *Director* one week, *Director of Photography* the next, *Gaffer* and *Equipment Hauler* the next, and so on. Directors never shot their own projects so we could develop much needed collaboration skills. We did, however, edit our own work on the legendary Steenbeck — cutting the negative with a razor blade and taping the film back together (with great care) so it wouldn't break when threaded into the projector. The pressure was intense, as there was no "undo" button and every slice of your negative resulted in the loss of ½ a frame in your sequence.

The one thing I've left out is all of these films were MOS — without sound! We were focusing solely on the moving image and directing the camera. Trying to capture performance and good sound while exposing a quality image on film would be junior year's challenge.

Sight & Sound Video: I hated this course. Well, one half of it. For the first half, we worked on the 12th floor television studio at 721 Broadway, in what must have been crews of twelve or more. Essentially, we were learning how to make multi-camera television, but without a live studio audience. The rotation included *Director, Camera Operator* (on one of the three studio cameras), *Sound Mixer, Chyron Generator*, and so forth.

The challenge that was arising for me across all of these production courses was generating enough content in "The Pete Chatmon Idea Factory" to meet the required number of assignments, without burning out. In a given year, I'd need at least twelve to fifteen different ideas to get a grade. When I was in a class that I was less enthusiastic about, I'd push to work on a storytelling technique rather than coming up with something awesome on the page, knowing that directing skills might be more useful than uninspired writing.

Now, the other half of this course, I loved. We were tasked with going out into the field and making short documentaries. After Tupac Shakur was killed in September of 1996, many tributes were painted across New York City, and I camped out with a camera in front of a mural on Houston Street. I interviewed dozens of passersby about what Pac had meant to them. I was energized by the cinema-verité of it all, interacting with real people who said unexpected things. I developed a dynamic cinematography style that could respond to the unpredictable realities of documentary. Ten years later, my production company would make its bread and butter on projects just like this.

Actor's Craft I: Some folks have called me an "Actor's Director" and if that's the case, I earned that title as a result of this class.

Have you ever had to do a log roll, act like a tree, or roar like a lion before presenting your truest emotions to a class full of kids looking at you like "WTF?" Well, if that doesn't make you respect the beauty of what an actor offers you in front of crews of ten to a hundred people, I don't know what does. Additionally, this course was a prerequisite for

Directing The Actor and Directing The Camera, both of which were on my target list of classes for junior year.

Intro to Dramatic & Visual Writing I and II: I mentioned above how the "Pete Chatmon Idea Factory" was being pushed to its limits with all of these assignments. This was the main class for which I was reserving my creativity. D&V Writing was split into two semesters and would be the class where, ideally, I'd write the short film that I would direct as my senior thesis.

I wrote a script entitled *3D* which focused on Doreen's Delicious Diner, a fixture in a Black neighborhood that was beginning to suffer from the growing realities of gentrification. What was once a *place with heart* became merely a *place to go* and my story followed the demise of the community through a waitress, her gas-pumping boyfriend who aspired to rap, and a con man who entered the diner with dubious intentions. A homeless man stationed in front of the diner who sold books when it was Black owned, but was no longer respected once gentrification hit, provided a Greek chorus. The title *3D* was not only an acronym for the diner, it also referred to the idea of looking at these issues and characters in a three-dimensional way. I had something to say, and was using every class as an opportunity to prepare myself to say it.

General Education Classes: I rounded out my electives this year with Economics and other liberal arts classes that escape me today. More importantly, I began focusing my remaining gen-ed opportunities on courses that would help me better understand the issues that concerned me. I decided to explore the Metropolitan Studies major. The curriculum focused on the study of cities and metropolitan regions in an historical and contemporary perspective, which I knew would provide answers to my questions on events like the great migration, white flight, and how the urban areas that might serve as settings for my films came to be.

Junior Year

Color Sync: It was the fall of 1997, and to tell you I was excited about this class would be an understatement. We were going to be shooting on color film (So long, black and white!) with sync sound (Hello actors that say words!). This meant generating yet <u>another</u> idea for what would be a six to eight minute film, but my excitement to write and direct would push my idea factory into action.

Gone were the days of shooting an assignment in four to five hours. No, for this project, entitled *$5 to Six* (it followed a $5 bill through the hands of six people in New York City), we would have the equipment from Friday afternoon until Monday morning, and be responsible for coordinating more logistics than ever before. It would be my first real Producer experience, as I had to beg and borrow to meet the production budget (about $700, which felt like $700,000), make a schedule (really the AD's job, but hey!), rent a truck (by finding someone older than twenty-five to put the rental under their name), figure out craft service and catering, secure different wardrobe and props, muster the strength to approach random business owners to ask if I could shoot on their property, and more. In regard to locations, I quickly learned the value of identifying racism and navigating the bullshit to achieve your goals. I'd had zero luck every time my two hundred pound, young Black male frame approached a location owner. After the third instance, fearing that I might not be able to make my film, I asked my producing partner, Hannah Alejandro, to be the point person for entering potential locations and asking to speak to the owner. I'd play her assistant. When we locked down our deli on the very next approach, I learned that while you can't change folks, you can adapt your tactics to get what you need. I was also learning that some of this shit will NEVER be on a syllabus. There's a Real World dynamic to filmmaking that can't be taught and requires instincts and Emotional Intelligence. I would later work to impart this to my students when I returned to NYU as an instructor.

SELF HELP:
THE ADJUSTMENT

EMOTIONAL INTELLIGENCE

The art of directing requires delivering notes, both large and small, to cast and crew. These "adjustments" ensure that the goals of any given scene are achieved. If we, as Directors, can identify these pivots for creative success in our characters and collaborators, why would we not apply this same analysis to ourselves? We are, after all, characters in our very own hero's journey.

The driving force behind applying this skill to your own experiences is Emotional Intelligence (EQ). According to Daniel Goleman, who helped popularize the concept, there are five components of EQ:

SELF-AWARENESS
SELF-REGULATION
MOTIVATION
EMPATHY
SOCIAL SKILLS

Self-Awareness is probably the most challenging of these components to harness. As we move through the rest of the book, I'll be making note of critical moments in my journey where I was able to direct myself, due to self-awareness, to make adjustments toward my desired goal.

The *$5 to Six* shoot was rife with peaks and valleys. This was the project where I first met Dorian Missick, who would go on to star in *3D*, *Chameleon* (a short I directed in 2003), my debut feature *Premium* (shot in 2005), and my 2016 short *BlackCard* that was picked up by HBO. He would also be the co-officiant of my wedding. Relationships, y'all. Anyway, I was coming into my own as far as working with actors, but this film also presented me with a few heartbreaking technical difficulties. We shot on the CP-16 camera, and after one particular slow-motion sequence, I would find out in post-production that the camera never regained a consistent 24 frames per second while rolling. This meant that everything we shot after the slow-motion bit, which was basically the first five pages of the script, was never in sync longer than a few seconds. It became impossible to synchronize the actor's mouths with the words, and I was left with a film that had no usable dialogue for the first five minutes. I was able to receive a grade for the course, as our requirement was only to present our dailies to the class, but after this experience, I was defeated and disheartened. It wasn't technically my fault, no pun intended, but the fragility of creating a successful project was revealed.

I learned firsthand why Color Sync was the "fork-in-the-road" class, as many students, after the demanding realities of their three-day shoots, gave up on their dreams of directing and focused on other parts of the process. That wasn't going to be me. I had quit the saxophone, soccer, and rapping in the past, but I would not be quitting on my dreams of becoming a Director.

Actor's Craft II, Directing The Actor, and Directing The Camera: After having taken two rounds of Actor's Craft and feeling confident in at least understanding the realities of what actors experience, I was ready to focus on directing.

Directing The Actor helped to develop our communication skills, distinguishing the difference between emotionally driven and result-oriented directions. It also preached that we should never give a line reading to an actor (though there are rare cases where I've come to disagree with that.)

Each Director would serve as an actor for their fellow classmates, so while we weren't necessarily working with the next Denzel Washington or Meryl Streep, we were replicating what we'd eventually be doing on our own sets. I remember being given direction by a classmate (who has since gone on to be a successful Hollywood Director), and making a mental note that I would *never* direct someone in the same way they chose to direct me. The subtext of the scene was not explored, the intentions of my character were not discussed, and ultimately I was lost as to what was desired from me as an actor. The lack of clarity made the experience not only aggravating, but confrontational. I knew that if I could at least avoid this approach, I'd be helping my cause.

Directing The Camera challenged us to develop our ability to tell a story via shot selection and sequencing. We would present our selected scenes to class, with a breakdown of our coverage. We would also have to create shot lists for the scenes of our classmates. It was a great way to work the muscles of blocking/staging a scene and picking a point of view from which to capture the action. I had done a good enough job in this regard on *$5 to Six*, but I challenged myself to step up my game tenfold whenever I got the opportunity to direct *3D*.

Producing The Short Screenplay:

Producing The Short Screenplay was invaluable. NYU worked to ensure the job of the Producer was understood to be a collaborative, creative position, too. The class taught me how to work smarter, as opposed to harder, especially in regards to learning how to ask the right questions, and thinking three or four steps beyond every decision — before making it. With this newly developed muscle, I could now put on my Producer's hat while writing, to make sure I wasn't creating scenarios that would be unnecessarily hard to accomplish once I stepped into the Director's chair.

Metropolitan Studies (continued): I was compiling enough Metropolitan Studies credits to consider a minor in the subject, but my 18-credit course load every semester since freshman year had been specifically designed to allow more freedom in my senior year. As a result, I stopped one class shy of earning a Metropolitan Studies minor. But again, I'll call this strategic quitting, all in the service of achieving a larger goal.

Nevertheless, Metropolitan Studies had taken me into a variety of tight-knit neighborhoods in Brooklyn and Queens, where I researched the communities and learned a great deal, specifically, about the Jamaican-American and Russian-American experiences. It also exposed me to the Asian/Pacific Islander experience. I remember one course where the professor gave a weekly assignment called "Bloopers." Students were tasked with making note of anything in the media (TV, films, books) that stereotyped people of Asian/Pacific Islander descent. It was interesting to see how other cultures could be the brunt of mainstream culture's insensitivity, and while I had a heightened sensitivity to jabs at my own, I barely noticed those directed at my fellow diverse communities. That blind spot landed on me and would find its way into my approach to writing. Moving forward, I promised to humanize all of my characters, making extra efforts to represent those traditionally left on the periphery of a white protagonist's world in mainstream projects.

Senior Year

Advanced Production: The fall of 1998 felt like I'd made the NBA playoffs. Advanced Production was the two-semester course I'd been planning for since thumbing through the curriculum guide after my mother dropped me off at my dorm. This was where undergraduate students finally had the opportunity to direct their thesis films. Twenty students enrolled in the class, vying for ten allotments of equipment, insurance, a two-week production period, a small stipend, and a six-month window beyond graduation of access to all necessary post-production facilities. At the end of the first semester, each student would pitch their project to the class in a presentation that usually included some kind of PowerPoint slideshow detailing their story, why they were passionate about making their film, their budget (and how much was already secured), any cast or crew attachments, as well as anything else that might make a student stand out as being more prepared than their nineteen other classmates. It was friendly competition, but underneath, we were all definitively rooting for one Director: ourselves. Those who were not selected by the professor typically dropped the class for the second semester, deciding that directing was not in their future. This was always a bit of a pet peeve of mine, as I felt if you are going to let not being "selected" be the reason you don't make your film, then you didn't deserve the allotment to begin with. Making a film requires a driving, relentless, almost insane passion to bring a story into the world, and if a professor, hired by some university, is the determining factor as to whether or not you will tell your story, then this game isn't for you.

Before I go any further, I need to return to that little issue of my unfinished film from junior year. The final component of the pitching process was to screen your prior work from an intermediate production class. Remember my technical problems, and the fact that the first five minutes of my film *$5 to Six* were out of sync and without usable dialogue? Well, the film department and Professor Mo Ogrodnik didn't care about that. A finished film would need to be presented. I sat down and watched this nine-minute film over and over again. The dialogue would kick in around minute five, and while you could get a sense of what was happening from the images, there was no way this would be presentable. After much deliberation, I landed on writing a voiceover to cover the beginning and be interwoven into the latter parts of the film. This was far from ideal, or desired, but it was proof that there are three stages in which you make your film: *there's the film you write, the film you shoot, and the film you edit.*

The unexpected by-product of the voiceover was that I could shorten almost every scene in the film, because the narration was providing information and context that no longer needed to unfold on screen. What took three to four minutes in my over-written script (just being honest) could be communicated in one or two minutes with the new voiceover. I chopped the final film down to a six-minute running time and while I was not super excited about the end product (in comparison to what I had envisioned), I was proud of myself for having stuck it through to find a solution to unforeseen technical problems. I, my friends, was a Director. I learned from this experience, and proved to myself that I could see a project through to completion, no matter what happens along the way. When I would return to the film school more than a decade later and teach the very same class, I was always saddened by how many students never finished their films.

With my presentation complete, anchored by a final cut of *$5 to Six*, I was selected as one of ten students to direct a thesis film in Mo Ogrodnik's Advanced Production Workshop. The final step, before heading home for winter break, was to complete the production calendar for when we returned in the spring semester. My budget was $24,000 and the amount we had on hand was: $0. I had a nice business plan that my Producer, Christina DeHaven, and I put together, but we had no commitments and hadn't been able to start fundraising until we knew we had the green light for the class. One or two students wanted to shoot in February, at the start of the production period, but the remaining eight or nine of us were jockeying to get the latest spot possible. Some, I could tell, due to sheer fright, others from their desire to procrastinate and just wanting to have the longest pre-production period possible. But, for me, we needed all the time we could get to raise the damn money to make the film. Literally. With

Johnnie Cochran as my inspiration (and no intention of leaving without winning), I presented my argument to the class, and fortunately, Christina and I were able to head into the holidays knowing that our shoot would be locked into the final slot. *3D*, from a script I'd started in my sophomore year in 1996, would be going into production from April 21–May 5, 1999.

We broke for winter break and I got down to business. The only question I had, for all comers — friend, foe, or family — was "where the money at!" In early January, I was able to pitch *3D* to the head of a major record label that I had interned for, and to my surprise, he was all-in. $24,000 for two credits: one for his production company and an executive producer credit for himself. That sounded great to me. I essentially gave him the pitch I'd done to get the allotment, but added a little flair while leaning more heavily on the elements that might entice him. "We could always add a soundtrack and elevate this to a level beyond your typical short film." I was getting better at this. I'll talk more about fundraising and pitching in Chapter 4 when I get to the making of *Premium*, my $520,000 feature, so don't think I'm going to leave you hanging.

Like this guy did me.

On April 21st, the day we checked out the gear from NYU, I drove the equipment truck to 57th Street in Midtown Manhattan to pick up the check. There had been several weeks of infrequent replies to my calls and emails, but it wasn't quite radio silence. If you think I had navigated post-production issues with *$5 to Six*, I was about to have first-hand experience with one of the biggest challenges in entertainment — financing and fundraising. In particular, dealing with shady people who lie about who they are and what they can do. I was too young and dumb to have demanded paperwork to guarantee this financial backing, and naive enough to think that a man's word meant something. This was a guy I had worked *for*, who my sister had worked *with*, but clearly, I had ignored Tribe Called Quest's warning: "Industry rule number four-thousand-and-eighty, Record company people are shady!"

The general manager of the label knew this was a fucked-up situation and being the semi-honest one out of the two, wrote me an $8,000 personal check that would essentially get me from checkout day, that Wednesday, until the following Monday. I remain grateful to him for doing that. The other $16,000, however, suddenly reverted back to being my problem. And, it stressed me so much that I broke out into shingles.

Production would be a mixture of creative affirmations and behind the scenes catastrophes. On the very first night of shooting, with the check still in my pocket, our generator caught fire, and our production was shut down by the Maplewood, New Jersey fire department. You couldn't write this shit. I had hoped to return to my local neighborhood as the hometown kid "destined for greatness," only to become a blurb in the local paper announcing that city hall had kicked us out of town. Major fail.

Forced to find a new location, Christina and I doubled back to a property we had scouted in Dunellen, New Jersey. It was a bed and breakfast — far from a diner — but they had an event room in the back, situated off of a kitchen, and I figured with zero options on the table, well . . . it would be perfect! That's a common occurrence in production. Knowing that the kitchen would not suffice for our location needs, I got on the phone and after multiple referrals, landed in a conversation with the father of someone who had lived on my block from first to third grade. Mr. Eatman owned a Burger King in Newark, New Jersey, and graciously granted us one night to shoot, after they closed for the day. Suddenly, we had almost everything we needed. The final piece of the puzzle came when I secured Je's Restaurant in Newark, a soul food spot my family had been going to for years, that was friendly enough to let us use the location as an exterior.

Other aspects of the shoot had gone somewhat smoothly. My crew was filled with fellow classmates hungry to step into new positions. My cast, carefully selected after a long audition process, has gone on to live on your television screens and in theater complexes. I knew one of the most important roles, "Jeff Sellers," would be played by Dorian Missick, who starred in *$5 to Six*, but the rest came from the large pool of up-and-coming talent in New York City, hungry enough to be looking for work on tiny student films.

Ultimately, after some tough decisions, and a few folks dropping out for "better opportunities," my cast rounded out as follows:

"Angie" — played by Kerry Washington, who was also graduating from undergrad, and about to start making her mark in indies like *Our Song* and studio films like *Save The Last Dance*.

"Reggie" — played by Al Thompson, who went on to an impressive career in commercials after roles in *The Royal Tenenbaums* and *A Walk to Remember*. He also was a leader in the digital world of webseries in the early 2010s, deserving far more recognition for what he created with ValDean Entertainment.

"Malcolm" — played by Charles Parnell, who would go on to appear in blockbusters like *Transformers: Age of Extinction* and television shows like *Briarpatch* and *The Last Ship*.

"Florence" — played by Angela Nirvana, who went on to appear in many classic independent films and other works.

"Da Cook" — played by my good friend, and natural, non-actor, Sean McPhillip, now an attorney.

"The Owner" — depicted in a photo and portrayed by David K. Irving, chair of the film department and my former Sight & Sound Film professor.

And, oh yeah, I played "Derick."

After successfully navigating two weeks of production, my final moments on set would be something I wish never happened. We were heading into the final scene of 3D, a Do the Right Thing inspired riot in front of the diner, that pushed Kerry Washington's character "Angie" to make the climactic decision of the film. Somehow, I had not been informed that Kerry had a "hard out" and needed to leave by a certain time, effectively making it impossible to shoot an already ambitious scene in the way I had prepared. I snapped. I had walked an insane tightrope for almost six months, and with my eyes on the finish line I felt like I might not complete the race I'd been preparing for since the fall of 1995. My solution? A profanity-laden tirade, not directed at anyone in particular, but surely an illustration of a Director in over his head, both creatively and psychologically.

We got the scene in the can, essentially by resorting to handheld tactics — cinema verité skills I'd learned in my earlier classes — but Murphy's Law, the rule that "everything that can go wrong, will go wrong," had proven itself accurate yet again.

I had missed my senior formal to shoot 3D, but I didn't mind. I'd accomplished what I set out to do at NYU, knowing that I still had some areas to improve if I were to become a professional Director. Clearly, I'd have to get control of my emotions, but I'd also have to get a better understanding of basic business practices and legal safe-guards, so I could avoid the trappings of con men and people with bad intentions or simply unable to deliver on what they promise. I also recognized that I'd need to develop a more thorough understanding of the psychological demands placed on a Director.

They say "You can't learn to control the horse until you can control yourself."

But first, I'd have to graduate.

Graduation

Over the years, I had watched several friends enter the professional world with successful thesis films, only to find themselves unprepared to answer the question, "What's next?" As graduation loomed, less than two weeks after wrapping production on *3D*, I pondered how to avoid the same fate.

The conventional wisdom for an independent filmmaker entering the year 2000 was still to "Go make a feature film." TV's Golden Age, as it would later be defined, had barely begun, with the premiere of HBO's *The Sopranos* on January 10, 1999. So, the idea of even directing for TV was not viewed with much enthusiasm by me, or my directing classmates. Film was the *only way*.

In mid-May, my sister Jennifer, and I headed to Corning, NY to babysit our cousins for a week. It was a nice break from the realities of making a thesis film, and since post-production would have to wait until I returned to my mom's apartment in Jersey City and raised

more money, I decided to get back to work as a Director by putting my Writer's hat on. I purchased my first copy of FinalDraft screen-writing software, taking advantage of the student discount that was soon to expire, and began the script for what would be my debut feature film, *Premium*.

I didn't quite know what lay ahead, but I was ready to drive the road less traveled. I'd later be surprised by just how much I had to pave my own way.

▶ **CHAPTER 2 KEYWORD: DISCIPLINE**

In the hopes I can say this without sounding like an elder, I believe the ease with which the profession of directing can be entered today has decreased the level of discipline in emerging Directors. Diving into any and everything with potentially unlimited, unfettered access has created, for some, a lack of mastery over individual crafts.

No matter how you design your own curriculum, or formulate your own approach to education outside of a university or trade school, make sure that you develop proficiency over the building blocks that lead to your dream.

It will make you stand out from the crowd, and you will be rewarded for your expertise.

RESOURCES

- **HOW TO:**
How To Budget (Page tbd) --------------

- **SELF HELP:**
*Worksheet 2 — The Six Building Blocks of Your Craft
(Page tbd)* --------------

- **INSPIRATION:**
Let's Shoot! with Pete Chatmon, Episode 13
Aya Cash on Becoming Comfortable With Discomfort
Available on Apple Podcasts, Spotify, and all Podcast Platforms

Wednesday Morning (2020)
***Directed by Pete Chatmon and starring Kelly McCreary, Spencer
Garrett, Colman Domingo, Blake DeLong, Joy Nash, Louis Ozawa,
Elena Campbell-Martinez, Remy Ortiz, and Monnie Aleahmad***
Available on Apple Podcasts, Spotify, and all Podcast Platforms

HOW TO BUDGET

The production of my NYU thesis *3D* was unique, because while we were anticipating (read: hoping) we'd be selected for an allotment, I could not realistically approach anyone to write a check for something that wasn't definitively moving forward. We also couldn't hedge our bets, because if the film did not get selected, the budget would have soared as a result of losing access to equipment, insurance, and all other NYU perks. So, this was how we arrived in the horrible position of having a green light in December of 1998, yet $0 in the bank for our April 1999 shoot.

The industry standard, however, as applied to independent productions (meaning you did not start shooting with a studio or distributor attached and a guaranteed release) is as follows:

1st: DEVELOP and WRITE a screenplay, either from an original idea or a pre-existing property that you've secured the literary rights to produce (magazine article, book, life story, amusement park ride, etc. . . .)

2nd: FINANCE / FUNDRAISE for the production of your screenplay. You'll need to make a budget and schedule for your project. If you're lucky, you may have already lined up an actor or two during development who will help attract investors to your project. Once you've got the money in the bank, ideally with enough to cover you through post-production and the marketing/release of the film, your project is given the "green light" to go into pre-production.

> ***When we get to the making of my feature film *Premium*, I'll talk a bit more about getting investors to green light a project with only enough cash on hand to complete production. . ..

3rd: PRE-PRODUCTION, which is where you start hiring the rest of your cast and crew, securing locations, finalizing the schedule, designing the creative approach to the project, etc. . . .

4th: PRODUCTION, where at long last, you shoot this project that you have been developing for what seems like forever!

5th: POST-PRODUCTION, where you edit the film, finding creative solutions to all of your production challenges. You will also do a sound edit/design/mix, color correction, original score, create titles, handle any visual effects, etc. At the conclusion of post-production, your film is ready to be delivered to whatever platform(s) will screen or exhibit the project. As this all draws to a conclusion, you should also be preparing promotional materials and finalizing a website for the project.

> ***Another point to add is that in today's world, there's often a PMD: Producer of Marketing and Distribution. This person may get to work during pre-production to ensure you are building an audience via social media as the project moves through the various stages. This helps to strengthen audience investment, so that by the time the project is released there is measurable demand.

6th: DISTRIBUTION, whether that's running the film festival circuit in hopes of securing a deal with a studio or an online release via platforms like YouTube, Vimeo, Short of the Week, or others.

WORKSHEET 2:
THE SIX BUILDING BLOCKS OF YOUR CRAFT

At the beginning of Chapter 2, I stated that film school is not a requirement for success or learning how to be a Director. Nevertheless, I believe that the best Directors understand every aspect of how a production operates — logistically, hierarchically, and psychologically. In the same fashion that the best CEOs know the inner workings of the business they've been hired to lead and inspire, a Director can fully protect her vision by being fluent in the demands of every department.

Below are the six building blocks of craft for the Director to master. I've listed them in the order you'll typically engage with them, as you move from script to screen. Thematic clarity and precise dramatic intention are crucial in making the most of each building block.

WRITING
ACTING
PRODUCTION DESIGN
CINEMATOGRAPHY
EDITING
MUSIC and SOUND DESIGN

Writing
It's important to understand story principles and how different storytelling devices are utilized, based on genre.

Acting
Before you ever get to set, your understanding of acting will ensure that you have well-rounded characters operating in the service of your story.

Production Design

While in prep, you will be scouting locations and/or working in concert with your Production Designer in regards to how your sets should feel. Locations and sets tell a story of their own and are often "characters" in a film or TV show — ignore this building block to the detriment of your story.

Cinematography

Many Directors lean heavily on camera and lenses and style of shooting, but if you're lensing a location that could have better represented your story, and performances that don't work in concert with your themes and dramatic intention — it can look good for no reason. All of these buildings work in concert with each other.

Editing

Knowing how you will edit your project will save valuable time on set. Don't shoot needless coverage. Knowing how to complement the thematic intent of your story by playing with pace, shot selection, and scene order will help you carve out the best version of your idea from the footage you've captured.

Music and Sound Design

These building blocks are often underappreciated, but the right score, song choice, or soundscape can elevate everything you've done above to levels beyond your wildest dreams.

Do your research and study all of the above crafts. Never stop being curious. And, always challenge yourself to make the most out of each department.

That, my friends, is directing!

FLEXIBILITY

THE REAL WORLD
AKA THE SCHOOL OF
HARD KNOCKS

With *3D* in the can, I was an NYU graduate with a Bachelor of Fine Arts degree. I sarcastically coined the acronym "Better Find Another," considering there was (and still remains) no direct route to becoming a Director (no matter the degree). But, hey, I was ready. With a piece of paper. And, soon enough, a film. Between odd jobs, the continued pitching of our prospectus to friends, family, former orthodontists, and the like, as well as contributions my mother was able to scrounge together, I was somehow able to complete post-production on *3D* in the winter of 2000.

▶ **CHAPTER 3's KEYWORD is: FLEXIBILITY**

Every April, NYU presents The First Run Film Festival, an event show-casing the finished projects of all students in the various production classes. Theaters are packed with classmates, professors, cast and crew, family and friends, and most importantly, industry representatives. Though I had missed the April 2000 event due to the long post-production period on my film, the upside now was that *3D* had picked up a little steam after a premiere at the Mill Valley Film Festival in Northern California. Perhaps, I hoped, I might be able to return to First Run in 2001 with some heat behind the film.

In December 2000, as I strolled the underwhelming event space of our second festival, one I'd essentially paid for the "luxury" of a screening (don't fall for that one, folks), I checked the voicemail on my first ever cell phone and heard a message that I'll never forget:

. . . Your film, 3D, is an official selection of the 2001 Sundance Film Festival.

I happily left the event and immediately called my Producer, Christina DeHaven. We were one of sixty-four films chosen, from 2,174 entries (*Variety*, December 10, 2000). It felt incredibly validating, especially because Sundance had been presented as the pinnacle of success for the student filmmaker. It was time to get working on an official poster, press kit, postcards, as well as look into booking rooms and researching what young filmmakers should prepare for when headed to a major international film festival. I purchased Chris Gore's *Ultimate Film Festival Survival Guide* and absorbed every detail.

We hit Park City, Utah in January of 2001, ready for action. Christina and I were joined by Dorian Missick, my best friend Joe Mettle (Director of Production for my company at the time), and my sister Jennifer (who had also served as costume designer on the film, alongside my mother). Coincidentally, I was also getting my first chance to hang out with my other sister, Tait, who was there handling a marketing event for a client. Tait and I grew up in different homes, unaware of each other, but once we met, we were able to build a relationship that's become a special bond, and in many ways, would help ease my transition into episodic television directing some fifteen years later.

We plastered the town with 3D posters and postcards, got plastered at the parties on Main Street, brushed shoulders with folks we'd seen on the big screen all our lives, and overwhelmingly, just soaked up what it felt like to be able to reach out and touch the industry we wanted to break into so badly.

HOW TO DESIGN A SHORT FILM

There are no hard and fast rules to making a short film, but as a Director of multiple shorts and audience member at dozens of festivals — I've noticed a few things.

First, designing a typical beginning, middle and end to your story can be the kiss of death. The average running time of the shorts that do get programmed has been skewing shorter and shorter with each passing year. This means the selection of your twenty-minute short overrules two to three other films that are in the five to eight minute range. Will your film be that much better? If it is, will it withstand the politics that come with any selection committee?

With this in mind, I recommend focusing on an event or moment that is critical to the growth of your protagonist. An experience that challenges the essence of who they are and how they see the world. Present a thematic question, explore your answer to that question with the events of the film, and leave the audience wondering how life might continue beyond the frame, after your story concludes. This cliffhanger device is particularly useful in the event your short takes off and people are interested in seeing a further exploration of your characters in a longer format (feature film, TV series, etc.).

As an example, the world in my short *BlackCard* is incredibly complex. It's layered with many characters and rules of engagement that drive the story, making it work as a comedic, satirical, dramedy that wears its politics on its sleeve. The film, however, focuses on a single afternoon with "Leonard" and "Lona," that culminates in a decision that will reverberate across the universe long after the credits roll.

Think as big as you want for your idea, but when designing your short film, grab a scalpel and focus on the one thematic element that best represents your vision.

3D played in one of five shorts programs, screening several times over the course of the festival to a great response. Our other star, Kerry Washington, was getting a lot of heat from the festival for her portrayal of "Niecy" in Demane Davis and Khari Streeter's *Lift*. It was clear things were beginning to take off for Kerry, as Jim McKay's *Our Song* and Thomas Carter's *Save the Last Dance* would soon confirm.

During the festival, one particular incident on a shuttle taught me the importance of losing my New York attitude, and opening up to people and opportunities.

The gentleman sitting next to me on this packed shuttle was more or less being a nice human and making eye contact with me, which,

in some places I'd lived, could be the beginning of a problem. Being smart enough to at least not react as if I were back home, I gave a nice enough "Hello" to get him to mind his business. Nevertheless, he insisted on chatting with me and we soon discovered that we knew each other and had been exchanging phone calls for the past six months. *Phone calls where I was the one seeking assistance.* After this experience, I made a mental note to adjust my disposition. I could (and would) still be wary of everyone, but they didn't have to know it. As time progressed, I would learn a lot more about managing emotions, especially in dealing with clients at my production company, investors for my films, and the large casts and crews of episodic television.

SELF HELP:
THE ADJUSTMENT

ATTITUDE

There's a version of the shuttle story where I would return to New Jersey and tell my friends how "crazy" it was that I ran into this gentleman in this fashion. We'd laugh, order another round, and move on to the next topic of discussion.

The adjustment, however, was to look at the shuttle experience as Take 1. Like any Director bringing a story to life, I analyzed whether or not what happened in that exchange was going to be conducive to me reaching my goal of finding a foothold in this industry. There was one clear answer: NO. If I repeated the same behavior, there was no telling who I'd miss the opportunity to connect with or offend next.

For Take 2, and all interactions moving forward, I could avoid the same potential pitfalls and put myself in a better position to succeed with the aforementioned attitude adjustment.

Every interaction on your journey offers valuable information that can help bring your story to life. The challenge is to be self-aware enough to critique yourself and committed enough to change.

In February 2001, a few weeks after the festival, I received a phone call from Lynn Auerbach at the Sundance Institute. I was back in New Jersey, living at home with my mom, sending email and snail mail follow-up to all the folks I had met back in Park City, including the gentleman from the shuttle. The Sundance Institute is another tentacle of the organization that develops art and artists, putting filmmakers in a position to gain a spotlight on their work designed to assist with the development and ultimate financing of a project. Lynn Auerbach told me they were interested in my voice and wanted to see if I had any feature length projects in the works. I laughed, proud of myself for the efforts made after graduating NYU two years prior, and of course replied, "Yes." I told her I would get the script for my feature *Premium* to her right away and after a quick polish, I sent it off for her review. I won't say the script was "there" yet, but I knew I would have to send something as quickly as possible to get in the pipeline and be considered. I was really on my toes after watching the missed opportunities of former classmates and colleagues.

As I waited for an update on whether *Premium* would be selected for the Sundance Writer's Lab that summer, NYU's First Run Film Festival was creeping up on us. The festival would occur in April of 2001 and *3D* was finally going to screen at the place where it all started! It was worth the wait because now, with all of our Sundance success, we were a featured part of the marketing used to publicize NYU's festival in the trades, magazines, and official newsletters. Sounds good, right?

Well . . . when the craft awards were announced, as well as the finalists for the undergraduate Wasserman Awards, *3D* was left off of every possible list and acknowledgement. I'm not going to lie to you, I was pissed, and somewhat insulted, considering our Sundance selection was ultimately being used to entice audiences to attend the festival. Because I was young, new to the game, and not fully aware of how things "worked," I set up a meeting with then chair of the undergraduate film department, Prof. David K. Irving — the man who taught my Sight & Sound film class in sophomore year and posed for a photo of the gentrifying owner that appeared in *3D*.

David kept a straight face as I ran down my prepared list of griev-
ances, driven by my unrealistic expectations and self-importance. I
don't remember verbatim, but I'm sure I said something to the effect of
"This department told me that Sundance was the pinnacle of student
filmmaking success and I did that!" followed by "How are you guys
going to spotlight my film to indicate the quality of the programming,
then not reward the film as a quality project?" When I finished, David
told me about many films in the past, including one that had even
won the coveted short film competition at Sundance, but returned to
First Run without being selected as a finalist or recognized for its craft.

Touché.

What was I going to say to that? Underneath it all, I was most angry
about not being able to take advantage of the professional opportunities offered by being a finalist. Those three undergraduate films would
travel to Los Angeles for another industry screening later in the year,
bearing the endorsement of the university, as well as being given an
opportunity to have a mentorship meeting with one of NYU's great
alumni. I'm talking about the Martin Scorseses of the world. Literally.
And, since I already knew that many of my classmates did not have
their next projects ready to go, whether conceived or in any stage of
development, I felt it was a missed opportunity not only for me, but

the university, too. That may sound crazy, but the strength of any program is reflected by the accomplishments of its students, and I knew that many of my cohorts were not ready to play ball and receive the support the University's infrastructure offered.

The most important takeaway, here, was that I was getting a glimpse of how things "worked." This was a firsthand example of the power of relationships. Whether right or wrong, I knew that my four years at NYU had been lived under the radar. Sure, I completed all of my work, often turning it in early, and answered questions when called upon, but I didn't really make a point to personally distinguish myself amongst the student body. There were no professors that could say "This is my guy," and I think that presented its challenges when competing against classmates that had developed that very important relationship currency. This is not to say that those films and filmmakers at First Run were undeserving, and in hindsight I don't necessarily think I was robbed, but my episodic television success is anchored by the relationships I've developed over a twenty-year period, and I recognize now that I was without any real network.

This would be something I would never forget. And never let happen again.

Over the next year, I would continue to go back and forth with the Sundance Institute. They'd send me notes on my script for *Premium*, then give me a new date by which to submit a revision for the next Writer's Lab. Without fail, I'd hunker down, address the feedback, and kick back a draft to the very patient Lynn Auerbach. I was not going to miss this opportunity. In regards to pushing my projects forward, I was developing an ability to keep going and going and going until given an absolute "No" as far as interest (this would prove super important in fundraising and introducing myself to new people in new industries down the line).

By the time Spring 2002 came around, two things had become evident. One, I was going to keep on submitting updated scripts if given the go-ahead. And, two, *Premium* was <u>not</u> going to be selected for development with the Sundance Writer's Lab. That, however, did not mean the end of Lynn's generosity and support in helping the project. For this, she was legendary. She provided me with a list of fifteen to twenty Producers to contact in Los Angeles, in the hopes of setting up meetings that might propel *Premium* toward the partnerships that could get the film made. If my film was too mainstream for the Sundances of the world, then perhaps the mainstream avenues would offer a road to success.

I headed to Los Angeles in June 2002, right after a surprise 25th birthday party. Excited to make my mark on Hollywood, I was joined by Dorian Missick (now attached to star in *Premium*) and Joe Mettle. I crashed on my sister Tait's West Hollywood couch. We were armed with the screenplay, an electronic press kit (EPK), and a short promo video that I had directed at a local gas station to introduce readers of the script to the world of the main character, Reginald "Cool" Coolidge.

Premium was a love story about "the love before the love." That one partner with whom you journey through so many ups and downs, hoping to make it work, but inevitably discover that it's not meant to be. It's often presented as sad, but my take on the story was to present it as hopeful, because whatever lies ahead for your next relationship will only benefit from what you learned from "the love before the love." The other pillar of the narrative was following a struggling Black actor as he pumps gas at his mother's boyfriend's station, all the while trying to build a career based on embodying roles that have integrity and showcase the Black experience in all of its nuance. His ex-fiancée, "Charli" (played by Zoe Saldana once we raised the money and cast the film), appears at the gas station thirty-six hours before her wedding to a local lawyer (eventually to be played by Hill Harper.)

I was driven by the dictum "write what you know." My girlfriend from high school and part of college had gotten engaged (one of my first friends to do so) and upon hearing this I wondered, "What if I wanted to stop this from happening?" As I designed the world of the film, I couldn't get past the fact that this "What if?" inclination really came from a juvenile, egotistical place. Essentially, it was me saying, "How are you going to marry this guy over me?" — a line that eventually made it into the mouth of "Cool." Ultimately, his brazen ego is given a wake-up call as a result of this childish impulse to prove something, acted upon at the risk of upending "Charli's" life. *Premium* was cathartic on another level, as much of what "Cool" desired to do as an actor reflected what I wanted to accomplish as a Writer-Director.

Our two weeks in Los Angeles went well enough (few ever really tell you how to have a good meeting, but I will, later in this book). Nevertheless, I suppose I didn't embarrass myself. I had a hook-up on a rental car and was able to "fake it 'til I make it" in a Mercedes Benz SUV. My sister Tait, arranged a lunch with legendary music executive, Andre Harrell, where I met Ted Witcher, the Director of one of my favorite films at the time, *Love Jones*. I ended up at a Mike Tyson fight party at director Bille Woodruff's house in the Hollywood Hills, sitting next to R&B singer Christopher Williams. Dorian and I visited legendary casting director, Robi Reed's house to watch a screening of the independent film *Shottas*. We were seeing behind the scenes as to how Hollywood worked.

There were plenty of producer and potential agent meetings in offices, but unfortunately, over what's now almost two decades, I don't remember the cast of characters. I do recall, though, one person who stood me up and never showed, who since has sought to hire me for a directing job (I'm smiling as I type this, and no, I didn't accept the offer). If you ride the wave long enough, the tide always turns.

The most important meeting, though, was really just a quick hang whose impact wouldn't be felt for another fourteen years. Dorian and I caught up with his cousin, Shaheed, at Fatburger on Santa Monica Boulevard. Shaheed was with his friend from their days at Clark Atlanta University, a young, emerging writer named Kenya Barris. In November 2016, when I shadowed Director Linda Mendoza during the third season of Kenya's first narrative show, *Black-ish*, as part of the

Disney/ABC Television Directing Program, it was this chance meeting in 2002 that had put us on each other's radar and initiated a relationship where I could be given the opportunity to finally transition into episodic television directing.

As our trip came to a conclusion, the results were quite clear to me, even though I had to read between the lines. Not everyone will tell you flat-out that they don't like your project, or it's not for them, or provide notes as to how you can improve it. But enthusiasm is easy to read, and in this industry, when people are interested, they do not play coy or hard to get. Oftentimes, an idea is "sold in the room." As I thought back to everything I'd heard in those offices, and more importantly, to what was revealed by people's varying lines of questioning, I recognized that while *Premium* had been too mainstream for Sundance, it was . . . drumroll . . . too indie for Hollywood. I'd have to wrap my head around that one.

But first, I'd need a job.

My initial job after graduating NYU was working at Baseline Studio Systems, which was purchased by Hollywood.com while I worked there. A new upstart, IMDB.com, had entered the game and the information that Baseline offered at a paid subscription was now available to the industry for free. The company tried to find ways to compete, but in May of 2002, I was laid off. So, this L.A. trip had been part work, part vacation, and part therapy, as I considered what would be next for me as far as surviving and making money. Because, as you can tell, filmmaking didn't pay the bills!

Christina DeHaven was working in the production office of NYU film school. Another classmate, Eric Juhola, was leaving his position to work professionally in the industry, and Christina would be moving up the ladder, leaving her former position in need of a replacement. Knowing my predicament, she informed me of the opening, filling me in on the requirements and expectations. I threw on my only suit and hopped on the PATH train into Greenwich Village for my interview. I was fortunate to land the job and very thankful for the opportunity, as my filmmaking pursuits would be counterbalanced by various jobs at NYU, both administrative and as faculty, for the next thirteen years.

My official capacity as "Assistant Production Coordinator" consisted of signing forms and vouchers for the students to deal with outside vendors (Kodak, B&H Superstore, Technicolor Film Labs, etc.), managing the relationships of those vendors (that had been set up by Christina in her position as Production Coordinator), and serving as a liaison between the film department and NYU's office of insurance, so our students would learn how to fully pre-produce their films to ensure success. As life would have it, this would prove to be the exact right job at the right time, as I raised my understanding of pre-production and . . . drumroll . . . was also able to borrow film and video equipment!

As 2003 began, I continued working on the script for *Premium* and began focusing on the idea of raising the money for the film independently. After my education on relationships at NYU's First Run Film Festival, I considered that any financial support would likely come from my local community in South Orange and Maplewood, New Jersey, and I began to focus on how I might become the big fish in a small pond of 15,000 people.

I decided to make another short film. The clock was ticking and *3D* had become something I'd directed four years ago. If you're a chef, you cook . . . if you're a writer, you write . . . and if you're a Director, to me, it's no different. You DIRECT. I wrote *Chameleon*, a short film about the double consciousness that Black folks employ to navigate life in America. I was further exploring the themes that most interested me and challenging myself to become a stronger Director, before embarking upon a feature film. *Chameleon*, of course, would star Dorian Missick, and in many ways served as a practice run on local fundraising.

I would find another partner for my team in Emily Konopinski. I ran into Emily as I was leaving a local barbershop, seven years since the days we shared George Chase's high school Super 8mm filmmaking class. She had recently returned to Maplewood after serving in the Air Force, and was super interested in the messages I wanted to tackle. She was also heavily involved in the South Orange and Maplewood community and its many organizations.

We raised around $3,000 from fifty people, including an emerging politician by the name of Cory Booker. Contributions ranged from $5 to $200 and we received coverage in *The Newark Star-Ledger* in regards to our two sold out screenings at Gallery 1978 in Maplewood. My profile was elevating in the community, and I knew these press clippings would be useful in the evolving press kit for *Premium*. I also envisioned that some of the people who supported the film might be potential investors for *Premium*, and if not, they could surely speak well to the experience of working with me.

Chameleon would go on to run the festival circuit, taking my vision to ten more festivals around the world. On the heels of this experience, I felt like I could defend, again, the ability to call myself a Director. My confidence to level up to a feature film also grew exponentially.

Now, it was time to get that money.

study of the homeless. While in prison, Atkins had written a 300-page script about his life, which his girlfriend offered to its include "The Hours and Times" and "Color of a Brisk and Leaping Day," is returning with "The Sleepy Time Gal," a

Jacqueline Bisset; the team of Scott McGehee and David Seigel, who contributed 1993's "Suture," are bringing "The Deep End," starring Tilda Swinton; and DeMane Davis and Khari Streeter, of '97's

Over," have a follo "Lift," starring Kerry ton and Lonette McKe

But director Timo Bui is unique in that h ited Sundance as the er/co-writer of his

DAILY VARIETY (GOTHAM), 1/17/2001

Sundance chain plan

By CARL DiORIO

The plug was pulled on long-incubating Sundance Cinemas before the joint venture could birth a single theater, but a glimmer of hope remains that a solo Sundance project or two might survive.

Construction projects that had been under way in Portland, Ore., and Philadelphia were canceled in November as Sundance execs acknowledged financial problems at joint-venture partner General Cinemas had effectively killed arthouse circuit plans. Local proponents of the Portland development believe there's a slim chance the project — 75% complete when work was halted — can be salvaged.

Sundance Cinemas was launched in 1997 by a for-profit

unit of Robert Redfo dance organization an Cinemas, a unit of dive hibitor GC Cos. Initial p for some of the theater operation by the end of' delays soon pushed th Jan. '99 with a projecti theaters would be in pla

Now, all that's off, t a suggestion that the org could find another backer for one or two Redford spokesman Rivers says two local some promise, but d dish details and caut talks are extremely pr

One proposal invol theater that was part sidio military installati Francisco. The other historic Aero theater Monica.

The Presidio is part

significantly. The WGA
that while VHS sales will
$8.1 billion this year to
on in 2005, DVD sales
to $11.2 billion in 2005
current $2.7 billion.

all the analysts agree
that the sell-through mar-
h includes videocassettes
, will be fueled by DVD
y over the next five years
video-on-demand pay TV
ther expand revenue
McLean said.

key issues raised by the
clude boosts in residuals
foreign and the Fox net-
abolition of the posses-
lit on films. Studios and
have indicated that they
t to pressures on profits
y fragmented TV markets
; production costs.

'GA, which faces a May
xpiration, and the Alliance
Picture & Television Pro
ve yet to set a date to begi
ons. The AMPTP has sai
early negotiations but th
said the Alliance has no
it will take the step
n economic issues to jus
ng early talks.

)YALTY

es. Under the new scheme
ions streaming on the In
uld be required to pay
known as sound-recording
ce 1996, federal law ha
all other Webcasters to pay
cording royalties.

r in the fall, a broad-based
m of recording industry
aunched SoundExchange
nsate labels and artists for
rformances of their songs
ast, as well as on cable
lite-based radio services.
Exchange will be run by
e consisting of the RIAA
for Independent Music, th
Federation of Musician
ican Federation of Televi
adio Artists, execs from the
r labels and musicians.

leged spy Wen Ho Lee and his family, for ABC. Shanti will super-
vise the production. Along with a team from the Annenberg School
of Communications at USC, journalist Robert Scheer will act as
technical consultant on the project.

In a separate deal, Hyperion, the book publishing unit of ABC,
has acquired the world rights to Lee's first-person account of his or-
deal.

Sundance sets shorts slate

By GREG REIFSTECK

HOLLYWOOD — The Sun-
dance Institute has announced the
short films to be featured in the
2001 Sundance Film Festival, to be
held Jan. 18-28 in Park City, Utah.

Sixty-four shorts, chosen from
among 2,174 entries, will be
screened as part of a shorts film
program or preceding a feature-
length film. A jury will present an
award to a short film of outstanding
achievement and merit.

"What strikes me about this
year's shorts competition is the diversity of nationalities represented," fest programmer Trevor
Groth said. "A number of these
films were created in the United
States by filmmakers from such
homelands as the Czech Republic,
Greece, Korea, Poland, Russia, Taiwan, Thailand and Vietnam, to
name a few. ... The shorts this
year represent what a melting pot
we truly are."

The following are the short
films selected: "3D" directed by
Pete Chatmon; "The Anchor Man,"
Christopher Summa; "And Now
Happiness," Tung Wang Wu; "And
She Wasn't" (Taiwan), Asio Liu &
Awei Liu; "Baby" (U.K.), WIZ;
"Because of Mama" (Russia), Ser-
guei Bassine; "The Big House"
(Australia), Rachel Ward; "Big
Love," Leif Tilden; "Bit Players,"
Andy Berman;

"Closer" (U.K.), directed by Tina
Gharavi; "Damages," Marianne
Dolan; "Delusion in Modern Primi-
tivism," Daniel Loflin; "Detroit
Jewel," Tom Megalis; "Did I Wake
You?," Venus DeMilo Thomas;
"Donuts for Breakfast" (New

Zealand), Felicity Morgan-Rhino;
"Drink Me," Lisa Barnstone; "Ellie
Parker," Scott Coffey; "Erased," Jay
Rosenstein;

"Football" (U.K.), directed by
Gaby Dellal; "Forest Views"
(Netherlands), Bart Vegter; "Four
P.M." (U.K.), Samantha Bakhurst &
Lea Morement; "Giina, an Actress,
Age 29," Paul Harrell; "Gone Un-
derground" (Germany), Su Turhan;
"Goulash," Mimi Zora; "Grandma,"
Sungyeon Joh; "Greatest Show on
Earth," directed by Anne Paas; "Gr-
rlyshow," Kara Herold; "Gulp,"
Jason Reitman;

"Helicopter," directed by Ari
Gold; "In Search of Mike" (Australia), Andrew Lancaster; "Infec-
tion" (New Zealand), James Cun-
ningham; "Jigsaw Venus," Dean
Kapsalis;

"Lint People," directed by
Helder King Sun; "The Little Big"
(France), Pierre Yves Clouin;
"Member," David Brooks;
"Metropopular," Amy Krider;
"Miguel," Henry Lu; "Mirror," Lee
Lanier; "Motorcycle" (Thailand),
Aditya Assarat; "Mountain Trip"
(Austria), Siegried A. Fruhauf;
"Mullitt," Pat Healy; "Muse 6,"
Sarah Rogaeki;

"Nine Lives (The Eternal Mo-
ment of Now)," directed by Jay
Rosenblatt; "Ode to a Hunter," Per
Fronth; "Offside," Leanna Creel;
"Outlet," Robert C. Banks Jr.;
"Pate," Agnieszka Wostowicz-
Vosloo; "Peekaboo Sunday," Laura
Levine; "Peter Rabbit and the Cru-
cifix," Anthony Dominici; "Pie
Fight 69," Christian Bruno & Sam
Green;

"Rejected," directed by Don
Hertzfeldt; "Shadowscan" (U.K.),
Turn to page 23

DAILY VARIETY (GOTHAM) 12/11/2000

Film shown at Sundance

By Maria Zingaro
Staff Writer

Since mid-January, life for the brother and sister team of Pete and Jennifer Chatmon of South Orange has been a series of making calls and taking calls, requesting meetings, following up and lots of waiting for replies.

The drill is a standard one for anyone looking to push a product. But in the Chatmons' case, what's not so standard is the product they're pushing — Pete's films.

A burgeoning filmmaker, Pete just passed a major career milestone. His black and white film "3D" was one of 54 short films selected out of a pool of about 2,500, all submitted in application to the prestigious Sundance Film Festival held Jan. 18-28 in Park City, Utah. And while, to an outsider, making it to such a prestigious festival may seem a destination in and of itself, for someone like Chatmon, who is looking to become an industry insider, Sundance is just the first foot in the feature-making door; his short film is just a very elaborate calling card.

This is not to say that Pete Chatmon's first complete movie — actually his senior thesis for an undergraduate degree in filmmaking from New York University — is not meaningful to him.

Not only did Pete direct the film but he wrote it, too. "My ultimate goal is to direct, but I know, at this point, no one is going to give me great scripts. I know that I have to write them in order to have them," he said.

Plus, he noted, the big film studios look for "self-contained acts," making the writer-director hyphenate a desirable attribute.

An urban character study, "3D" is a ...

Pete Chatmon

terse examination of how far people will go to get ahead. It's principal characters are so anxious to find a better life that they become vulnerable to the seductions of a con-man but, in the end, all wind up re-immersed in the realities of their neighborhood.

The Chatmon family resources which went into the project give further testimony to the value it has for its creator. Costing nearly $1,000 per minute to make, about half of the money for the 24-minute-long film came out of the Chatmons' own pockets. In part because of her contributions, Pete's mother, Jacqueline Chatmon, was made the film's executive producer.

But, nostalgia for the project aside, Pete Chatmon knows he's got very few opportunities to sell himself to the people who can help him to make a career. His short must be the showcase for his talents, so that's how he shops it around. Sundance was merely a venue for this — albeit one offering nearly unimaginable exposure.

Of course, there will be others, too. He is waiting for word of acceptance from about 10 other film festivals — all offering further opportunities to See DIRECTING, Page 3

Directing is Chatmon's dream

(Continued from Page 1) make the connections which will potentially advance him in his profession.

"You try and build up an infinite number of people in your corner who can help you when you need it," he described. "You meet and, maybe two years later, they will help you on another project."

Here is where sister Jennifer comes in. In an industry that virtually demands everyone have his or her own public relations rep, she stepped up to help her brother. "Rather than me call with a different name, it was easier to have her call," Peter explained, only half in jest.

With a degree in music business, also from NYU, and some contacts of her own from having worked in her industry of choice, Jennifer was a natural for the job.

"Next to yourself, the next person who's going to have that same vested interest is going to be a family member," she said, explaining her reasons for being a part of "3D" and her brother's career. An aspiring singer herself, Jennifer said she'd expect the same of Pete if she needed the help.

"We work out of his room, but it's very big business," she described.

As part of the job of neverending networking, she also got to go to Sundance and schmooze, but she's been along for some of the less glamorous times as well — like the night Pete filmed from 8 p.m. until after the sun came up. "That night was a test of everyone's character," Jennifer described.

So, with Sundance behind them and some other festivals yet to come, the Chatmons are preparing for Pete's next project — a full length feature film — and are trying to garner the necessary funds.

Right now, Pete is working on his pitch for the script. And as anyone who has ever seen "The Player" — the Robert Altman movie depicting life in Hollywood behind the scenes — knows, the pitch alone can decter-mine whether or not a movie is e made.

His next production, P explained, trying out his la attempt, will be a love story featur an actor whose commitment to girlfriend is tested when he land plum role.

"It's a coming-of-age story t thorough a romantic relationship," J nifer quickly added.

If he gets the funds he needs, F hopes to set the film in his hometo "That will be great for South Oran There's neer been a feature shot sol in South Orange," he said.

He's optimistic about his chan too. "I plan to be shooting the r feature by some time in 2002," said.

NEWS-RECORD

of Maplewood and South Orange

Party set to raise funds for film being shot locally

By Shaun McCormack
Staff Writer

Double 7 Film is inviting local residents to join them July 13 at Cent'Anni Ristorante on Highland Place to celebrate the second short film from South Orange writer and director Pete Chatmon.

The party and fund-raiser is being held for "Chameleon," a short film focusing on "intra-racism" and a black man's internal personality struggle.

"The story is about a man climbing the corporate ladder and, no matter how far he climbs, he realizes he can't change who he is," Chatmon said.

Charlie, the 25-year-old protagonist, has two distinct personalities; one for the personal life he shares with friends and family and one for the corporate self he shows to colleagues, Chatmon said.

Some people say we are either one or the other; that one part is real and the other is a façade.

"I'm arguing that we are all of these different things," Chatmon said. What it means to be black or white or corporate or blue collar is not that cut and dry.

Artwork included with "Chameleon's" business plan spells this out.

It depicts a man who is literally split in half. The man is clothed on his right side in formal business attire. His left side is covered with urban street clothes: a basketball jersey, athletic pants and a sneaker.

He carries a briefcase in his right hand and a boom box in his left hand.

The illustration refers to the confusion and "double consciousness" W.E.B. DuBois wrote about in "The Souls of Black Folk" and the "social chameleon" Chatmon feels he himself represents.

Shooting will begin in August. "Chameleon" will be shot in South Orange, Chatmon said.

A 1995 Columbia High School graduate, Chatmon studied film at New York University's Tisch School of the Arts.

His thesis project, "3D," a comedic drama — Chatmon calls it "dramedy" — about the lengths people will go to for fiscal success, was an official selection at the 2001 Sundance Film Festival.

The film was shown in 20 other festivals, but Sundance was the most prestigious.

According to the business plan for "Chameleon," Chatmon is "driven by an unrelenting passion to redefine 'black film' under the label of Double 7 Film," where Chatmon is chief executive officer. Chatmon is hoping to raise funds for "Chameleon" with the July 13 event in Maplewood.

Production budgets can climb through the roof, even with short films, so the group needs help, he said.

"We're trying to put the word out in the community because the film is very relevant to what's going on here," said Chatmon.

Even after New York University donations and benefits Chatmon has secured, the cost estimate for "Chameleon" approaches $16,000.

Personal donations, in-kind donations and tax-deductible donations will be acknowledged with correspondence, invitations to screenings and special events, a VHS copy of the completed film and a screen credit and thank-you in the end titles of the film.

THURSDAY, JULY 3, 2003

NEWS RECORD

of Maplewood and South Orange

NEWS RECORD of Maplewood and South Orange

THURSDAY, JULY 17, 2003

Chatmon to shoot film in village

By Shaun McCormack
Staff Writer

Spike Lee is to Brooklyn as Kevin Smith is to Red Bank: filmmakers synonymous with the communities they represent.

Local filmmaker Pete Chatmon has hopes to create that kind of association between himself and the South Orange-Maplewood community.

"I want to create that same kind of thing for this community," he said. Projects he's finished and projects he plans for the future are rooted here.

Chatmon is a product of the South Orange-Maplewood school district, attending grades K-12 in district schools.

He credits Columbia High School

and his filmmaking teacher, George Chase, with his drive to pursue the craft.

"I kind of felt that I could express something there," Chatmon said of Chase's class.

"You only had to do one project every quarter, I was doing eight or 10," he said.

Being exposed to the creation of movies had a huge impact on him. "I'm glad I got that exposure," he said.

Chatmon began seeking out ways to get involved with the industry.

He learned Chase had gone to New York University. He found out some of his favorite filmmakers — Spike Lee, Martin Scorsese and Oliver

Stone — also graduated from New York University.

Chatmon applied to New York University and was accepted into the university's prestigious Tisch School of the Arts. He's worked connections through the school to keep costs down on his upcoming film, "Chameleon."

See VILLAGE, Page 3

Pete Chatmon takes an artist's perspective as he examines the scenery of an upcoming shoot at the South Orange Train Station for his latest film, 'Chameleon.' The Columbia High School alumnus says he owes much to the film classes he took at that school.

Village to help set tone of 'Chameleon'

(Continued from Page 1)

"One hope is that all the local artists here can get involved in one way or another," he said.

Chatmon has already involved Columbia High School graduates Emily Konopinski, Class of 1998, and Joe Mettle, Class of 1995, in his projects. Konopinski and Mettle are working as producers on "Chameleon" and Mettle is the presi-

dent of Chatmon's double 7 film company.

At some point, Chatmon said he'd like to get Columbia High School graduate and Grammy Award winner Lauryn Hill — of Fugees fame — to work on the music for one of his future films.

The immediate plan is to start filming "Chameleon" on Aug. 1, 2 and 3.

There are plans to shoot inside the large office building across from

Carvel on the south side of South Orange Avenue. Chatmon's own home will likely be used for other scenes.

Chatmon expects "Chameleon," when it is finished, to have the look of the film "Eight Mile."

"It's the muted colors. The muted dull blues, grays and greens. I want it to be like that so the viewer focuses more on the story" and less on the look, he said.

NEWS-RECORD

of Maplewood and South Orange

THURSDAY, NOVEMBER 6, 2003   mymaplewood   — PAGE 5

Local filmmaker uses suburban backdrop to examine racial roles

Independent short 'Chameleon' to be screened locally this week

By Shaun McCormack
Staff Writer

What happens when the character you've created to survive in one reality collides with the person you are in another? What do you do when the "blackness" you suppress is unearthed and put on display in white America?

South Orange filmmaker Pete Chatmon will try to answer these questions Saturday during the screening of his short film, "Chameleon," at 1978 Springfield Ave.

"Chameleon" tells the story of protagonist Charlie, a black man struggling to find himself in a white environment.

The movie was filmed Aug. 1, 2 and 3 in and around South Orange.

"We came up with the final outputs to DVD two nights ago," Chatmon said.

The film was edited indie-style with Final Cut Pro on Apple Powerbooks.

These are the kinds of things you have to do on this type of budget.

"We only raised about a quarter of the money we intended to, so we're still in the hole a bit. That was a big trial, just getting everything done for less, getting people to work for zero versus little, but that goes to the strength of everybody involved," Chatmon said.

A lack of cash wasn't the only inconvenience.

"We got kicked out of Mountain

Station because we didn't have a permit. Transit police came and kicked us out. That made it a little tough as well. We got a couple of shots and had to move it to another location," Chatmon said. The crew was unable to get a planned shot of a character boarding the train, but Chatmon said they were able to work around it.

Chameleon has been submitted to about 25 different film festivals, including the Sundance Film Festival.

Chatmon's last film, "3D," was shown at Sundance, "so we're hoping to have some success."

Those interested in seeing "Chameleon" can do so Saturday at 1978 Springfield Ave. The screening starts at 8:30 p.m. Admission is $7.

▶ **Chapter 3 Keyword: FLEXIBILITY**

You may have your own ideas about how things are going to work out, but the universe is likely to be on an entirely different page.

Your flexibility will allow you to stay on the path as your journey evolves!

RESOURCES

- **SELF HELP:**
Worksheet 3 — Writing Your Bio and Origin Story
Carole Kirschner offers a FREE e-book, Telling Your Story In 60 Seconds if you sign up to receive occasional email updates. Visit www.carole-kirschner.com *for more info.*

- **INSPIRATION:**
Podcast:
Let's Shoot! with Pete Chatmon, Episode 03
Dorian Missick on the Journey From Blockbuster Video to ABC's "For Life"
Available on Apple Podcasts, Spotify, and all Podcast Platforms

Recommended Readings:
- ***"Chris Gore Ultimate Film Festival Guide" by Chris Gore***
- ***"Never Eat Alone" by Keith Ferrazi***
- ***"48 Laws Of Power" by Robert Greene***

Leaders of Industry
Social Media allows you a window into the worlds of people doing what you aspire to do. Follow those people, engage with their content, and see what you can learn. Adopt or adapt what works for you.

Make a list of ten leaders and follow them now!

CHAPTER 4

HONESTY

WHO'S GOT $520,000? ANYONE? ANYONE?

Perhaps I ended that last chapter too soon. Before I could really focus on fundraising, the script for *Premium* needed to be polished. I'd seen Spike Jonze's film *Adaptation* (2002) and while they poked great fun at Robert McKee's infamous *Story* seminar, word on the street from many of my filmmaking friends was that this three-day session was not to be missed. Besides, industry heavyweights from Steven Spielberg to William Goldman to Peter Jackson had all raved about the course, so if it helped them, I knew it could help me.

▶ **CHAPTER 4'S KEYWORD is: HONESTY**

In March 2003, I swiped my credit card for almost $500, further compounding my debt and interest, but more importantly, excited to embark upon this journey into deepening my understanding of story. Attendees packed the New York Directors Guild of America Theater on 57th Street for ten-hour sessions across Friday, Saturday, and Sunday. We listened intently as Robert McKee dissected the individual elements of story. Once identified, we'd be able to use those elements more deliberately in exploring the themes of our scripts. The last day included a scene-by-scene analysis of Michael Curtiz' *Casablanca* (1942). It being one of my favorite films, with characters and a story I was extremely well versed in, I was excited to delve into the beat-by-beat breakdown. McKee essentially used this classic as a case study for how to tell a good story, and as you were given insight into the architecture of the script, you were forced to recognize the shortcomings of your own writing. It was an eye-opening Jedi mind trick.

I left the *Story* seminar finally acknowledging something I should have admitted a while back. The script for *Premium* was not up to par. You have to be able to look at your work honestly and say, without a doubt, "I've done my best." If you can't say that, I suggest you go immediately back to the drawing board. I opened my FinalDraft screenwriting software, highlighted over 100 pages of good dialogue clothed in basic plot and hit delete. I chose this flair for the dramatic because I wanted to make the point to myself, "You are starting over." I didn't want to just create a new document with a new file name. I was no longer going to try and satisfy mainstream technique to the detriment of what I really wanted to say.

HOW TO WRITE WHAT YOU KNOW

Writing a screenplay is an incredibly difficult task. No one leaves the symphony saying, "I should write a concerto," yet we all have that friend who thinks because they've seen all the movies and exhausted Hulu's television library, that, well . . . they've got what it takes to write the next great screenplay. And, let's be honest, perhaps "that friend" can be found when you look in the mirror.

Unfortunately, it's only when you get beyond the basic premise and into the depths of your script that you realize how brilliant the best writers have to be in order to deliver a finished product. This is why the solution recommended most often to new writers is to "write what you know."

Screenplay format and structure may not be your strong suit when getting started, but you've lived a life, compiled your own experiences, and mining this "material" for a script removes the challenge of creating an entirely new world. It also gives you a bit of a head start into the marathon of screenplay writing.

The most important step, however, is to study the craft of the screenwriter to learn how to take what you've experienced in life and transform it into something cinematic. Poetic license exists for a reason!

HOW TO // ASSET CHECKPOINT ONE:

The four different assets identified in these checkpoints serve as a guide for you to keep track of the materials I created to raise $520,000. Some items are optional, but they all help to communicate your vision. Clarity is the most important part of building a team, whether it be artistic collaborators or financial investors.

■ **Completed Script [the blueprint]**

Over the following month, I wrote the screenplay that I wanted to read, trusting that it would resonate with others. Next, I created an electronic press kit (EPK) because I didn't anticipate passing the *Premium* script around to potential investors. Without a trailer of any sort, I wanted something visual to enhance my presentation of the project. It had been four years or so since I'd shot *3D* and many of the actors I worked with on that project were beginning to climb and find their feet in the lobby level doors of the industry. My *Chameleon* cast mates were on the rise as well. I shot interviews with the cast and crew from both projects, intercutting footage of them in their Hollywood projects with their performances in my films. Anthony Artis, an NYU colleague and friend, served as EPK cinematographer. This would be our first collaboration, as we were building a creative partnership and trust that would lead to our *Double Down Film Show* podcast.

One of the anchors of the press kit was my vision for "A New Wave in American Cinema." I wanted investors to understand that we were doing more than just making a film — we were starting a movement. I was also making my first effort to brand myself, a keyword I'll address in more detail in Chapter 12. The idea that a film could be "Black" as a genre was something that had always irked me. There are a variety of differing opinions on this, but fundamentally, the idea of genre dictates that certain storytelling devices are going to be honored and expectations are going to be met in any project fitting within said genre. In the Western, we know that there will be a high noon showdown at the end of the film. In the horror film, we know that the promiscuous people will be the first to die. In a romantic comedy, we know that there will be a meet-cute, as well as some outside force that's going to challenge the possibility of the relationship succeeding between the two main characters. If we agree that genre has expectations and rules, what exactly is being said about Black people by creating the all-encompassing filter of "Black film"? Obviously, race and culture affect character, but they do not supersede genre. My goal was to show that the stories of Black characters exist everywhere.

All of the people interviewed in the EPK spoke to my vision and how *Premium* would represent "A New Wave in American Cinema." This project was an opportunity to be involved with the development of a new voice, with a storyteller who would continue to grow, and with someone who represented ideas that you, as an investor, also believed should be out in the marketplace.

HOW TO // ASSET CHECKPOINT TWO:

- Completed Script [the blueprint]
- **(17) Minute EPK [to highlight experience and illustrate promise]**

With the script and EPK in hand, it was time to turn my attention back to finding a producing partner. I scoured every film organization's calendar for any panel or group event to determine if there were folks that I might partner with in seeking independent financing for *Premium*. I passed out my fair share of business cards, but I wouldn't find success until I looked a bit closer to home on NYU's Job Bulletin. This resource, run through the Alumni Affairs office, was where the industry posted opportunities for recent graduates, and fellow students posted about projects they were looking to partner on, create, produce, etc.

The post that stood out to me was from a recent graduate named Kevin Frakes. He had worked with some mutual friends, including Al Thompson, who had been in my NYU thesis film and spoke highly of him. I immediately got the sense that he was a smart, persistent go-getter with whom I'd be able to vibe. As we talked over Thai food at Lemongrass Grill on University Place, it was evident that we'd be able to complement each other's skill sets as we attacked the raising of funds for *Premium*. Kevin was completing an MBA at Yale's School of Management, with a specific focus on film financing slates, which made him a bit of a unicorn as far as understanding both the creative and business sides of what we were embarking upon. It's been no surprise to watch as he's produced indie films as well as the *John Wick* franchise in the years since. With our burgeoning partnership in place, he brought on a producer whom he had worked with, Lynn Appelle, who crafted our first budget to produce the film.

I cannot remember the specifics, but I believe that first budget was between $1.5 and $1.75 million. You always start by throwing everything *and* the kitchen sink at the wall, hoping that you secure this "best case" scenario financing, knowing you can apply a scalpel to every line item that exists on your next draft. For the next year or so, we approached different funding opportunities, from independent production companies to high net-worth individuals with an interest in the entertainment industry. After more than a dozen dead ends, and with a reduced budget of $750,000, Kevin introduced me to Sriram Das, a classmate at Yale, who was interested in being an executive producer and has continued to produce films under his Das Films banner. With this piece of the puzzle in place, we decided to formalize our partnership and create an LLC for the production of *Premium*.

I had maintained a relationship with Lynn Auerbach at the Sundance Institute and decided to reach out again for her advice and insight.

After one more review of the script, which she felt was the strongest draft to date, she made the suggestion that the target budget for most first-time filmmakers should be $500,000. Kevin and I reluctantly agreed to back our budget into that number, and we called Lynn Appelle to make yet another slice and dice pass on our budget. As we cut costs in more than half from our original number, the goal was to put it all on screen, in service of the story. Robert McKee would have been proud.

With our new and improved final budget in place of $520,000 (we had a few legal and casting fees to add), and Sriram onboard as an executive producer with a $100,000 investment, Kevin, Lynn, and myself were confident we could step out into the world and begin to raise the money.

HOW TO RAISE FUNDS

A lot of filmmakers consider fundraising a scavenger hunt in finding money and tapping shoulders in direct pursuit of a check. I've come to find, however, that fundraising should be considered as an awareness campaign.

How many ways can you make it possible for your team to have organic outreach with as many individuals and communities as possible?

A crowdfunding campaign is a great example. Your real goal, in my opinion, is getting as many people as possible to share the link to your campaign. Then, by virtue of getting the word out to as many people as possible, you end up having a greater cross-section of potential investors, supporters or contributors for your project. Fundraising for an independent film in 2004 and 2005 was no different than what crowdfunding would become over the next decade and a half.

We decided to break the budget down into units and use those units as the pieces through which an investor could participate in the film. With Sriram on board, we had identified the $100,000 investment as the trigger for executive producer credit. We felt comfortable with this number because it would allow, at most, five executive producers, ensuring the credit would retain its value and prevent the film from being overburdened by producers. If that was going to be our number on the high end, we had to figure out what our entry point would be. Our instinct was to make the minimum unit available for purchase at $5,000 — larger than anything that I could pay — but my hunch was that someone interested in supporting the film might find the $5K amount digestible, even if outside of their normal investment portfolio.

With 104 units available for the entire film, our next step was to determine how we'd define involvement on all of the other levels. Kevin had a great idea, which was to make the purchase of one to ten units ($5,000 to $50,000) receive a "Founding Producer" credit. Building upon that, we determined that eleven to nineteen units ($55,000 to $95,000) would receive an "Associate Producer" credit. Lastly, at the top, we had the executive producer credit at twenty or more units ($100,000 or more).

HOW TO IDENTIFY INVESTORS

When it comes to fundraising, it's important to consider your investor demographics. I had determined that there were probably four different types of people that would potentially invest in a film written and directed by me. In no particular order, those people were:

Bucket 1: parents of friends or local folks who knew me from a young age, and would be excited by the opportunity to help propel me toward this dream that they knew I had been focused on since 1993. . . .

Bucket 2: folks who were interested in telling a story about a struggling Black actor trying to build his career, while maintaining integrity in an industry that often is involved with stereotypical portrayals. . . .

Bucket 3: people with an affinity toward love stories who wanted to be involved with a film that spoke to this idea of "the love before the love" or the most important person that you don't end up with. . . .

Bucket 4: folks with an appetite for risk who wanted to have something more unique and sexy to talk about on the golf course or in the helicopter or in the boardroom, as they compared what they did with their disposable income with similarly wealthy friends. . . .

I prepared a pitch designed to speak to each of those different buckets at the drop of a dime. My job became researching every potential investor via the internet or any mutual contacts who might have been able to give me information. Once we met in-person, I'd make the best judgment call possible as to which of the four buckets would be most interesting to them, and excite them to want to hear more about *Premium* to potentially invest.

Another component that's important to mention in this awareness campaign is that not every investor will necessarily be a financial investor. There will be investors who are interested in you and the project, but unable or unwilling to put their money toward the opportunity. Their investment will be putting their time and their name behind helping connect you to those who can invest directly in the project. Time and time again, as we moved toward our fundraising goal, I was surprised by the people who offered their network to me in an effort to help spread the word and raise money. I'm talking about people inviting friends to their homes and giving me the floor to present. I'm talking about people inviting potential investors out to dinner and footing the bill for these meals. It was really heartwarming to build a community around this campaign of financing "A New Wave in American Cinema."

HOW TO // ASSET CHECKPOINT THREE:

- Completed Script [the blueprint]
- (17) Minute EPK [to highlight experience and illustrate promise]
- **$520,000 Business Plan and Subscription Agreement [prepared by our production counsel, the Business Plan outlined how the film would get to market and how investors would see any return on investment while the subscription agreement was the document that any investor would sign to confirm their participation in the project]**

This next decision might seem counterintuitive, but I decided to have a party. There was only so much shoulder tapping that could happen locally. And if I was going to build awareness, I figured a party was well within my wheelhouse and something that I could accomplish. To make it unique and keep it on brand, I knew that it couldn't just be any regular old event — it would need to be something that was based around the film itself. And, with my birthday coming up, I figured that'd be the best date to take advantage of, as folks always like to come out and celebrate with you on your special day. I circled Saturday, June 5, 2004 as the target date, and sent an email blast out to

over 2,000 people with a subject line asking "Is 6 Weeks Enough Time To Get Ready For The Premium Party?" It had to be, because I had just written the event in stone.

"The *Premium* Party" was designed to bring as many people from all of my various communities together as possible. The recent NYU graduates . . . the folks who liked to hit the Manhattan bar and lounge scene on weekends . . . and the friends who didn't really do either, but might come say a toast for my 27th birthday. It was more or less like any other party, but at midnight, we were going to show a film. We showed the EPK, which may have been a bit of false advertising for a "film," but I was willing to take whatever incoming fire might come over that bit of wordplay. I had to sell myself. The pricing of the event was $10 before midnight and $15 after, incentivizing people to get there in time to see the EPK. Having learned a little bit about marketing, branding and presentation, I reached out and connected with Eye-5 Marketing, a company that provided hostesses (mostly models and actresses) to work the event, ensuring that the party would have a "grown and sexy" vibe.

The "*Premium* Party" performed overwhelmingly well. I had risked a bit of money in paying for the hostesses and agreeing to an aggressive bar guarantee in order to get the venue for free, but at this point, I was willing to roll the dice on our project on any strategy that would amplify our awareness campaign. 400 people attended our event, which was an affirmation that we could throw a good party and people wanted to hang with us. It was also a bit of a challenge — can we do this again? And, if we do it the right way, how much more successful might we make it?

I looked at the calendar and picked a date four weeks out from the party we'd just wrapped, knowing I'd need to make a "film film" this time around. With the EPK, they'd been introduced to the project and my team, both in front of and behind the camera, but I wanted people to feel what we had in store with the finished product. I also wanted to have something that would be useful down the line for conversations with potential investors.

I wrote a script that allowed Dorian Missick to go through all of the varying conflicts that his character, "Cool," faced in the script for *Premium*.

Confessions of Cool was a seven-minute short film shot on a white cyclorama stage, which is basically infinite white space with curved walls that don't read on camera. The audience learned that he's an actor. That he's working at his mother's boyfriend's gas station. That he is adrift in both life and love. They also learned the fatal flaw that he'll have to conquer if he is to move into a space of growth by the conclusion of the film. I tapped Anthony Artis on the shoulder again (he'd done a great job shooting the EPK) and he was down to shoot *Confessions of Cool* during a four-hour window I had booked at a New York City studio. I'd be lying if I said spending more money I didn't really have upfront didn't concern me, but again, it felt like a calculated risk after the turnout at the first party.

Any sequel should be an improvement, so I also knew we'd need to elevate the marketability of the event. I reached out to another friend and rising talent, Anthony Mackie, who was doing promotion for Spike Lee's new feature, *She Hate Me*, in which he starred alongside Kerry Washington. I asked Mackie if he'd be open to having us promote the film at the *Premium* party. At midnight, we would show the trailer, which he could introduce, immediately followed by the premiere of *Confessions of Cool*. Once he agreed, he got the artwork to us, and Emily Konopinski called on a local favor to have a flyer created for the event.

The *Premium* Party: Take II was another success. The response to *Confessions of Cool* was the best I'd ever had to anything that I'd written and directed. I was energized, excited, and had renewed confidence that we could meet our goal — somehow. We also had, in my opinion, all of the necessary assets to communicate with investors and supporters alike.

HOW TO // ASSET CHECKPOINT FOUR:

- Completed Script [the blueprint]
- (17) Minute EPK [to highlight experience and illustrate promise]
- $520,000 Business Plan and Subscription Agreement [prepared by our production counsel, the BP outlined how the film would get to market and how investors would see any return on investment while the subscription agreement was the document that any investor would sign to confirm their participation in the project]
- **Confessions of Cool, seven minute short film [introduced viewers to the world of *Premium* and the themes being explored in the film]**

Our awareness was at a higher level than it had ever been. We were continuing to run programs and events through the South Orange-Maplewood School District, ensuring that folks remained aware of us after *Chameleon*. Our hope was that when prospective people reached out and tapped a shoulder to learn more about *Premium*, or me as a filmmaker, they would only need to make one or two strategic phone calls before finding someone who could vouch for me. They would find

someone who hung out in New York nightlife and could say, "I went to this party and I saw what that film was about, and it was great." Or they might know another filmmaker who would say, "I know Pete from the independent film community," or they might find someone who went to NYU, and they could offer, "Oh, I know him from NYU."

The next big event I planned was "The *Premium* Presentation" on November 11, 2004. With the awareness campaign rolling, I wanted to do a formal presentation to specifically place us in front of as many potential investors as possible. We secured Goldcrest Postproduction's screening room/event space in New York City's Meatpacking District. The venue sat fifty-five people, so Kevin, Lynn, Emily, and I designed a guest list of folks who we felt had the means to purchase a $5,000 unit in the film. That list was rather short, maybe ten or twelve people, so I called on several friends to be "plants" to fill out the room, ensuring potential investors would be surrounded by people who would speak highly of me and the project.

Kevin and I set a fundraising closing date of March 31, 2005. Investors at our presentation and everyone we'd meet moving forward would have until this date to write their check. Along the way, we'd secure "commitments" for whatever unit amounts they wanted to purchase of the available $5,000 units, allowing us to illustrate fundraising momentum before the closing date.

The other thing that Kevin and I did to enhance our ability to succeed was identify a fundraising green light mark for *Premium*. This was the point at which we would release the funds and move into pre-production. Our green light number was $380,000 of the $520,000 budget (roughly 73% of total funding needed). All of the committed investors signed documents acknowledging their understanding of this threshold.

The "*Premium* Presentation" went well. We showed the EPK, followed by *Confessions of Cool*. We worked as a team, with Kevin speaking to the investment opportunity and the numbers, while I focused on the creative aspects of the film. That was very important, as potential investors are not going to feel secure if one person is talking about everything. If you were to be investing in a soft drink, you don't want to hear about the formula for the drink, the bottling for the drink, the packaging for the drink, the marketing for the drink, and the distribution of the drink from one person. Ideally, you want to hear from five different experts dedicated to successfully overseeing each aspect of the assembly line.

We walked out of the "*Premium* Presentation" with two commitments, somewhere between $15,000 and $20,000, as well as some folks interested enough to say "Hey, keep me posted." That was a solid victory in my book, and now the focus became moving forward with these initial logs on the fire to see if we could set the project ablaze.

The presentation also yielded my first real non-monetary investor. My buddy Wayne Bryant, who'd been aware of what I was doing with *Premium* for many years, responded to the elements of our pitch and energy in the room in ways that our periodic phone calls could never communicate. Excited by our "New Wave in American Cinema," Wayne introduced me to his friend Tom Hopkins, and we had a very expensive sushi dinner in the Meatpacking District that Wayne graciously paid for. Over the course of that meal, Tom and I clicked — he already had interest in producing — and we made a date to connect again with his producing partner, Tony, and of course, my producing partner, Kevin.

Tony, Kevin, Tom, and I would have one of the more expensive dinners I've ever paid for at Spice Market, also in the Meatpacking District. You gotta fake it till you make it, and let them order the expensive dish without batting an eye. Kevin offered them comfort in seeing that we were a good team, and I'm sure the pedigree of his Yale School of Management MBA didn't hurt. Over dinner and endless rounds of drinks, we presented them with our roadmap to making *Premium*.

Any negotiation is a dance, as people begin to reveal their actual interests. Understanding the breakdown of our $5,000 units and accompanying credit, Tom and Tony were clear that they wanted to have a production company credit, in addition to any executive producer credit. Kevin and I left the dinner and brainstormed a way that we might satisfy that request, while maintaining the integrity of our business plan. After so many "noes" and the ever-shrinking budget, we had failed to imagine a scenario where an independent production company would want to be involved in our little indie film.

We decided that a production company credit would be worth a $200,000 investment. Why? Because a single executive producer credit was $100,000. And, if the two of them could double that, bringing in about 40% of the budget, then it seemed fair that their production company be acknowledged for that value.

We also decided that however they wanted to arrive at a $200,000 investment would be fine with us, whether that meant splitting the investment between the two of them, or bringing in additional investors to reach the $200,000 total. In order to incentivize that, we offered points from our producers' backend, so the more investors that they brought in toward the $200,000, the more backend participation they would receive. Our return on investment was already structured to be very advantageous to investors because we were not in this to make money — we just wanted to make a film and introduce ourselves to the industry. This offering was another good faith example of the spirit of the project, while being designed to inspire action by investors. A dance indeed.

I'd like to briefly return to the keyword of this chapter — honesty. I remember being asked by an investor, "What's the worst that could happen?" After considering how honest I would be, I decided to "Keep it 100" and responded by telling him, "The worst thing that can happen is you have a DVD that sits on your shelf, that no one's seen but you and the people you love, but it will be connected to a project that you were excited to be involved with, a voice that you wanted to help get out to the world, and an opportunity for you to be a factor in how people converse about issues close to you."

He invested $30,000.

When our closing date of March 31, 2005 arrived, we had commitments totaling $310,000, leaving us $70,000 short of our green light mark. We'd come too far to watch this thing fall apart. Kevin, Lynn, and I debated what we could do to comfort our investors (with honesty) in our ability to still move forward into pre-production without sacrificing our vision. Our answer was to waive each of our salaries, leaving a $25,000 shortfall. We identified line items within each department that we could slash, prioritizing the principle of putting

the money on screen, and ultimately arrived at a production budget that could be achieved for $310K.

I sent an email to each committed investor asking for their written approval to move forward. Surprisingly, everyone replied, "Yes," in full agreement with our strategy. On April 4, 2005, we green lit *Premium* and began spending the re-allocated $310K, eyeing a start date of June 5, 2005.

I was now a feature film Director.

▶ **CHAPTER 4 KEYWORD: HONESTY**

Along your journey, people will feed off of your positivity. It's your job to maintain excitement about the project and the path ahead. That's why you're the leader. The Director.

Nevertheless, there will likely come a time when you'll have to manage expectations and share hard truths with your team, partners, investors, or audience. Do not run away from these moments.

The sun won't always be shining, and you will be respected for what you do on the rainy days.

RESOURCES

- *SELF HELP:*
Worksheet 4 — What's The Worst That Could Happen? (Page tbd)

- *INSPIRATION:*
Podcast
Let's Shoot! with Pete Chatmon, Episode 07
Robia Rashid and Mary Rohlich on That One Time They Were On Opposite Sides of a Creative Decision
Available on Apple Podcasts, Spotify, and all Podcast Platforms

Your Presence is Requested For An Evening With
Pete Chatmon and Double 7 Film.
Please Join Us For Cocktails & Conversation and
Find Out More About the Cinematic Revolution Redefining the Film Industry.

The **PREMIUM** Presentation
Including a Screening of Pete Chatmon's Latest Film
CONFESSIONS OF COOL
Begins at 8pm

Cocktails & Hors'douvres Will Be Served

Wednesday, November 10, 2004
7 - 10pm

Goldcrest Screening Room
799 Washington Street
between Horatio and Gansevoort Streets
NYC

RSVP by November 1, 2004
212.492.5148
or
rsvp@double7inc.com

For Additional Inquiries Please Contact Double 7 Film
info@double7inc.com OR 212.492.5148

The PREMIUM Presentation ...
A New Wave in American Cinema

7 - 8 PM
THE TRAILER

Cocktails (provided by Dewar's)
Hors'douvres (provided by Celebrated Foods)

8 PM
THE MAIN ATTRACTION

> An Introduction by Acclaimed Screenwriter & Playwright Richard Wesley
  - Chair of the Department of Dramatic Writing at New York University
  - Writer : "Uptown Saturday Night", "Let's Do It Again"

>> Double 7 Film: The Movement – 15 Minutes

>>> CONFESSIONS OF COOL
Written, Produced, & Directed by Pete Chatmon – 6 Minutes

>>>> PREMIUM : Invest in the Future of American Cinema

Upon Conclusion
THE OUT-TAKES

Conversation
Gift Bags (provided by The Robert Graham Collection & New York Moves Magazine)

Brought to you by Double 7 Film & GamePlan Marketing

www.double7inc.com   www.dewars.com   www.gameplan-nyc.com

Premium Electronic Press Kit — https://vimeo.com/531379905
Password: EPK

Confessions of Cool — https://vimeo.com/4577617
Written, produced and directed by Pete Chatmon. Starring Dorian Missick.

WORKSHEET 4:
WHAT'S THE WORST THAT COULD HAPPEN?

The keyword for Chapter 4 is "honesty." For the purposes of this worksheet, I want you to think about the hard truths that many questions will require of you as you navigate your career.

You can tell lies in almost every aspect of your life (not recommended!), but to be a successful Director you are responsible for the truth. You'll never get out the gates if you can't identify the truth of a story, scene, or performance, as well as how that truth trickles down into the building blocks of directing.

So, how can you prepare yourself for the hundreds (maybe thousands) of questions you will answer over the course of a project? Ask yourself:

WHAT'S THE WORST THAT COULD HAPPEN (WTWTCH)?

WTWTCH if I don't fully prepare my blocking and coverage? I will not make my day, and the production will potentially lose hundreds of thousands of dollars. Production will not be happy, and I will lower my chances of being invited back to direct again. Plus, the word of my lack of preparation will get around town.

WTWTCH if I don't break down the script and prepare thoughtful, motivated directorial notes for each actor in every scene? I will be exposed as being unprepared and perhaps lose the faith of the talent, making it very difficult to get nuanced performances. And guess what? The talent on one show or film knows all the other talent you may work with in the industry.

WTWTCH if I don't prepare for this meeting? I will miss an opportunity to build rapport and develop a relationship in a town where who you know is everything.

You probably noticed that each scenario ends with the warning of word getting back around town. That's because reputation is everything, and word travels fast in our creative communities.

Whether you're directing/prepping a project or trying to get hired for a directing job, always consider WTWTCH in every scenario and I guarantee, your preparation will be more thorough and your results more exceptional.

PREMIUM —
THE MAKING OF
MY FIRST FEATURE FILM

In the first week of April 2005, I walked into Lou LaVolpe's office at NYU to request time off to shoot *Premium*. I knew that I could navigate most of the pre-production process while sitting behind my NYU desk, but I would need ten weeks off for the peak of prep, four weeks of production, and at least part of the picture edit. Music, sound design, and the other final steps could be accomplished while working my full-time gig.

▶ **CHAPTER 5's KEYWORD is: SACRIFICE**

Since I'd started the job in 2002, I'd proven myself to be a dependable employee. Lou and I had bonded over our early morning arrivals to work, which may have also played a factor in him going to bat for me. Beyond that, he was a filmmaker too, and I think excited to see me move a step closer toward the dream all filmmakers share.

Lou's blessing required the sign-off from my immediate boss, Christina DeHaven. I bet you can see where this is going. Do you think the producer of my NYU thesis and friend since freshman year was going to say "No?" Lou and Christina got the ultimate green light for my sabbatical from the area head, Rosanne Limoncelli, relaying to her that they would be able to get through the summer's lighter workload without much impact due to my absence. I had also committed to doing everything possible to set up whoever might be assisting with the workflow as to how to do my job.

Pre-production was an interesting juggle of creative responsibilities. I switched my Writer's cap for a Director's beret and began to think about how I would take *Premium* from script to screen. The blueprint is definitely your screenplay, but there are many details left to be determined, once the focus turns strictly into performance and visual realization of the text.

We were also beginning the process of crewing up. This was where Lynn Appelle really stepped in, as Kevin and I, both new to feature film production, were unfamiliar with the exact timelines for hiring a DP, production designer, costume designer, and everyone else to complete the department heads and remaining crew. We wanted the fewest number of paid weeks of work, while ensuring there'd be adequate time to prepare.

HOW TO PREPARE FOR A FEATURE VS. A SHORT FILM

Some may say that directing a feature film is nothing more than directing multiple short films at once. And, if you would have asked me in 2005, before I directed my debut feature *Premium*, I would have said the same. Once production commenced, however, I quickly came to disagree with this sentiment.

Directing a feature film requires much more stamina than you might anticipate. You are likely to be tracking a storyline over a longer period of time than you have in your short films. This will affect every department of production — wardrobe (multiple changes, and multiple outfits if you have stunts), production design (numerous locations that must also tell a story), hair and makeup (continuity over a longer period of time and multiple events), visual effects (unavoidable with today's workflow), and let's not forget camera (stylistic motifs that work in concert with the story as it develops) — as well as all of your other areas of craft.

You will be directing around the clock, and it will feel like the film you've been dying to make is now, in turn, intent on consuming your entire world. You will wake up super early every day, immediately think about how you will get through this day of production, prep the next day's work after you wrap and until you fall asleep, and deal with all of the unforeseen challenges that, in many cases, will blow your mind. Your diet will suffer and your brain will be tapped out. You will also need to drink water. Plenty of water.

So, how do you prepare?

You will treat prep like a precious jewel and plot out every nook and cranny of your film, all the while knowing you'll need to save space, and allow for the creative epiphanies that occur on set when collaborating with talented artists. You will not think that because you've made a short film, you can just level up and plow through the process. You will think about all the potential questions that might arise from your cast and crew along the way, finding answers for things you hadn't considered.

And if you can, you'll ask as many other feature films Directors as possible for advice!

The final piece we were simultaneously navigating was the casting process, as we needed to round out the talent that would surround Dorian Missick's "Cool." Apple was a Thai restaurant, around the corner from my NYU job at 721 Broadway, where I had at least a dozen actor meetings, during my lunch break, set up by our casting director, Sig De Miguel.

On a production of this scope and budget, with a first-time feature Director at the helm, you're unlikely to get an actor with experience to come in and audition in the traditional sense. They've done more work than you and have prior experience that you can view to determine if you think they are a fit for your project. I redefined my idea of an audition and found these meetings to be an opportunity for me to determine whether or not we vibed, and whether or not I could see myself having an opportunity to elevate the script with them. Independent projects are a house of cards that can easily collapse, making it very important that you have people on board who don't become a virus to the morale of your cast and crew. One person complaining about craft service, or the amount of money they're not getting paid, or the inexperience of the crew can lead to a mutiny.

In the beginning years of the project, we had Kerry Washington committed to be in the film, but scheduling became an issue as time moved on, opening the role of "Charlie" back up to casting. I'd had my eye on Zoe Saldana after seeing her work in *Drumline* and was a huge fan, so I immediately told Sig that I really wanted to try and get her in *Premium*.

One of the many benefits of casting directors is that they know what's going on behind the scenes with talent, and in our case, how an actor views working on independent films. Sig knew that Zoe had worked with Hill Harper on another indie, Jordan Walker-Pearlman's *Constellation* (2005), and had a great experience, so we figured they might be excited about the opportunity to play an engaged couple in *Premium*. From my point of view, this would potentially complement what happened in the script, as Zoe and Hill would arrive as somewhat of a unit, leaving Dorian as an outsider to their pre-existing relationship. Perhaps some of that dynamic would find its way into the DNA of the production and ultimately the portrayals of the characters.

The rest of the cast came together via direct offers to talent, a few of whom I'd had lunches with at Apple. Sig had done a wonderful job of directing us toward our ultimate cast selections, which included Tonya Pinkins, Eva Marcille, Sean Nelson, Novella Nelson, Keith Nobbs, Frankie Faison and Bill Sadler. An amazing cast!

On Sunday, June 5, 2005, we started principal photography. We were scheduled for a twenty-two-day shoot with two six-day weeks, followed by two five-day weeks. Our hope was that by starting aggressively then transitioning to a more traditional schedule, we'd be able to pound through the 105 pages we had to capture, while maintaining morale and not overworking the crew.

During the shoot, I continued a practice I'd started in prep, which was providing weekly updates to all of our investors. They deserved to be aware of what was going on with their money and with the film, especially since they had approved the project to move forward beyond the initial green light level. I wanted them to feel confident and be aware that we were not going to sacrifice quality or execution. The unexpected upside of the special green light was that now we were able to bring potential investors to set, presenting them with a much easier decision to make than merely looking at the text of a business plan. They could watch a funny, layered dinner scene with Dorian, Zoe, and Hill being shot and make an investment with a clear vision of what they were buying.

Our biggest assistance in this effort was Craig Woolridge. I met Craig through my South Orange and Maplewood community, where he'd been aware of my filmmaking efforts through our local events and projects, starting with *Chameleon*.

Craig was interested in producing, and with our budget gap needing to be closed, Kevin, Craig, and I agreed upon a scenario where if he could secure $40,000 toward the film, he would receive an associate producer credit. The strategy we'd landed on with our other executive producers was put into play again. Craig quickly got to work and made it happen. Kevin secured the final funding through Rob Barnum, Josh

Newman, and Cyan Pictures, ensuring that we were fully capitalized and able to breathe a little easier as we moved toward the finish line.

Premium was shot on Super 16mm film, demanding a specificity and efficiency from our cast and crew that you don't necessarily require these days when shooting HD video. Each Kodak roll of 400 feet was expensive to purchase, as well as develop, while only providing eleven minutes of footage. We would live or die by our three to one shooting ratio (every shot had been allocated a maximum of three takes in order to fall within our budget for film stock).

When we were at our best, it was beautiful to watch these super talented actors bring my words to life, many of whom I'd watched on TV and film for years. It was amazing to witness the dedicated crew turn an empty, white walled apartment into Tonya Pinkins' character's home — fully wallpapered, furnished, and designed to communicate decades of life. Then, after shooting out the location, the art department struck the entire set and re-painted it white, all in time for a new tenant to move in just twenty-four hours after we'd wrapped. We stole shots on New Jersey transit trains, raced Mother Nature to accomplish night shoots with more pages than logic might have said were possible, and somehow navigated the tensions that can arise between people working closely together under stressful conditions and very little money.

When times were challenging and we were hanging by a thread, struggling to complete a scene or secure a same-day location in the midst of shooting, it felt like my entire world would collapse, and my dream of being a feature film Director might disintegrate before my eyes.

But we powered through. I learned that a short film and a feature film are two entirely different enterprises. The mental and physical stamina required to keep the creative, logistic, and psychological trains on the track for a larger crew, across an extended timeline, is incredibly taxing. But diving in head first is the only way to take a step toward your creative passions. To see if you will sink or swim. To discover that failure is not an option.

When our twenty-two-day shoot concluded, I breathed a sigh of relief, but it was short lived. The moment our assistant director Brian Bentham yelled, "That's a wrap," meant I'd merely be changing the location of my job. The next day, instead of reporting to set, I'd be heading to the Harlem apartment of my talented editor, K.A. Miille. We'd spend the next four weeks editing, editing, and re-editing — doing everything possible to craft the best film we could — polishing up things that may not have been captured so well during production, and finding solutions for the mistakes of a first-time feature Director. Our collaboration was great, and I returned to work with K.A. nine years later, when I was looking for an editor for my short film *BlackCard*.

Once we locked picture on *Premium,* I sent another update to our investors, letting them know where we stood and what remained to be done. Almost immediately after sending this email, I was contacted by one of our producers, Steve White. He wanted to discuss a project.

Steve arrived at Cafe Pick Me Up on the Lower East Side — the first place we had met to discuss a potential investment in *Premium* — with a gym bag of interview tapes of soldiers from the 761st "Black Panther" Tank Battalion. These African-American men were WWII veterans who, after returning to the harsh realities of Jim Crow America, put their dollars together to hold a reunion every year since 1948. Each reunion was an opportunity for them to find comfort and solace in their brotherhood, especially since many of these men did not share their traumatic experiences with their families.

After a 2002 *New York Times* article about the dwindling ranks of the battalion no longer being able to afford future reunions, Steve generously stepped in to support them, and also began capturing their experiences on tape. When I came knocking on his door in 2005 looking for *Premium* investors, Steve was searching for a Director to make this documentary. What I simply envisioned as financial support for *Premium* was actually an extended audition for the job.

I took the tapes home and watched all thirty hours of footage over the weekend. That Monday, I immediately reached out to Steve and said,

"I'm in. I would love to be involved with this. Please let me know what you need me to do." He tasked me with putting together a budget, so I reached out to . . . drumroll . . . Christina DeHaven, and over the next few weeks, we crafted a budget to make a feature documentary. She made it possible for me to have a job to return to after directing my first feature, and I returned the favor with a new feature film for her to produce.

As my next feature was slowly coming together, post-production on *Premium* was coming to a conclusion. We still needed to find a distributor, but I was elated that a project I'd begun six years prior, in May of 1999, was inching closer to completion.

The once insurmountable hurdle of raising the money and producing a feature film had been cleared, now we just had to make sure we got this thing out to the world, and started making some money back for our thirty-five investors.

▶ CHAPTER 5 KEYWORD: SACRIFICE

You will be forced to make a myriad of choices as a Director that your friends and family may not understand. Balancing that full-time job (outside of your dream profession), as well as the responsibilities that come with maintaining relationships, will require you to make choices as to how you allot your twenty-four hours each day.

Sacrifice will be required, but it pays off over time. Keep your eyes on the prize.

RESOURCES

■ *SELF HELP:*
Worksheet 5 — Scheduling Your Day for Optimal Success
(Page tbd)

■ *INSPIRATION:*
Podcast
Let's Shoot! with Pete Chatmon, Episode 12
Paula Huidobro on Learning How To See and Pay Attention
To The World
Available on Apple Podcasts, Spotify, and all Podcast Platforms

The Archive
Premium — https://itunes.apple.com/us/movie/premium/
id1051984569
Written, produced, and directed by Pete Chatmon. Starring Dorian
Missick, Zoe Saldana, Hill Harper, Tonya Pinkins, Eva Marcille,
Sean Nelason, Novella Nelson, Keith Nobbs, Frankie Faisin, Wil-
liam Sadler

IN THE MIX

Live on the set of "Premium." Frankie Faison, Tonya Pinkins, Dorian Missick Our outstanding Crew! Celeste Gregoire & Pete Chatmon Zoë Saldaña & Pete Chatmon Lynn Appelle, Kevin Frakes & Sabrina Tubio-Cid Frankie Faison and Daughter, Emily Konopinski & Pete Chatmon Pete Chatmon watches the scene unfold Greg Staley & Pete Chatmon Keith Nobbs, Pete Chatmon & Dorian Missick The set of Phil's Fill Up Frankie Faison as "Phil"

DOUBLE 7 FILM PO Box 1003 South Orange, New Jersey 07079 e info@double7inc.com www.double7inc.com

DESIGNED BY TRACEY BEY OF TRACE PAPER DESIGN

WORKSHEET 5:
SCHEDULING YOUR DAY FOR OPTIMAL SUCCESS

Directors often tell me there's not enough time in the day to accomplish everything on their list, and to a degree, this is true. My approach, however, is to scale back what you need to accomplish into manageable, incremental units.

For example, when I get a script for an episode of television, I look at how many prep days I have remaining until my production meeting, divide the number of scenes in the episode into the number of remaining days, and then block and design coverage for x-amount of scenes per day. That allows me the bandwidth to have all the other meetings that occur during prep, watch cuts, read prior episodes, etc. — without feeling overwhelmed.

Strategic time management can open up creative opportunities that you may never have imagined. Below, I've provided my daily scheduling template, allowing room for you to sketch out your own day. Try breaking things down into the following seven units and see what you can accomplish!

Early Mornings: I wake up, work out, drink coffee, and devote a fresh mind to whatever project is of the highest priority. The clarity of a well-rested mind should be exploited!

_____

8 a.m.: Emails. I reply to what's time sensitive, read the trades, and nurture my network.

_____

10 a.m.: I return to any to-do items from my early morning priority project. Make more progress!

---

12 p.m.: I cleanse my mind with something different. If I'm writing . . . I'll watch something. If I'm directing . . . I'll read a book. You get the point. Pivot to something new to energize your creativity.

---

2 p.m.: I'll either return to my priority project or work on something in development. This might mean writing an outline for a new script, sketching new ideas, or refining a pitch deck.

---

4 p.m.: Emails! I don't ignore my accounts during the day, but I wait until now to reply, if I can.

Evenings: Devote your time accordingly, but choose wisely. Always move the needle forward.

THE DIRECTOR'S CUT: ACT I

CURIOSITY.
DISCIPLINE.
FLEXIBILITY.
HONESTY.
SACRIFICE.

I needed to harness and master the principles of these keywords in order to navigate *The Set-Up* portion of my journey. Specifically, over a thirteen-year period (1993–2005) en route to achieving my dream of directing a feature film:

Curiosity helped me discover filmmaking. . ..

Discipline strengthened my development during the early years of learning and practice, allowing me to acquire additional skillsets I hadn't expected to need as a Director. . ..

Flexibility allowed me to deal with the inevitable curveballs and challenges that were presented. . ..

Honesty got me over the hump when tough conversations were presented. . .,

Sacrifice held everything together.

Refer back to Chapters 1-5 in Act I for specific *How-To, Self-Help,* and *Inspirational* tools to propel you along your path as a Director.

1977-2005

ACT I: THE SET-UP

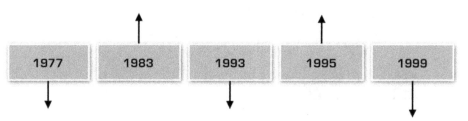

- Pete and family move to New Jersey from Brooklyn
- Pete discovers what it means to be Black in the suburbs

- Pete graduates from Columbia High School with an acceptance for NYU's Tisch School of the Arts Film Department

| 1977 | 1983 | 1993 | 1995 | 1999 |

- Pete is born in NYC, an empty canvas, ready to find his calling

- Pete watches Spike Lee's *Do the Right Thing* and connects with cinema stronger than anything thus far on his brief journey
- Pete picks up a Super 8mm camera in George Chase's filmmaking class

- Pete Graduates NYU with his tesis film, *3D*, starring Kerry Washington
- Pete begins writing *Premium*, his debut feature film

The Director's Cut

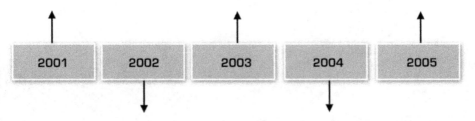

- *3D* is an official selection of the 2001 Sundance Film Festival

- Pete directs the short film, *Chameleon*, raising his profile with an interview in NJ's *Star Ledger*

- Pete shoots *Premium*, starring Dorian Missick, Zoe Saldana, Hill Harper, Frankie Faison, Tonya Pinkins, and Bill Sadler
- They prepare to run the film festival circuit in pursuit of distribution

2001   2002   2003   2004   2005

- Pete travels to Hollywood for the first time for producer meetings connected to his feature script, *Premium*
- Pete meets Kenya Barris
- Pete starts his administrative position at NYU as Assistant Production Coordinator in the film department

- Pete teams with Kevin Frakes and raises $520,000 from 35 investors to shoot *Premium*
- Investments range from $5,000 – $100,000

ACT II:
THE CONFRONTATION

[2006-2014]

REPUTATION

BILLS TO PAY: 12 YEARS OF EMPLOYMENT AT NYU

My first assignment in the fall of 1996 in my Sight and Sound: Film class was to construct a sequence of parallel action. Parallel action is an effect created when two or more actions in two or more different locations are presented by cross cutting between them. This alternation between actions proposes to the viewer that these events are taking place at the same time.

▶ CHAPTER 6'S KEYWORD is: REPUTATION

Well, from Summer 2005 until Summer 2015, I was on a parallel action, collision course of my own, that consisted of three trains running on three separate tracks:

- *The Pete Has to Get Paid Train* (I'd only paid myself $15,000 over six years to write, produce, and direct *Premium*. . . .)
- *The Pete Wants to Make Art Train* (I wanted to continue telling unique stories spotlighting the Black experience. . . .)
- *The Pete Will Have to Change the Way He Views the World Train* (I'd have to accept that the above two trains don't always work together, and I'd have to find creative ways to make money, so in turn, I could finance my own art. . . .)

Ultimately, I'd need passengers to join me on each of these trains. All three departed South Orange Station at 8:08 a.m. on an August day back in 2005.

Returning to my full-time job at NYU as Assistant Production Coordinator was quite the pivot from calling "cut" and "action" on my debut feature film. It was a bucket of cold water over my head, awakening me from a beautiful dream. Yes, it was all part of the journey as my ten-week sabbatical had a definitive end date, but the feelings that came with sitting back down at my desk were real, and it felt, for a moment, like I'd been sent to the filmmaker's penalty box.

HOW TO POLITIC

Oxford Languages defines politics as: *the activities associated with the governance of a country or other area, especially the debate or conflict among individuals or parties having or hoping to achieve power.*

For those who think this may not apply to them, I point you toward the two most important words in that definition: *Other areas* — which really means, ALL areas.

Anytime you put two people together in an environment — politics commence. Who gets the bigger piece of meat in the days of living in caves? Who gets the top bunk bed? Who rides shotgun? Who will win the jury prize at the film festival? Who will direct the season premiere?

In recognition of the existence of politics everywhere you go, it's useful to consider the following in every exchange you navigate:

What are the needs of the other person?

You're more likely to get what you want, if you're able to help the other person move closer to their goals.

What are the customary practices in the world you're entering or operating?

Are you reaching for low hanging fruit or asking for something the other person may perceive as beyond your abilities? If so, be sure to have built a case to support your ability to perform whatever task you are aspiring to do.

Have you developed and nurtured the necessary relationships to support your goals?

Ideally, the person you're interacting with will be well aware of your abilities, but as you move up the ladder, you will find yourself in conversation with people who are unfamiliar with your skills. Having allies and colleagues who can speak to your potential is key. Sometimes, a stamp of approval can seal the deal. No one walks alone.

Discount politics all you want. Just know that you will be selling yourself short at the same time.

I was twenty-eight years old. I knew that dedicating another six years of life to produce my next feature film, while earning a sub $35K salary, would not be looking at my future with an eye towards fiscal responsibility. I also knew that I would never be able to raise funds in the same fashion I had for *Premium*. That was a one-time event, and if the film were not a commercial and/or critical success, it'd be very difficult to get future investors. My next film would have to be "sellable."

Perhaps, with what I'd learned, I'd be able to explore a topic I was passionate about, in a package that the gatekeepers would gobble up. In the meantime, though, I was slow to take my own advice, and continued writing draft after draft of a feature I started in 2004, entitled *What About Us?* — a dramedy about a fictitious town that received monetary reparations for slavery. I'm pitching this project today as an episodic television series.

My staff job at NYU paid my bills, but was unchallenging and unfulfilling. As a result, but mostly out of my love for all things storytelling, I found myself going above and beyond my basic duties of signing forms, calling vendors, and answering students' pre-production questions. I happily shared my knowledge, experience, and perspective with anyone that asked. Many times, I offered outright. Slowly, word began to get around that for almost any film related inquiry, "Your best bet is to talk to Pete, the guy at the production office window." I'd cemented a reputation in the South Orange and Maplewood Community with my exploits to produce *Chameleon* and *Premium*, now I was finally developing one within the ecosystem of NYU's Tisch School of the Arts — years after walking the halls as a student.

An unexpected opportunity revealed itself when Joan Horvath approached me to teach a second section of her class, Acting for the

Camera Workshop. Joan had sought student recommendations to see if there was anyone they felt might be a good fit as a teacher. Asher Goldstein, a student of hers and constant presence at my office window, mentioned me. He would later be a producer on Daniel Destin Cretton's 2013 debut feature *Short Term 12* and 2019's *Just Mercy*.

Joan and I met to discuss the principles of the class, as well as my background and passion, and while I was not an actor, nor did I have a master's level degree, I relayed to her that I understood the value of the class, what the end goals were to make each student feel like they'd spent good money on their expensive education, and that I could knock it out the park. I didn't say how excited I was about potentially adding a stop on *The Pete Has to Get Paid Train,* as I had learned long ago not everyone needs to know the full extent of your motivations.

The Open Arts curriculum committee approved me as a co-instructor, alongside another former student, friend, and recent graduate, Hannelore Williams. "Open Arts" meant that Acting For The Camera Workshop existed outside of the Kanbar Institute of Film and Television, and the class was open to the entire university, both undergraduate and graduate. It was an interesting mix of life experiences and disciplines, with the joining factor being that the students had a genuine interest in developing on-camera tools. Students workshopped one scene over the course of the semester and completed the class with an edited reel, shot by a teacher's assistant who typically had a focus on cinematography. Our TA was Antonio Cisneros, who later shot Hannelore's *Queen Hussy* webseries that I directed in 2011, as well as the ABC Digital/Juvee Productions webseries *American Koko* that I directed in 2016. I can't reiterate enough how important relationships are to your journey.

There's a saying, "Tell me, I forget . . . show me, I remember . . . involve me, I understand." This became my mantra over the next two years that I co-taught this course. I challenged myself to become the best teacher possible. I learned how to guide not only one student with a question, but the rest of the class, so they could take the fractions of information that I was presenting to propel one student's growth and do the math to figure out the answer for themselves and their own projects. It was a difficult dance at times, but I loved it. I've always found that the height of any craft exists at the intersection of talent and passion with practice and persistence, driven by a dissection of details and dedication to execution. I was becoming a better communicator because of teaching, and while I didn't know what might lie ahead of me creatively, I knew that this ability to lead a classroom and guide a unit toward a shared goal would come in handy.

But before all of that, I was thinking about my next target. The teaching money was a nice little bit of pocket change on top of my NYU desk job. Since I was able to survive on that salary, I used 75% of what I made from teaching to pay off the credit card debt I'd accrued while developing *Premium*, as well as some of the student loan debt I'd been carrying since 1999, making the desk job money stretch a little further moving forward. I figured I could add another stop to *The Pete Has to Get Paid Train* by moving toward the goal of teaching the classes that I had taken during my time at NYU. With Open Arts under my belt, I became focused on securing a teaching position within the Kanbar Institute of Film and TV. Many of my NYU professors had been working professionals, so it seemed like the perfect model to follow. Why not?

In 2009, when NYU added a Production Supervision Committee to the process of approving students' films to shoot, I was invited to join. The reputation I'd built at the production office window — being helpful to every student — was paying off yet again. While not a teaching position, this committee gave me a chance to work in tandem with other professors and build a name for myself with the community of folks whom I sought to join as a peer.

My first full-fledged teaching assignment within the department was Pre-Production Colloquium, a class designed to prepare students for the process of dealing with the aforementioned Production Supervision Committee. I was the perfect fit, as it was a new class and the existing faculty was spread thin across the already existing curriculum. Timing is everything. In some regard, my relationships and reputation were allowing me to slip into academia through the back door. I taught Pre-Production Colloquium for three semesters, improving my teaching skills while deepening my relationships with faculty. All of this would pay off in 2011, when the university welcomed Joe Pichirallo, the first department chair in decades not promoted from within the department.

It was a changing of the guard. Joe had started his career as a reporter for *The Washington Post* before transitioning into the film business. He worked his way up from creative executive at HBO Pictures, to setting up Searchlight Pictures, to Executive Vice President at Focus Features, and head of the feature film unit at Will Smith's Overbrook Entertainment. His films included *The Secret Life of Bees, Lakeview Terrace, Antwone Fisher, One Hour Photo, Hollywoodland*, and more. He was open to mixing things up a bit, and as a result, didn't necessarily find a faculty in full support of new ideas. From the outside looking in, there seemed to be a feeling amongst some of the faculty that a new regime was being thrust upon them without any inclusion in the transition to new philosophies. There's a reason a president selects their own cabinet every four years.

SELF HELP:
THE ADJUSTMENT

ALLIES

It's often uncomfortable to talk about politics, but as I said earlier, it's an important currency of success in any industry. So, shake it off and keep reading!

At this moment in time, thanks to what I'd been learning on my journey as a Director raising money and putting various teams together, it was clear to me that being an ally to Joe would be helpful in my pursuit to teach more classes within the department. I loved the students and the opportunity to share what I'd learned, so why wouldn't I align myself with someone who could put me in a position to perform? And, knowing how contentious some of the dynamics were amongst the faculty, why not be a breath of fresh air for someone working to navigate a new environment?

Unbeknownst to me, I was also getting a front row seat to what being an episodic television Director looked like. You arrive with what may be the "top job" on paper, but your success will be dependent on the buy-in of your "faculty" — the cast and crew. Applying constant analysis to your experiences and making the proper adjustments will help you avoid potential pitfalls down the line.

I welcomed Joe into the family I was just beginning to join myself, offering to be of any help that I could. I told him what I'd accomplished as a Director, what I'd done at the university, and where I saw myself fitting in down the line. I wanted to be useful in whatever design he had for the department and, specifically, hoped to teach the production courses that had been so instrumental in becoming the filmmaker I was at the time.

As I'm sure you can imagine by now, considering your time with me on this journey, I was *not* tossed a job to teach a production course! I was, however, unexpectedly invited to join the incoming freshmen application review committee — giving me an opportunity to vouch for under-represented students that might be overlooked in their quest to study at one of the world's premier film schools. Earning a spot in the freshman class had gotten exponentially more competitive in the years since I applied in 1994. When Joe asked if I also wanted to join the First Run Film Festival Committee — I had to hold in a bout of ironic laughter. Of course, I said "Yes," relishing the opportunity to also vouch for films and filmmakers that, like myself back in 2001, may not have developed strong relationships during their time at the university.

I finally landed my production class when Joe assigned me to Intermediate Narrative Workshop in 2012. This course, formerly known as Color Sync Workshop, was the same class where I produced *$5 to Six*, marking my first collaboration with Dorian Missick and my education in Murphy's Law. How full circle was that?

I quit Pre-Production Colloquium, so I could focus on my twenty-four students and their films. I maintained my 9 to 5 desk job at NYU, and was in the early stages of building the infrastructure for my production company. Additionally, I continued my campaign to teach advanced level production courses, as that was where I felt I'd be most effective and the experience the most rewarding. As I had progressed further and further into my professional career, I was always annoyed by the lessons I learned the hard way that I felt a faculty member should have prepared me for as an aspiring Director. Filmmaking will beat you down, but it only keeps you down if you're clinging to the belief that talent is enough. It's not. So many Directors quit pursuing their dreams because they're unprepared for a bumpy road that requires proving yourself, when perhaps you feel you shouldn't have to, and developing skill sets like Emotional Intelligence and political acumen in order to stay afloat. Any student in my class would learn what the job of Director is really about and what would be required of you for the best shot at success.

In 2013, I was finally selected to teach an advanced level production course. Narrative Workshop was the one semester version of Advanced Production Workshop, where I produced my thesis film, *3D*. I felt that the accelerated pace of this class, cramming two semesters of information into one, though viewed as a challenge, was something I could turn into a positive. It allowed me to successfully teach more about directing in fewer weeks, because the students would be looking to absorb and apply everything possible in order to develop, prep, and shoot their films within the twelve-week period.

Seven years after pursuing teaching, I had reached my goal, adding multiple stops to *The Pete Has to Get Paid Train* — mostly by taking advantage of opportunities as they came, and focusing on how I might maximize what these new worlds offered. As always, I thought, "What's next?" and plotted to climb further, applying for a Full-Time Faculty position. I'd developed the resume and built the relationships, especially since the selection committee would be composed of the faculty I had become a part of.

I remember the interview like it was yesterday — ten people at the long end of a conference table grilling me on my experience, why I wanted the job, how I'd be a good fit, etc. It was like a scene from a movie. You could feel the tension between the old guard and the new — the inevitable reluctance to pass the torch to newcomers who had acquired their skills through non-traditional avenues. Remember, I had essentially slid in through the back door. Nevertheless, I felt that I'd done everything needed to earn my seat at the table and performed well in the interview, but ultimately, I didn't get the job.

Which may have been the best thing to ever happen to me.

Had I gone down that road further, I could have fallen too deep into academia to be able to jump, at a moment's notice, at the opportunities that would soon arise as my production company began to grow (which I'll talk about in a few chapters). Months later, this new outlook compelled me to turn down an offer for a Full-Time Faculty position in the NYU Singapore film department. Silver linings and moments of clarity come at times you'd least expect.

My ultimate exit from teaching, at least at the university level, was accelerated by the challenges connected to the final class I was assigned, initially called Life On Set. This colloquium was another part of Joe Picharillo's new direction for the department. It was a requirement for all incoming freshmen, designed to introduce students to the nuts and bolts of film production, while also preparing them for the Production Supervision process that would be an integral part of their NYU education. Life On Set replaced a legendary course that had existed for more than a decade, and while the idea was in the right place, the implementation of this new curriculum caused quite the shakeup amongst the faculty, leaving people to choose sides, and putting the future of the class in the balance.

I was totally unaware of the legacy and the unfolding drama when I accepted the class. Having been told it was an opportunity to "put my stamp on a course," I jumped at the chance. But after several semesters of intra-faculty conflict, a decision was made that ultimately seemed designed to appease the warring factions and mend relationships as the department moved forward.

Life On Set became Art and Practice.

I was joined by the instructor of the legendary class that had been removed — Professor Tom Drysdale. Now co-instructors, and soon to be friends, Tom and I spent weeks developing a syllabus, and over time, came up with what we felt was an amazing class. Tom poetically described what we'd created as a course that would "keep the students' heads in the sky, but their feet on the ground," and to this day I run into former students who tell me just how much they appreciated what we delivered to them week after week.

After a semester or two of continued controversy surrounding the class, however, I decided I'd had enough.

I quit.

My production company was beginning to support me full-time, and the NYU politics just weren't something I wanted to continue navigating. I felt I'd reached my destination as a teacher in that particular universe and if I were going to continue, I would do it on my own terms, whether through a master class, book, podcast, or even social media. Besides, I could always return to the university at another point in time, when a committee might deem me experienced enough. That's sarcasm — kinda.

The biggest takeaway from this decade of my journey was seeing, first hand, the inner workings of politics. If you ever have an opportunity to immerse yourself in these dynamics, I *highly* recommend it, as it's pretty amazing to watch. I learned how to avoid alienating people, how to win friends, how to play the long game, and how to weigh the impact of every decision and every move I'd make — *before* making it. I also learned what *not* to do, and while I knew I would make my own mistakes in the future, I promised myself to cash in on what I'd witnessed to save myself some time, money, and heartache.

▶ CHAPTER 6 KEYWORD: REPUTATION

Reputation is defined as "the beliefs or opinions that are generally held about someone or something."

You have the ability to craft the vision that people develop of you, your perspective, and your projects. How will they speak about you when you're not around? That's up to you and what you do in every aspect of your communication with people — both in person and online.

Nurture and protect this with everything you've got.

RESOURCES

■ *SELF HELP:*
Worksheet 6 — The 5 Pillars Of Reputation (Page tbd)

■ *INSPIRATION:*
Podcast
Let's Shoot! with Pete Chatmon, Episode 18
Raamla Mohamed on Learning To Write In Any Environment
Available on Apple Podcasts, Spotify, and all Podcast Platforms

WORKSHEET 6:
THE FIVE PILLARS OF REPUTATION

Before you can nurture and protect a reputation, you've got to build one! Over time, I've come to find that reputations rest upon the following five pillars:

(1) Aptitude: *A natural ability to do something.* Are your talents identifiable? Does your work speak for itself?

(2) Attitude: A way of feeling or acting toward a person, thing, or situation. Do people think you are positive, supportive, and collaborative? Does your attitude inspire them to want to assist in the professional pursuit of your artistic talents?

_____

(3) Affect: The outward display of one's emotional state. Includes nonverbal communication, such as body language and gestures. Are you giving off the vibes that you want to or that you think you are? Do you wear your heart on your sleeve in all situations, including those that are challenging? Is your affect diminishing someone's desire to spread the word about you?

_____

(4) Accessibility: Being easy to speak to or deal with. Are you approachable? Are you receptive to feedback — both positive and negative? When finally "in the room" with someone, would you embarrass the person who recommended you, due to your lack of accessibility?

_____

(5) Adaptability: The quality of being able to adjust to new conditions. When it's time to pivot, can you recalibrate or do you get flustered? Lose your temper? Shut down? When you're finally on set, thanks to your hard work and plenty of recommendations, will your lack of adaptability cement you as a one-episode Director?

_____

In the empty lines above, rate your proficiency in each of the pillars from one to ten (ten being the highest.) Next, reflect honestly on where you need to do some work and jot down two or three action items that you can implement to enhance your reputation and increase the number of people who would love to see you succeed.

REPETITION

PREMIUM — THE ROAD TO DISTRIBUTION

As I was pursuing my teaching career at NYU, all the while working my desk job, I was also completing post-production on *Premium*. The biggest hurdle would be finding a composer for the original score.

> ▶ **CHAPTER 7's KEYWORD is: REPETITION**

Everything that I had already learned on my previous films was put back into practice. I was updating investors, working on a poster, postcards, and website, and navigating the many creative elements of post-production that remained. I even joined MySpace for the sole purpose of promoting the film — an important introduction to social media and how to maximize the platform.

I met Eric Lewis through his then manager, Nancy Hirsch. After an amazing performance at Cleopatra's Needle on the Upper West Side, followed by a lunch at a SoHo diner, I hired Eric to compose the score for *Premium*. I knew this guy was a genius, long before he changed his artistic name to ELEW, and I felt very fortunate our paths were able to cross. I remember after we landed on the centerpiece of the score — a piece entitled "Cool's Theme" — I was driving home to my mother's house, playing it on repeat and crying.

That was not an experience I'd ever had, but whatever he did with that piano drilled down into all of the emotions I had poured into "Cool," his character, the film, and my life over the previous six years.

It was simply beautiful. ELEW would later compose the score for *761st*, *BlackCard*, *Wednesday Morning*, and perform at my wedding in Mexico in 2019.

For the remaining post-production elements, we made a deal with Goldcrest Post-Production, the same place where we held "The *Premium* Presentation," back in November 2004. Our arrangement provided one-stop shopping, allowing us to complete our sound design, sound mix, color correction, digital intermediate, titles, and everything in between — all under one roof.

The world premiere for *Premium* was at the 2006 Miami International Film Festival (MIFF). To my dismay, I had become the only person I knew to have had a short film premiere at Sundance, but whose feature film was not selected. I was surprised, and I'll admit it, pissed and hurt. Nevertheless, MIFF had just hired a new festival director, Nicole Guillemet, who had previously served as the co-chair at Sundance, and knowing this, I felt we'd be in good hands as she would be looking to make her presence known with an amazing event.

Premium represented the United States as one of twelve films in the World Cinema Competition. Upon receiving our selection announcement, I fell further into repetition mode and reached out to Megan Quitoni, a friend from high school who worked at Harrison &

Shriftman, a Miami-based public relations company. I knew PR would make or break this project. Word of mouth had been important for my other films, but *Premium* was driven by investments (not contributions), and our investors would need to start seeing some money back ASAP. The only way that could happen would be if we sold or licensed the film. The right PR strategy would essentially be returning to yet another awareness campaign, but this time for both audience and distributor eyeballs.

I went back to my executive producers and sold them on the idea of an event to coincide with the world premiere. We threw another *Premium Party* at the super trendy Shore Club in Miami. Harrison & Shriftman secured Grey Goose Vodka as our sponsored liquor. We packed the event with local celebrities, and coordinated with MIFF's publicity team to ensure the invite to our party went out to every tastemaker on their list who was in town for the festival.

Costs began to increase as we were contractually obligated to provide first class flights and hotel stays for Dorian Missick, Zoe Saldana, Hill Harper, and Eva Marcille. It was a calculated risk, however, because I knew the impact of a picture and the "thousand words" that the right image would offer. In fact, our prized moment from the entire event was a shot with Dorian, Zoe, Hill, and me that went out over the

photo wires (Getty Images, Wire Image, etc.) that I know was instrumental in pointing distributors toward our film. I jokingly refer to it as the $25,000 Kodak Moment, because after all was said and done, that's how much the event, as well as the personal publicity I paid for to amplify my presence, ended up costing us.

We secured a distribution deal with Codeblack Entertainment — one of two distributors that ultimately competed for the film. We were most excited about the fact that they offered a limited theatrical release, in addition to DVD, because at that time, many of the deals were straight-to-video. As the film was presented to ancillary markets, we were also able to secure a Showtime cable premiere, and a release window on Netflix, which had started streaming select titles in 2007.

We were finally sending money back to our investors, and I felt like we'd crossed the finish line. I was a professional Director with a film available for purchase out in the world! I had envisioned this back in 1993, though I had no idea what the journey would entail.

While I was enjoying this minor victory, my friend Candice Sanchez McFarlane started to get in my ear about writing something that would be sellable and less challenging to fund, especially given the

lessons learned after eight years on *Premium*. She'd heard my complaints, and threw it right back at me.

Knowing she was right, I nodded my head and said, "Let's talk."

▶ **CHAPTER 7 KEYWORD: REPETITION**

Fortunately, once you figure out the ingredients to success, there will be sections of your journey where you can work from muscle memory.

Enjoy these times, but don't get lazy. You'll be navigating uncertain waters soon enough.

RESOURCES

■ *INSPIRATION:*
Podcast
Let's Shoot! with Pete Chatmon, Episode 17
Barry Alexander Brown on Avoiding Creative Death
Available on Apple Podcasts, Spotify, and all Podcast Platforms

761ST AND TRIBECA ALL ACCESS

It was Spring 2007. Before Candice and I could really dive into brainstorming a more "marketable" screenplay than *What About Us?* (my dramedy about monetary reparations for slavery), I had to finish up what I'd started with *761st*. I'd been simultaneously moving through both production and post-production on the documentary as we pushed *Premium* toward distribution. My editor, Adam Hark, had come up with a creative solution to completing the film while I continued working my full-time desk job at NYU and teaching classes after hours.

Using Apple's early instant messaging platform, iChat, he set up a camera in his Jersey City editing suite to capture his monitor, allowing me
to view and give notes in real time, speaking softly to avoid getting
caught by my NYU colleagues.

▶ CHAPTER 8'S KEYWORD is: RESILIENCE

The thirty hours of tape that Steve White had given me when we met
back in 2005 became the canvas of the film. The heart of our narrative followed the WWII exploits of our dozen Black tankers between
October 10, 1944 and May 8, 1945. This was not enough to build a
film, however, so we were actively shooting new material, in order to
tell the story. In documentary production, you are essentially "writing with the camera." You can't explore ideas on your laptop as you
have to get out there and shoot, conduct interviews, and shoot b-roll,
occasionally returning to the editing suite to discover that something
doesn't work. I was becoming a better writer, as our limited budget
would not allow us to endlessly investigate all the ideas that came to
my mind. Specificity and economy were key.

761st was built upon a two-pronged narrative. First, it would be a
document to illustrate the indisputable heroism of these Black men
who fought valiantly overseas for freedoms they did not enjoy back
home. Second, it would be an exploration of why the United States
government made such a highly coordinated, concerted effort to avoid
publicly acknowledging their heroism, especially in a so-called meritocracy like the military. The obvious answer, in my opinion, was to
avoid creating heroes and elevating pride in multiple generations of
Black folks. Living under the realities of second-class citizenship would
prove harder to swallow if we saw ourselves as not only Americans, but
as heroes. It pained me to see these soldiers finally acknowledged in
their 80s and 90s, stricken by deteriorating health and age, when the
photos from the 1940s that we'd compiled for the film showed strong,
capable, intelligent men that would have inspired their entire community at a time when it was so desperately needed.

It was also important to me to make sure viewers could understand what it felt like to fight and essentially live inside these tanks. We visited Jacques Littlefield, a gentleman in Portola Valley, CA, who founded the Military Vehicle Technology Foundation, which featured over 200 armored fighting vehicles, including those used in WWII. I was able to get inside the M4 Sherman Tank and show just how claustrophobic the experience was for the four soldiers assigned to each vehicle. These steel tanks were free of any and all creature comforts, providing no relief from subzero temperatures, and more often than not delivering concussions and other injuries during heated warfare, as projectiles detonated in and around the tanks.

We went to the Aberdeen Proving Grounds in Maryland to get a better understanding of what the American Sherman Tanks faced against the superior German Panzer and Panther tanks. We filmed another reunion in Fort Hood, Texas, and reached out to Gen. Colin Powell, who accepted our interview request almost instantly. I read his autobiography in one sitting to prepare for our conversation.

Interviews and video footage would still not suffice in painting a complete picture of the 761st Tank Battalion, so Emily Konopinski and I traveled to the National Archives in College Park, Maryland, to make copies and scan every bit of supporting documentation that existed.

News articles, After Action Reports (many stained with dirt and blood), and maps would help to place the audience in the moment. These materials, animated by Adam Hark in Adobe AfterEffects, would underline and underscore everything that the soldiers shared in their first-person accounts. Our ace in the hole through the entire process was producer Wayne D. Robinson, official historian for the 761st Tank Battalion, who ensured that all of our facts were accurate and the entirety of the context of every event was understood. The soldiers were detailing moments that occurred over 60 years ago, so he was also able to make sure we caught any comments that may have been incorrect, ensuring the facts were bulletproof and no one could take any shots at the documentary, and in turn, our heroes.

HOW TO DESIGN A DOCUMENTARY INTERVIEW

Whether you've been assigned an interview list or you've secured a "big get" who will elevate your project — the preparation remains the same. I like to consider each interviewee a "character" in the project. My job is to find a way to communicate their worldview to the audience in the shortest time possible. It's no different than exposing the truth of your fictional characters, except that you will need to use your people skills to get there.

Here are the steps I would recommend you take before each interview:

Do your research.

Yes, we have conversations everyday with people who we don't know, and you may be one of the great conversationalists of our time, but you have a goal with each interview, and you will need information and finesse to achieve it. Research reveals new angles to explore in your interview, as well as details that might help you build rapport with your interviewee. Sitting down in front of a camera and getting right to the truth can be an awkward proposition for many — your prep and research can help make things feel more natural and comfortable. . . .

Review the themes of your project and consider how the interview will serve as either a point or counterpoint to your narrative.

Does this "character" support your thesis or argue for the other side? Do they co-sign what has been said by everyone else or reveal that someone is lying? There is a point to every interview and it's up to you, as Director, to discover that point and share it with your audience. . . .

If possible, do a "pre-interview."

This is an opportunity to talk about the project and what you're looking to explore with the interviewee. It might also yield information that you can further investigate when you shoot. . . .

Prepare your questions.

Considering the time allotted for your interview, as well as the amount of depth you expect for each answer, prepare questions that will guide the conversation toward your desired result. I like to give each interview a thematic title so I can stay on track, should the conversation veer into unexpected territory. An unexpected answer is not an incorrect answer, and if you're prepared and on your toes, you may find thematic gold in these diversions. . . .

Be nimble.

But, also push back when you need to. I'd note though, that you are not a prosecutor, and oftentimes your audience will see when someone is lying or creating a false narrative as a result of how they interact with you and your line of questioning. . . .

Have fun.

You're learning about the world and yourself with every interview. A sense of genuine curiosity and interest always helps to relax an interviewee and create a more authentic experience.

This process has worked for me over the countless Branded Content videos I've directed, to the fifteen minutes (*literally*) that I was allotted to interview Gen. Colin Powell for *761st*. I enjoy the intimacy of documentary interviews because with each interaction, I get a new window into the human experience, which only helps me elevate my craft as a fiction writer.

My biggest mistake on the documentary was not creative, but in budgeting. More accurately, it was not being fully aware of how to budget to my creative vision. One of the first things I knew I wanted to do was avoid the boring, newsreel style use of stock footage that I'd seen in many military documentaries. I was adamant about not utilizing the same handful of shots of tanks, tankers, soldiers, and the like over an entire feature film. I wanted to try and create reenactments of sorts, carefully selecting moments that would mirror the soldiers' first-person accounts. This worked great as we made the rough cut, which executive producer Steve loved, but as we turned the corner to actually securing the high-resolution files of each clip, we did the math and had the rudest of awakenings. We were going to be $75,000 over budget if we used the stock footage as intended (coupled with a few other post-production necessities). Stock footage is typically available for licensing in ten second minimums, the reality, of course, being that you are only going to use a clip for two or three seconds. Multiply that across all of the stock footage storytelling Adam and I had spent weeks crafting, and I finally understood why all those films I'd ever watched used the same damn clips! I met with Steve to apologize for my mistake in budgeting, explain how we arrived there, and thankfully, we were able to finance the overage. Ultimately, we both felt the film was better for it, and I appreciated his sense of storytelling in agreeing to stay the course.

There were other lessons along the way. On our first traveling shoot with the Panasonic HVX200 camera that we purchased, I served as the DIT (digital imaging technician) and was responsible for downloading the media from the card and backing it up on the hard drive. I'd practiced several times before we went on the road, to make sure I understood the workflow, but after our first interview I failed to do it correctly, while successfully deleting the media on the card. With one stupid move, the interview we had just completed was gone. I asked the interview subject if we could continue and then proceeded to ask the same questions I'd just deleted, but in a different fashion. When he caught on, I admitted what had happened. Can't blame me for try-ing — it was super embarrassing.

There was also the time a hard drive failed on us while in Fort Hood, Texas. After the above experience, I had learned how to successfully transfer the media to a drive, quadruple checking to ensure that it had worked, but on this occasion when we came back to dump more footage, the hard drive had nothing on it. Like, everything that I had confirmed was safely transferred and stored was literally *gone*. We would later spend almost $3,000 to have that footage recovered which . . . drumroll . . . never ended up in the documentary. That speaks directly to my "writing with the camera" comment earlier. The good news, though learned in the absolute hardest fashion, was that anything I ever shot after these two heartaches would be backed up in triplicate on hard drives. My new motto became "If I don't have it saved in three places, I don't have it!"

Perhaps the most important lesson, though, was learning that "cinema of good intentions does not make good cinema." This comment was shared with me in a conversation with Dean Sheril Antonio at NYU. No matter what the topic of your project may be, you cannot let the impor-tance of the subject supersede your responsibility to tell a compelling story to the best of your cinematic abilities. Failure to do so will leave you with an uninterested audience and something that feels more akin to an afterschool special than a carefully crafted film. This is something I carry with me until this day, especially since much of what I tend to write has some element of historical fiction interwoven into its themes.

With *761st* in the can and an independent release strategy on the horizon (we would self-distribute DVDs via Amazon's CreateSpace service), I was finally ready to dive into screenplay brainstorming ses-sions with Candice Sanchez McFarlane. For months, we had kicked ideas back and forth via email, but nothing really clicked. Starting in the Fall of 2007, we set up a weekly call on Monday nights — 10 p.m. Eastern for me in New Jersey, 7 p.m. for Candice in Los Ange-les. Candice felt a heist film would be the ideal genre to explore, so we began our now standard process of watching every genre related film we could get our hands on, in order to study what's been done and find new spaces within that genre where we could perhaps elevate and innovate. Spike Lee's *Inside Man* resonated with us, and we felt that there was an opportunity to further explore one of the main details in the central crime of the film. Clive Owen's character, "Dalton Russell," found a target in Christopher Plummer's "Martin Case," a man guilty of having stolen property from someone else who could not, in turn, scream, "Give me back my stolen property!" We asked ourselves, what if it wasn't the perfect target in that sense, but a story where the protagonist was motivated to commit the "crime" for reasons that were revenge or payback for a historically significant wrong that had been perpetrated upon that person directly? What if the "crime" itself could be argued wasn't a "crime" after all? We decided to focus on challenging the basic idea of what's right and wrong, particularly in a country where so much wealth has been built upon the backs of Black people.

We landed on what would become *$FREE.99*, a heist film about a small town detective who gets a crash course in history, crime, and politics when a lone bank teller turned robber puts the fate of the entire community in his hands. For sixteen weeks, Candice and I would hop on the phone for two to three hours every Monday, throwing all of our ideas at

the wall until something stuck. Our biggest challenge was constructing a crime that, if everything aligned, could actually be pulled off. We hated how in so many of the heist films that we analyzed, a thorough chat over post-screening drinks could unravel the entire premise.

Satisfied with our script outline, and tired from the mental gymnastics it took to hash it out over late night phone debates, we put the project aside and figured we'd take a few months off before getting to the script. We both had full-time jobs to navigate, as well as other side projects that had been put in timeout and needed our attention.

Toward the end of 2007, I received a phone call about Tribeca Film Institute's new program, Tribeca All Access. It was similar to Sundance's Writer and Director Labs, to some degree, and I was told I might be a good fit for their category of independent filmmakers looking to direct their second feature film. Ready, as always, I submitted the script for *What About Us?* and waited.

In early February of 2008, I got word that, while they liked the project, *What About Us?* wouldn't really be the best fit. I got the sense that for them too, marketability would be important. These programs need success stories, as much as the filmmakers need a shot, so it's important for them to have a track record of projects moving through the program and into the marketplace. They asked if I had anything else to submit and I mentioned *$FREE.99*, to which they countered, "If you can get that to us in three weeks, then we will take a look at it." With that kick in the ass, I immediately called Candice and asked if she was game to put our heads back down and plow through a screenplay.

We decided, of course, to do it. Three sleepless weeks later, we submitted and were selected to participate in April 2008's Tribeca All Access program. The week's events consisted of twenty 30-minute pitch sessions with independent producers, production companies, and the independent production arms of the major studios — many of which would fold in the coming months (Picturehouse, Warner Independent, etc.).

My experience with fundraising for *Premium* came into play, coupled with Candice's expertise from the marketing and advertising worlds. We studied each company and the representatives they'd sent to meet with us. We tailored our pitch to the person in front of us so we could have the best chance to connect, build a rapport, and sell them something that would fit whatever their mandate for content was at the time. We bounced off each other — an effective team — I spoke to the creative aspects of the project, while Candice drove home the thematic elements. At the conclusion of the week's events, an awards dinner and ceremony was held at Buddakan, a trendy restaurant in New York City's Meatpacking District.

I won The Creative Promise Narrative Award and was super excited, as I felt it would provide a little more currency to *$FREE.99*, and help in my goal of making my next project with industry support, as opposed to private investment. The cash prize and "Missy at Home" artwork from Renee Cox were the cherry on top.

April turned to May 2008. I still wanted nothing more than to be a working Director, making the films I wanted to make, hoping each film would make whatever amount of money necessary for me to make the next. I was also slowly raising an interested eyebrow toward television, as a friend of mine, Seith Mann, was beginning to make inroads into episodic television work via the Disney/ABC Directing Program.

In August, I made my second trip to Los Angeles to chase the dream. Again, I stayed with my sister Tait and her boyfriend (now husband) David, in Santa Monica. I was no longer a Director in search of producers for my first feature. I was now:

- Director of *Premium*, an award-winning feature film that starred a skyrocketing Zoe Saldana (she had moved on to *Star Trek* and *Avatar*) . . . .
- Winner of The Creative Promise Award from the Tribeca Film Institute for a new screenplay . . . .
- Writer-Director of the screenplay *$FREE.99* (looking for funding) . . . .
- Writer-Director-producer of *761st*, an independently produced and distributed documentary feature . . . .

With all of the above, I felt ripe for the industry's picking. After six years, I'd figured it out on my own and returned with the treasure, and then some. If I had been in the music business, I would have been a rapper who'd made a successful mixtape, sold a bunch of records out the trunk, and was now ready for an imprint deal with a major label. Because if you can make it happen with no traditional help, conventional wisdom says that with some marketing behind you, plus everything that comes with deep pockets and long relationships, you're gonna kill it.

I worked my contacts and was able to set up a few meetings. I met with The Gersh Agency, Innovative Artists, Evolution Entertainment, Principato Young, and a handful of other places, but I encountered the same lack of enthusiasm as when I had been looking for money. I ultimately signed a management deal with a gentleman who was never able to provide any results, but I figured I should at least have *someone* out in the world *supposedly* doing something to advance my career vs. having no one at all.

What was interesting to me was that the industry was totally unaware of the changing landscape that was happening on the ground, driven by the filmmakers who would come to lead Hollywood in the next five to ten years. Almost every person I met told me I could not be a Writer-Producer-Director, and that, in fact, I'd have to choose one. I don't know if that was a fear of the multi-hyphenate, or just a nice way of letting me down, but in apartments and homes across the country, filmmakers like Ava DuVernay and Joe Swanberg were figuring out just how many hats they could wear so they could get their vision out to the world in an industry where their voices weren't deemed valuable. This was a by-product to the collapse of those mini-majors and smaller production companies that Candice and I met in their final breaths during Tribeca All Access — remove the infrastructure, remove the gatekeepers, and a Director with hustle and passion will figure out a way, by any means necessary, to say what they've got to say.

I returned to New Jersey, disappointed but undaunted. Perhaps a heist script, anchored by an historical Black event, was not what the industry was looking for. Nevertheless, I'd managed to improve as a Writer, and I would always have the script in my back pocket whenever proper financing for the film might be thrown my way.

I made a commitment to increase the volume of my opportunities, which meant writing as many scripts as I possibly could. Working with Candice had proven the value of a co-writer — I worked both faster and smarter, making each draft feel like the equivalent of two or three drafts after all the debate and conversation connected to each decision along the way. I reached out to Shani Harris Peterson, a talented film-maker and friend, whom I had met at the San Francisco Black Film Festival back in 2003, at a screening for my short film, *Chameleon*. We had similar sensibilities, and she was down to collaborate on a romantic comedy concept I'd been developing with another friend, Marissa Nance, who was Candice's boss when we were first introduced. I can't reiterate enough the importance of your community and relationships.

Shani and I wrote the script for that romantic comedy in a few months' time. We spent the next few months trying to attach actors with whom we had relationships, as well as production companies — all to no avail.

It was clear to me that I'd need to cement myself as a Director, if the writing projects were going to find any traction. It wasn't time to quit — in this instance, I'd need to pivot.

I sat down at my desk at NYU and started plotting my next move.

▶ CHAPTER 8 KEYWORD: RESILIENCE

Your resilience is called upon at the point in the journey where most people simply give up. For them, it's the point at which "The Confrontation" becomes too much.

You, however, know that this is an inevitable part of the process and will weather the storm by calling upon all the keywords you've mastered along the way.

Reassess, recalibrate, and remember — you're built for this!

RESOURCES

■ *INSPIRATION:*
Podcast
Let's Shoot! with Pete Chatmon, Episode 09
Keith Powell on the Moment Oprah Saved His Job
Available on Apple Podcasts, Spotify, and all Podcast Platforms

A PRODUCTION COMPANY, A PODCAST, AND A MONTHLY EVENT

By the time January 2008 arrived, I'd already figured my best bet to get directing jobs would be to create them myself. If I couldn't sell my own stories as screenplays, perhaps I could build my company by selling my personal journey to other people and convincing them to hire me to tell their story. Commercials would be my target. Branded Content would be my entry point, though at the time, everything was just called a "video." My production company, Double7 Images, was off to the races!

> ▶ **CHAPTER 9'S KEYWORD is: PIVOT**

Music videos were the furthest thing of interest, as I had sworn off directing them after another horrible experience with the same asshole who ghosted me on the funding for my short film *3D*. Let's just call this my young, dumb, and naive chapter, as he ended up stiffing me for $10,000 — a long story that will be very short. I moved on, knowing I might end up in jail for finding other ways to procure payment if I kept encountering practitioners of bad business.

My early clients were typically friends. There was the Volvo dealership in East Hanover, New Jersey, owned by the Haiken family, whom I had known since elementary school. There were short documentaries on members of my artistic community, and product promos for friends with restaurants in my hometown.

The budgets were almost nonexistent, typically about $5,000 per job, regardless of the scope. It would typically be me directing and producing, two shooters, and a production assistant doing any and everything that popped up. My goal with each project was to buy a new piece of equipment, so I could own enough gear to do future jobs with fewer people, allowing me to keep more of the money. I bought lenses first, as all of my friends had the new Canon DSLR cameras. I'd be able to use my lenses immediately on their cameras until I bought one of my own. I purchased a 50mm, 85mm, 24-70mm, 70-200mm, 24-105mm, and a Holga pinhole lens for some cool shots. When I'd saved up enough money, I joined their ranks and made my first big camera purchase — the Canon 7D and a tripod.

I could not afford production insurance in those days, so I really had to own as much gear as possible, because no rental house is letting anything out its doors because you've got a nice smile and an important project on deck. Next, I bought a Sennheiser 416 shotgun (the same microphone I used at NYU), a wireless Lavalier mic, and two 1x1 lite-panels. I needed to be able to answer the call for a job at a moment's notice. If a client had a project that needed to be shot tomorrow, or even the same day, and edited with a super quick turnaround — we could do it. My team of creative mercenaries, labeled the Double7 Squad, included Anthony Artis, Benjamin Ahr Harrison, Tristan Nash, Eric Van't Zelfden, Giga Shane, Leyla Rosario, Dylan Verrechia, Nicole Sylvester, Hannelore Williams, Tobin Ludwig, Eddie Simeon, and Wayne McElroy. The icing on the cake for clients was that we could do all of the above for much cheaper than the production companies we identified as our competition.

HOW TO IDENTIFY THE MARKET

When I discussed marketing and branding in my NYU film production classes, I would ask my students a question that always went unanswered.

What's the connection between Kingsford Charcoal and you?

Puzzled looks would flash around the room until I connected the dots. Kingsford Charcoal was the by-product of the remaining wood from Henry Ford's Model T assembly line. Rather than waste those stumps, branches, and sawdust, he suggested they process the scraps into charcoal. This introduced a new product line and a revenue stream that was lying in plain sight.

The point of this question was to nudge my young Directors toward considering the by-products of their own craft and the projects they'd created. In an entertainment industry that was slowly becoming more and more democratized, it was a discussion designed to redefine the idea of exploitation. If our goals were to work with movie studios or television networks that would be "exploiting" our talents in the service of their products (read any contract and you'll see this wording), why not "exploit" yourself and make money off of everything your skills might allow you to do?

Once you identify those skills and the services/products you can offer, you will have successfully *identified the market* for yourself. The next step will be to find the best way to fold your skills and products into something that best meets the demands of your market.

Using myself as an example, here's how I outlined everything discussed in this chapter, and why:

Starting a production company:

If I can create a media and events campaign for myself to raise $520,000 to produce a feature film, surely, I can apply those same skills to helping businesses and brands sell their products or services, no? And, won't this potentially put money in my pocket during the down periods where I'm trying to sell the next script or raise money for the next project? Time to exploit.

Starting a podcast:

If I can interview hundreds of people across the Branded Content and feature films I'm directing, surely, I can hold a conversation with industry leaders and talented craftspeople in front of and behind the camera, no? And, won't this allow me to further master my craft, broaden my network, and potentially elevate me to influencer status? Time to exploit.

Hosting a monthly event:

If I can throw parties to build awareness for *Premium* and our fundraising efforts, surely, I can throw a monthly event that builds upon the community of our podcast, no? And, won't this also serve to market our production company and myself as a Director? Time to exploit.

All of the above were merely by-products of efforts I'd been making since 1993.

Ask yourself what skills you have to exploit, and get to it! You'll be more creatively fulfilled than waiting for some industry entity to pluck you from obscurity. You'll be building your resume. You'll also be building your brand, so when the industry does come knocking, it will know exactly what your voice is and have a clear idea of how to . . . finally . . . best "exploit" you.

As I viewed the landscape in these first years of the Obama presidency, it seemed that companies had finally accepted a website as a necessary component of their business, but video, not so much. With web 2.0 platforms like WordPress and video sharing platforms like YouTube and Vimeo, my hunch was that if we could convince clients there was an impact and a value in telling their stories with video content as well as photos, then we could make ourselves the solution to the problem we diagnosed.

The story I sold and told to potential clients was the origin story of how I came to stand in front of them. I shared how we were a company built upon the efforts I'd employed to raise half a million dollars for *Premium*, my first feature film. I did not come from a rich family. I did not know rich people, but we constructed a branding campaign to build awareness around what we were looking to produce. We created events and made videos and other assets to give us as many entry points into the conversation as possible, and we worked to build a community of folks who were invested in supporting and helping us reach our goal of making the film. You read Chapter 4. My point was that if we could do that for our project, then we could surely help a company develop a conversation around their product, their brand, or their service. Our motto was "Putting Story First."

I rounded up the usual suspects — or suspect, in this case — and brainstormed business strategy with Candice Sanchez McFarlane. Our working relationship on *$FREE.99* revealed to me just how valuable a partner she was in story and storytelling. Her work at the worldwide advertising agency OMD, focused on Fortune 100 brands, would prove invaluable in identifying the problem or challenge for a client and constructing something creative to provide a solution. We continue to bounce off each other in the same ways today, when we walk into rooms with executives to pitch our television ideas.

We created Double7 Boutique, a new division of Double7 Images that would broaden our services to include research, market analysis, and design of the creative campaign, on top of what we were already providing with video production. With every job, at this point, having a budget somewhere between $5,000 to $10,000, there was no way to increase revenue if we didn't expand. By designing each project to be a campaign, or a suite of multiple videos and other assets, including photos, we could, in turn, increase our production budgets because clients were getting more for their money.

My friend whose family owned the Volvo dealership also happened to co-own Classickicks, a boutique sneaker store on Elizabeth Street in N.Y.C., in the former offices of Def Jam Records. Jen Haiken attended different middle and high schools after our elementary days, but she married another friend from high school, Nick Santora, and since all of our local friends supported their business, I popped my head in from time to time to update my sneaker collection. After what must have been my tenth or eleventh purchase, Candice and I decided to pitch them on a proposition — we will give you the full scope of our services, at no cost, but we would have final cut on the campaign, as it would be our calling card moving forward for new business under the Double7 Boutique banner.

They were game. After conducting a focus group of potential customers, Candice and I constructed the perfect campaign to tell their story. We discovered that some "non-sneakerheads" were hesitant to enter the shop for fear of not being "cool enough," while other folks didn't know how much the store had to offer as a lifestyle destination. We made three videos following three different types of customers on a real shopping expedition, where they interacted with the product and selected items that appealed to them. One video followed two 20-something women who discovered cool tracksuit and sneaker options, the second followed a late 20s skater-type who found some stylish Vans, and the third was Dorian Missick, who found a cool "Do The Riots Thing" T-shirt that he purchased. You know what I'm going to say here again — relationships.

We also shot a photo essay chronicling the release of Kanye West's original Nike Yeezy. This was similar to the Frame & Sequence project I'd made back at NYU in 1995. Each boutique sneaker store was given only eighteen pairs to sell, so we captured photos of the customers that lined up early (many overnight), their priceless reactions once they got their hands on the shoes, and of course the folks outside who bought a pair, just moments later, at exorbitant markups. The last bit of content we made was our entry level branding asset called "The Video Signature" which was essentially a thirty to forty-five second video of Nick and Jen explaining who they were and why they loved what they do. This would be embedded as a link in the signature of their emails, allowing anyone that they corresponded with to get a sense of them as a person before ever meeting them.

Prior to the shoot, I knew it would be important to get some press on Double7 Boutique. As always, I was taking what I'd learned along my journey and reapplying it to the next target. I reached out to my network to see if anyone could help us promote our venture, and Adam Hark, our editor on *761st*, replied. He was working at Fox as an editor and had a relationship with someone running a segment called "Young Guns" on the Fox Business Channel. Adam connected me with the producer, and after I pitched her on what we were doing, she visited Classickicks to do a profile on Double7 Boutique while we were shooting the campaign. As far as I was concerned, there was only one

point for this press — to put a price tag on this free campaign that we'd done for Nick and Jen.

That number was $35,000.

The three minute profile ran on the Fox Business Channel website and we shared it across every platform available, allowing us to successfully introduce Double7 Boutique as a company that could match the execution of a traditional advertising agency, but at a fraction of the cost. Without the expensive ad buys of traditional rollouts connected to television and print. The web would offer opportunities to us all.

With our press and price tag cemented, we went back to the well again and decided to throw a presentation to as many folks as we could round up who operated in the commercial and advertising spaces. The only thing different from what we'd done with "The *Premium* Presentation" in November 2004 would be the demographic of our audience. We weren't seeking investors for a film this time — we needed clients who saw us as integral to the success of their business. What I see in hindsight, however, is that I misread the landscape. The advertising and marketing industries were changing, just like Hollywood. The traditional agencies were threatened by what upstarts like Double7 offered, and to keep clients they began developing their own in-house teams to operate in the branded space at a cheaper cost. Nevertheless, we had cemented our origin story and secured amazing press to help us get the word out about the Double7 advantage. We'd find our core clientele soon enough.

An interesting occurrence at this time would be the raised eyebrows I'd get from many of my Director friends. In regards to the hours spent on my fledgling company they'd say, "You're a filmmaker, why are you making little videos for small businesses?" Yes, I had just come off the success of Tribeca All Access and *$FREE.99*, but after the journey of making *Premium,* I knew I had to find other ways to get paid. Besides, developing and fundraising for a film is not a full-time job, you can only do so much in a day, let alone a week or a month. My full-time desk job often left me with idle time. My teaching jobs were only a few hours per week, outside of my meticulous class prep. So, if I worked smarter, surely, I could maximize my hours of the day and propel myself forward on all of these parallel paths, no?

It's important to note here that I had a very specific vision and purpose, and the only thing that mattered was following my own compass. The last thing to give any concern to is what other people think. The way I see it, sweat equity is free and the muscles I was working were very important to my growth and integral to the work I do today as a Director of episodic television.

I was building a larger network. I was mastering multiple crafts because I was shooting more and editing more and directing and producing more — which would only help to enhance my skills. The transition that I would make seven years later in 2015 would be powered by the moves that I made to build this production company.

In August of 2012, I stepped away from my full-time desk job at NYU. It was my ten-year anniversary in the position and I did not intend to be celebrated for a fifteenth. I felt comfortable that the teaching

opportunities would continue, and was willing to bet on my ability to continue growing Double7, which was putting more and more pocket change in my bank account.

To that end, I had locked in a job with a "friend" and with our contract in place, knowing I'd be able to cover the costs once the project was complete, I decided to upgrade my camera package to the Canon C100 and Atomos Ninja 2 Recorder. DSLR cameras like the Canon 7D were becoming less professional as their image quality was being surpassed by more prosumer models, which also had better connections for microphones, and if I was going to be relying more on Double7 for income, I definitely needed to deliver a higher quality product.

This "friend" was someone I had co-produced "The *Premium* Presentation" with back in November of 2004. He had secured the liquor sponsor as well as a venue for a later event. But, on this project, he ended up stiffing me for $8,000, and I've never spoken to this guy since.

SELF HELP:
THE ADJUSTMENT

ANGLES

Rather than just be mad about what had transpired with this "friend," I decided to analyze the dynamics of our working relationship. If I were to never get the $8,000 I was owed, there had to be a definitive lesson — an angle — that I could take away from the situation.

That would be my payment.

As we delivered edits on the video, I noticed that this "friend" maintained contact with the client, but I was the gateway to all things creative. I viewed the proposals, hired all of the crew, directed the production, and managed the implementation of client notes during post-production. Without me, there would be no deliverable. If we upped and disappeared, he had no way of completing the job, and for the next project, he'd need to find a whole 'nother team of talented people with all of the equipment necessary to shoot and deliver a campaign.

The takeaway here was that he needed me much more than I needed him. And, if he needed to replace an entire team with gear, I just needed to replace one person — HIM. If I could find the clients and manage the relationships, Double7 could be the soup to nuts solution for a variety of businesses, and I could surely manage those relationships better than this guy could. This asshole stiffing me was just what I needed to turn the corner.

As I worked to build clientele and pay off the $8,000 debt for this equipment that I now owned, I went back to what had always worked. I thought about how I could build awareness around Double7 Images, as well as myself. Anthony Artis, who had shot all of the media connected to our fundraising for *Premium* and was beginning to work on his *Shut Up and Shoot Documentary Guide* (later published by Focal Press), decided it would be cool to do a podcast.

This was at the beginning of podcasting, before it was a household thing. He'd be able to come from the technical side, and I would cover the more creative aspects of filmmaking. We launched the *Double Down Film Show*, an hour-long podcast that ran from 2009 to 2011. We produced 83 episodes, in the beginning interviewing all of the friends that I had from the projects I'd directed including Dorian Missick, Zoe Saldana, Cliff Charles, Sam Pollard, and Dean Sheril Antonio. This allowed us to hone our process and get almost a dozen episodes under our belt before we reached out to potential guests who we didn't already know. My goal was to use the podcast as an opportunity to strengthen my brand and develop new relationships, so when I might want to reach out for a project down the line, the connection would already exist.

As an example, in December 2011, we interviewed Issa Rae, fresh off the success of her Kickstarter campaign for the *Awkward Black Girl* webseries. Six years later, in 2017, I directed *Due North*, the show-within-the-show for Season 2 of *Insecure*, which got me into the DGA. Then, the following year, I directed "Familiar-Like," a Season 3 episode of *Insecure*. That relationship was built firmly on what began on the *Double Down Film Show*, as well as running into Issa a couple times in New Orleans for Essence Music Festival while doing client work for Double7. And, if that's not enough, Issa was the first guest to agree to be on my new podcast, *Let's Shoot! with Pete Chatmon*, launched in June 2020 during the Covid pandemic.

At its peak, the *Double Down Film Show* had 40,000 listeners. I often kick myself in the ass for not continuing the show, particularly after looking at Joe Rogan's $100 million Spotify deal for his podcast, but c'est la vie. Anthony and I had become too bogged down with other projects and made the decision to wrap it all up after Episode 83.

I guess you could say I quit again.

Another brand building strategy was the launch of our "Short Shorts" monthly film event. I partnered with Forrest Smith, a promoter in New York City who was also interested in film, TV, and photography. "Short Shorts" took place the last Tuesday of the month at DROM, a lounge on the Lower East Side, where we would bring together the film community, to get them from behind their computers so they could connect in a physical space and potentially find collaborators for future projects.

I was in charge of finding the films (typically eight to ten per event) where the Directors would introduce their work, respond to a brief Q&A, and have an opportunity to mingle with the crowd before and after at the bar. Once "Short Shorts" concluded, the space transitioned into "The Eclectic Ride," Forrest's weekly music industry party. We ran "Short Shorts" for eighteen months, allowing me to keep my eye on the filmmaking competition (not kidding), further build my brand, and make a little extra money off the price of admission.

In 2013, still itching to create and knowing that the only barrier to making a documentary is a camera and access (much simpler than shooting a heist film like *$FREE.99*), Candice and I teamed up on a documentary project called *Click Here: Or How I Learned to Stop Worrying and Love Making Movies*. I had noticed that with the changing landscape I'd begun to put my finger on in 2008, a lot of Directors were becoming very anxious about how to find their place in an ever-shifting industry. My position was "Don't worry about it, just make something" and get it online en route to perhaps landing a more traditional platform, like Issa eventually did with *Insecure*. Or, on the flip side, if it only ever lives online, there are multiple ways to find success there and build a career. Stop worrying! Opportunity was everywhere, it just required a shift in perspective and changing who you ultimately pointed the finger at as the Boogieman holding you back. In the past, you could always say it was this or that gatekeeper that impeded your progress, but with cheaper cameras and gear, free distribution via YouTube and Vimeo, and free marketing via your own website and social media, well, the new gatekeeper was the man in the

mirror. The opportunity was (and still remains) there for you to take the steering wheel and drive the whole enterprise. You can't keep saying no one will give you a car or a lift down the road.

We shot two weeks of interviews, compiling twenty-eight amazing conversations for *Click Here* from the likes of Reed Morano, James Belfer, Emily Best, Alicia Van Couvering, Franchesca Ramsey, and others, before running an unsuccessful crowdfunding campaign via Seed & Spark. We raised $10,000 of our $50,000 goal. It was hard work and we learned a lot about crowdsourcing. Much like the podcast, I wish we had kept at it and figured out how to secure the funds, as the conversations in that documentary really powered me into the next stage of my career and would have been awesome for other storytellers to hear. I've included links to snippets at the end of this chapter.

As I'd already learned on this journey time and time again, opportunity can arise from the places you'd least expect. Here's another example. Over the 18 months of our "Short Shorts" event, we showed the work of filmmaker Tim O'Neill several times. Tim was editing videos for a friend, and as the communications agency that she worked for expanded, he recognized that the projects they were looking for him to produce were better suited for a production company.

Tim introduced me to Allison Rhone and after a few emails back and forth, we sat down for a coffee in December of 2013. I told her about my background and explained Double7's capabilities. Her employer, Egami Consulting, seemed like an ideal partner for us as they were expanding their video services. We were uniquely positioned to help them offer enhanced branding solutions to all of their clients.

Just a year and a half since my "friend" stiffed me for $8,000, I was looking directly at the opportunity I'd identified to build our business. I would be both the Project Manager and Creative Director of every job. The *Double Down Film Show* built an audience . . . which helped me find filmmakers for "Short Shorts" . . . which ultimately led to the relationship that birthed this new business partnership.

We produced so many jobs with Egami that it's hard to count, but they were always amazing to work with and challenged Double7 to grow, as we were faced with bigger and more frequent projects for the likes of Proctor & Gamble, My Black Is Beautiful, Tide, Cover Girl, and more. Tenishia Jackson Warner, Founder, and Mike Warner, Chief Relationship Officer, were the ultimate partners, and Allison Rhone remains a friend to this day. Black-owned businesses helping each other grow was the icing on top of the cake.

In the Fall of 2014, thanks to Egami, we landed the job that would change my life. Fittingly, it was a campaign for Oprah's "The Life You Want" Tour — an eight-city project for which we shot content to be distributed on Instagram's newly released video platform. Timing had struck again. We produced content for Proctor & Gamble sponsored brands, turning around fifteen short videos in just a couple hours each day and three wrap-up sizzle reels covering the totality of the two-day event. I was learning to work with brands under extremely time sensitive windows, and as the intermediary between Egami, the brand executives, and my creative team (including Anthony Artis, Tristan Nash, and Peter Reinstein). Little did I know, I was developing the necessary skills to work in episodic television.

It was our biggest contract to date, and after all of the parallel paths I'd taken to get there, I was starving to return to what I loved most — directing something in my voice. I wanted to see what I could do with all of the skills I'd been developing in creating literally *thousands* of videos for our clients. I looked at the money I would earn from "The Life You Want" Tour and decided to set aside $10,000 to make something.

Anything.

If I'd had a feature screenplay, it would have been that, but *$FREE.99* was too large in scope and I wanted to act now.

I remembered a short screenplay that my friend Tony Patrick had written. Tony was an actor in my 1997 NYU short film *$5 to 6* (the one with the sync sound problems), and after graduating from the

Dramatic Writing Department, had sold a feature to Hollywood for one of the last great spec deals before the industry started shifting. I had read Tony's script for *BlackCard* back in 2004, and often found myself thinking about it at random moments, more than a decade later. The story was set in an alternate universe where Black folks were required to carry an identification card, similar to freedom papers, that could be pulled at any given moment by a shadow organization called The Commission. Agents from The Commission were tasked with keeping people within the current guidelines for Blackness. This was right up my alley.

I asked Tony if he'd be open to letting me direct it as my next project. I'd pay for everything. He'd get a producer credit and retain ownership over the characters and the world he had created. And we'd work in unison to get the script to the place I envisioned before shooting.

Tony said "Yes" and I was back in the director's chair.

▶ CHAPTER 9 KEYWORD: PIVOT

There are times to buckle down and plow ahead, but occasionally, you've got to look at the results of your efforts to reach your target goal and pivot to something entirely new.

This is where *Curiosity* (Chapter 1) really comes back into play. The right pivot at the right moment can yield the results that have been eluding you.

Don't be afraid to make a change — as long as it's calculated.

RESOURCES

■ *SELF HELP:*
Worksheet 7 — Three Questions to Ask Before Pivoting (Page tbd)

■ *INSPIRATION:*
Podcast
Let's Shoot! with Pete Chatmon, Episode 15
Molly McGlynn on Rejection Being How You Become a Filmmaker
Available on Apple Podcasts, Spotify, and all Podcast Platforms

The Archive
■ *Click Here Video Snippets* — https://vimeo.com/manage/folders/3140728

WORKSHEET 7:
THREE QUESTIONS TO ASK BEFORE PIVOTING

There's no perfect time to make a transition, but don't jump off the deep end into the wilderness with no rations or plan to survive, either. Make sure you've prepared realistic answers to the questions below, as well as an actionable path to achieve them — *before* pivoting to your next goal.

(1) Have you studied the career path for Directors in this space? What will be your first steps over the next three months? Six months? One year? Five years? How long does it typically take for a Director to find her footing in this new arena?

_____

_____

_____

(2) Does your portfolio speak to your ability to deliver in this space? How will you speak about the work you've done in the past to communicate your ability to excel in this new arena in the future?

_____

_____

_____

(3) Have you developed a network that can support you with information and relationships as you begin this transition? List the ten people you expect to be of the most assistance and why.

_____

_____

_____

EXPECTATION

BLACKCARD: THE PSYCHOLOGICAL PIVOT

It was the Fall of 2014. I was 37 years old with $10,000 burning a directorial hole in my pocket. Before I had even reached out to Tony about the script, I thought long and hard about my journey over the past fifteen years since graduating NYU. Investing that amount of money in myself required a bit of a gut check, and I wanted to ensure I had the best frame of mind as I stepped into *BlackCard*.

▸ CHAPTER 10'S KEYWORD is: EXPECTATION

I took a moment to focus on and appreciate the following hard-earned milestones:

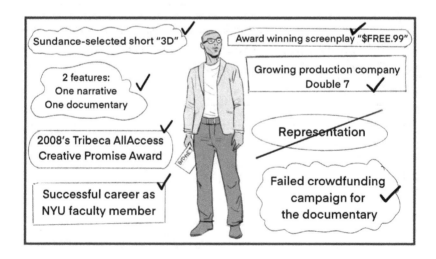

(1) Sundance-selected short film, *3D*, featuring the now world-famous Kerry Washington. . . .

(2) Feature films . . . one narrative (*Premium*) and one documentary (*761st*). . . .

(1) Major acknowledgment with 2008's Tribeca All Access Creative Promise Narrative Award, in addition to multiple awards and prizes on the film festival circuit. . . .

(1) Award-winning screenplay, *$FREE.99*, as well as three others written and ready to be sold. . . .

(1) Successful career as an NYU Faculty Member. . . .

(1) Growing production company with Double7 Images. . . .

(1) Failed crowdfunding campaign for the *Click Here* documentary. . . .

(0) Representation (no agent, no manager, no lawyer). . . .

I had checked quite a few boxes, in fact, more than many of my counterparts that were working professionally. Nevertheless, my idea of success had not been achieved.

I asked myself a series of probing, existential questions:

- *What's not working?*
- *What if everything I'm doing is wrong?*
- *How can I pivot?*

What wasn't working was that I had bought into the definition of "success" on someone else's terms. And, with every milestone that didn't lead to representation or the traditional career path I'd also bought into, I became more and more bitter. Bitterness was the root issue, and it took some mental gymnastics, mixed with brutal honesty, to arrive at this conclusion. I recommend therapy.

Everything I was doing wasn't wrong, as I was clearly finding a way to make a living as a Director, albeit differently than I'd envisioned in 1993. But, over the past ten years since I'd written, produced, and directed *Premium*, I had slowly relinquished my unique vision in exchange for projects I thought would "succeed." After *$FREE.99*, every subsequent script had become more and more a triangulation of themes I wanted to explore, mixed with genres I thought would sell, watered down with characters I felt the studios would like. In reality, I would not have been happy if those projects had succeeded, and in many ways, I'd actually dodged a bullet.

The pivot was simple. If I was going to spend $10,000 of my hard-earned money on *BlackCard*, then the film would be what *I* wanted to see and nothing else. Yes, that "I" is boldface and italicized. After the past 15 years and "no results," what was the point of continuing to dilute my vision?

The directing career I have now is anchored on the following decision:

My expectations would only be shaped by what I could control.

A basketball player can't win every single game, but he or she can most certainly play their absolute best, exercising their skills to exhaustion, while also identifying new weaknesses to overcome in the games that follow. My expectations for *BlackCard* were to tell a story in my voice and to the best of my abilities. At the end of the day, the only guarantee was that, if I rose to the challenge, I could watch a YouTube or Vimeo link that represented my talents as a Director in the year 2015.

HOW TO PUT YOUR MONEY ON SCREEN

Another title for this tip might be "How to Write to What You Know You Have in Your Pocket." When producing a passion project, the most important thing to consider is budget and how much money you can sensibly put toward your effort. *Don't go broke over your art, please.*

To that end, I believe that each project is anchored primarily by whatever themes you are exploring. You can adjust your vision and the scope of your project to successfully explore those themes with the resources you have.

Here are a few suggestions to get control over your budget. Creative adjustments to your script will allow you to complete the project in a fashion where viewers appreciate your storytelling, rather than comment on everything that you failed to pull off because you didn't have the funds.

Characters

More actors mean more mouths to feed. It also means more people to pay (if you're working under any of the SAG agreements available to productions of all scales). Can you tell your story with fewer actors? If you have fewer actors, the individual roles can be more thoroughly explored, and in turn, more enticing to talent. You may also be able to accomplish more each day, as a result of limiting the hair and makeup time across a larger cast. And with no disrespect to any department head, as I value them all, you might even be able to eliminate the need for Hair and Makeup, depending upon your needs for the project.

Wardrobe

Can the actors wear their own clothing? If so, that makes everything simpler and cheaper. You might also be able to eliminate the role of Costume Designer. In *BlackCard*, however, it was important that "The Commission" organization in the film appeared impressive, and part of that was their wardrobe needing to communicate an elite status. Because of that, I hired Tysha Ampadu as our Costume Designer, adding money to the budget, but providing significant savings in other areas, as we benefited from her years of experience and relationships with different boutiques and department stores. All of the incredible outfits in the film were secured with the tiniest of budgets, when considering what we *should* have paid. That is what I mean by "putting your money on screen." Speaking further to relationships, Tysha was someone I had first collaborated with on a music video in 2008, had as a guest speaker for one of my NYU classes in 2013, and always remained in touch with as a friend the entire time.

Locations and Production Design

Do you really need multiple locations? Can you shoot this on a sound-stage, like I did with *Confessions of Cool*? Can you use your apartment? Shoot on exterior locations that require relatively inexpensive permits? The unfortunate budgetary reality of all locations that you don't own is that you will need to provide Liability Insurance to any location owner and, yes, that too will cost you. A short-term production policy may range from several hundred to several thousand dollars, depending on what your script calls for. On *BlackCard*, we were able to secure the office location for "The Commission" thanks to our client, Egami Consulting, charging us the grand total of $1. Relationships.

Crew

The more you know how to do (or are willing to learn), the better chance you have at completing your project within a smaller budget range. Can you shoot? Edit? Drive the van? Cut the bagels? Act? Anything you can do to bring down your headcount will bring down your budget — just be sure not to sacrifice the overall quality of your project. As an example, if you have a performance heavy script and you are *not* an actor, this may not be the right time to step in front of the camera.

Post-Production

Your best bet is to edit the project yourself, or like any of the above key crew positions, find someone looking for an opportunity, who is enthusiastic to work on something for little to no money. You may also be able to barter one service or product for another. On *BlackCard*, I paid my Editor what I could to cut the short, but I spent two weeks essentially working as her assistant editor, setting up the project files and bins so she could work as efficiently as possible. I then paid my Sound Designer with an extra MacBook Pro I had purchased, but not needed, for the Branded Content campaign that made it possible for me to fund *BlackCard*.

Remember, money (or lack thereof) doesn't have to stop you from creating. In fact, I believe that the highest levels of creativity are powered by having to create from a place of desperation.

After several meetings and revisions, Tony and I arrived at the shooting script. I'd already rounded up the usual suspects, including Christina DeHaven, who would now produce a third project with me after *3D* and *761st*. I cast Dorian Missick as "Leonard" and off the strength of his trusted, creative opinion, talked to his wife Simone about the project, ultimately casting her as "Lona." Five years later, she'd be #1 on the call sheet on CBS's *All Rise* and have me brought in to direct the Season 1 finale (though Covid-19 would prevent that from happening).

The rest of the cast was comprised of talented New York actors who I admired and had relationships with from the independent film circuit. Hisham Tawfiq (*The Blacklist*), Stephen Hill (*Magnum P.I.*), Erika Myers (*Friends from College*), Malikha Mallette (*Daredevil*), April Matthis (*New Amsterdam*), Valence Thomas (*Men in Black 3*), Michael Markham (*The Decades of Mason Carroll*), Vladimir Versaiiles (*Orange Is the New Black*), and Nasser Metcalfe (*Tennessee*) all brought their A-games.

The crew consisted of the folks that had powered Double7 for the past ten years. Dylan Verrechia (cinematographer), Drew Renard Droege (production designer), K.A. Miille (editor), Tysha Ampadu (costume design), ELEW (music), and Sam Miille (sound design).

The $10,000 budget swelled to almost $30,000, but I knew going in that this would happen. I had prepared for it, but I wanted to make sure everyone focused on using creativity to solve problems, as opposed to my money!

As March 2015 drew to a close, I was taken by a Miles Davis quote I'd read that crystallized everything I'd gone through since picking up that Super 8mm film camera in 1993.

"Man, sometimes it takes you a long time to sound like yourself."

Truer words had never been spoken.

▶ CHAPTER 10 KEYWORD: EXPECTATION

When life fails to meet your expectations, bitterness, anger, and unhappiness often follow.

Adapt your perspective to accept the fact that there is no timeline for your directorial dreams. Maintain the positive outlook and energy required to build a team around your vision. Ensure that every step in your journey is a victory by redefining what each opportunity offers to your growth.

RESOURCES

■ *INSPIRATION:*
Podcast
Let's Shoot! with Pete Chatmon, Episode 14
Seith Mann on Being a Complete Filmmaker and How Timing Led To "The Wire"
Available on Apple Podcasts, Spotify, and all Podcast Platforms

The Archive
■ *BlackCard – The Short Film* — https://petechatmon.com/project/black-card/
■ *BlackCard – 10 Behind The Scenes Snippets* — https://vimeo.com/manage/folders/3140708

(FUND RAISING)
— No HUMANS
— BLACK SVVS FOR FREE ($400.00 IN BUDGET)
★ — SPONSORSHIPS — & FREE Budget Title : BLACK CARD

— INS: Short Term vs. Year long
    ↳ Co-production ????

Script Dated : 7/7/2014 — WARDROBE →
Budget Draft Dated : Aug 25, 2014
Production # :
Start Date : TBD
Finish Date :
Total Shoot Days : 3
Post Weeks : 2

Producers :
Director:
Location : New York, NY
Prepared By : C. DeHaven
Unions: SAGAFTRA - Short

Acct#	Category Description	Page	Total
1100	STORY & SCENARIO	1	0
1200	PRODUCERS UNIT	1	0
1215	TRAVEL & LIVING EXPENSES	1	0
1300	DIRECTION	2	0
1400	CAST	2	0
1500	CAST TRAVEL & LIVING *Hotel & Ground Transpo*	2	1,100
	Total Above-The-Line		**1,100**
2100	PRODUCTION STAFF	4	150
2200	ART DIRECTION	4	600
2400	SET OPERATIONS	4	1,500
2800	ANIMALS & PICTURE VEHICLES	4	600
2900	WARDROBE	5	500
3000	MAKEUP & HAIRDRESSING	5	100
3200	LIGHTING & GRIP	5	500
3300	CAMERA	6	350
3400	PRODUCTION SOUND	6	75
3500	TRANSPORTATION	7	1,070
3600	LOCATION	7	900
3800	PRODUCTION FILM & LAB	8	600
	Total Below-The-Line Production		**6,945**
4500	EDITORIAL	9	200
4700	POST PRODUCTION SOUND	9	0
4800	POST FILM/LAB	9	1,500
	Total Below-The-Line Post		**1,700**
6600	LEGAL & ACCOUNTING	10	0
6700	INSURANCE	10	0
	Total Below-The-Line Other		**0**
	Total Above-The-Line		**1,100**
	Total Below-The-Line		**8,645**
	Total Above and Below-The-Line		**9,745**
	CONTINGENCY (BTL) : 5.0%		487
	Total Fringes		**0**
	Grand Total		**10,232**

The Entertainment Partners Services Group, MM Budgeting

THE DIRECTOR'S CUT: ACT II

REPUTATION.
REPETITION.
RESILIENCE.
PIVOT.
EXPECTATION

I needed to harness and master the principles of these keywords in order to navigate *The Confrontation* portion of my journey. I thought I'd found "success" with the realization of my feature film *Premium*, but I was broke and becoming creatively unfulfilled with my professional and artistic pursuits. Over an eight-year period, I stayed the course and found the way back to my voice, setting the table for the creative revival I'm experiencing now.

Reputation helped me build allies. . . .

Repetition reinforced the value of what I'd already learned along the journey. . . .

Resilience was needed to dismiss the idea of quitting. . . .

The Pivot helped me successfully redirect my efforts. . . .

Expectation, or rather, losing it, was the glue that held all of the above together and propelled me into *The Resolution*.

Refer back to Chapters 6-10 in Act II for specific *How-To, Self-Help,* and *Inspirational* tools to propel you along your path as a Director.

2006–2014

ACT II: THE CONFRONTATION

- *Premium* premieres in the World Cinema Competition at the Miami International Film Festival
- Distribution negotiations begin
- Still in debt after paying for NYU and the 7 year journey of making *Premium*, Pete begins to focus on becoming faculty at NYU Film School

- Pete wins the Tribeca All Access "Creative Promise Narrative Award" for the heist screenplay, *$FREE.99*, co-written by Candice Sanchez McFarlane
- Pete directs his first major music video for the title track to the film, *Welcome Home Roscoe Jenkins*, starring Martin Lawrence
- Pete continues writing additional screenplays, including *What About Us?*, *Your Next Ex*, and an untitled biopic on Sam Cooke
- *Premium* has a Showtime cable premiere and is available via Netflix and on DVD at big box retailers

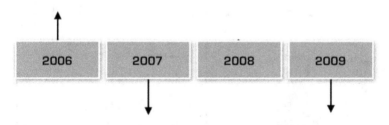

| 2006 | 2007 | 2008 | 2009 |

- Pete begins work on is second fature, the WWII documentary *781st*, narrated by Andre Braugher
- *Premium* has a limited theatrical release via CodeBlack Entertainment

- Pete returns to Los Angeles for agent and manager meetings
- There is no interest in representing him
- Still in debt, Pete identifies a shift in the commercial industry and repositions his production company, Double7 Images, to create branded content

The Director's Cut

Pete interviews for an adjunct faculty position at NYU
He is not hired by the university, but continues to teach part-time
To elevate his branding and increase his audience, Pete creates a podcast with Anthony Artis called *The Double Down Film Show*

- Pete launches *Short Shorts*, a monthly film event on the Lower East Side of Manhattan that will run for 18 months
- *The Double Down Film Show* ends after 83 on hour episodes
- Pete resigns from his administrative position at NYU as Assistant Production Coordinator in the film department

- Double7 Images secures a branded content compaign for Proctor & Gamble, producing Instagram videos for Oprah's *The Life You Want Tour*
- Pete uses $30,000 from his fee for the campaign to produce and direct the short film *BlackCard*, returning to his roots as a filmmaker making passion projects for his own creative growth
- Pete executive produces *Wilmington On Fire*, directed by Christopher Everett, a feature documentary that chronicles The Wilmington Massacre of 1898, a bloody attack on the Black community by a heavily armed white mob with the support of the North Carolina Democratic Party

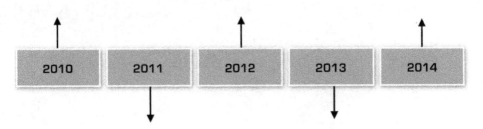

| 2010 | 2011 | 2012 | 2013 | 2014 |

- Double7 Images slowly grows, creating video and photo campaigns for small businesses
- Pete is given additional classes to teach at NYU

- Pete focuses on expanding Double7 Images, partnering with InteractiveOne and Egami Consulting to increase the scope of his production services

Scenes from the "water bottle tour." General meetings are an important component of the Director's journey. I tag these photos as #lobbies on my @petechatmon Instagram account. I also use the hashtag #directorslife for photos that chronicle the journey. (Disney | ABC Television)

Meeting with HBO Max about new projects on their drama slate as I worked to transition into more episodic dramas. #lobbies #directorslife

Prepping episode 302 of "Insecure" on the Atlanta to Los Angeles flight immediately after wrapping episode 306 of "Greenleaf." #directorslife

Table read for episode 112 of "Single Parents." The cast, producers, writers, department heads, network, and studio gather for a live reading of the script before final revisions and production. The most current draft of the production schedule sits next to my iPad. #directorslife

Director's Office for episode 306 of "Greenleaf." Every show welcomes you with a prep book, floor plans for sets and locations, and in some cases, a bottle of wine, mug, water bottle, and candle! #directorslife

I grab a similar picture on every show and label it #obligatoryslateshot on my @petechatmon Instagram account. #directorslife

Placing fire engines, ladder trucks, and aid cars with assistant director Kris Krengel for episode 314 of "Station 19." #directorslife

A friendly reminder from the producers of "Station 19." I got the wide shot. #directorslife

A rare lonely moment in video village. Reviewing blocking and shot lists on episodes 201 and 206 of "The Last O.G." #directorslife

Rehearsing on "The Last O.G." with Tracy Morgan, Cedric The Entertainer, and Allen Maldonado as showrunner Saladin K. Patterson looks on. #directorslife

My view from the process trailer as we prepared to tow Tiffany Haddish and Taylor Mosby around Harlem in "The Last O.G." #directorslife

Re-blocking a scene on episode 201 of "Mythic Quest" after rehearsal revealed a better approach. We shot this on the CBS Radford lot so our production designer Valdar Wilt created this signage to mask the fact that we were using crew parking as a location. #directorslife

Rehearsing Lynn Whitfield and Keith David on "Greenleaf" as assistant director Veronica Hodge-Hampton looks on. #directorslife

On the last day of a 2-episode "Grown-ish" block the producers and crew surprised me by wearing my signature army hat!

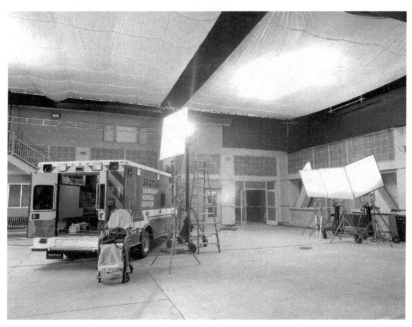

Placing the ambulance for episode 1706 of "Grey's Anatomy." Introducing vehicles and stunts requires an extra level of preparation and attention to detail to get your shots and make the day. #directorslife

A Porsche Cayenne rigged with the "Russian Arm" to get our RussFest shots for episode 605 of "Silicon Valley." This equipment allowed us to drive at high speeds and capture shots from multiple angles. (Cuddeback Lake, California) #directorslife

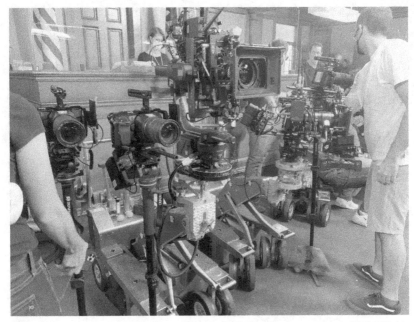

We had up to 27 cameras available for episode 203 of "All Rise." Producing Director Michael Robin designed this system to create a safer environment for shooting during Covid-19. #directorslife

My view in video village. I had to develop heightened levels of concentration in order to make notes on what was happening in each of the 12 frames! #directorslife

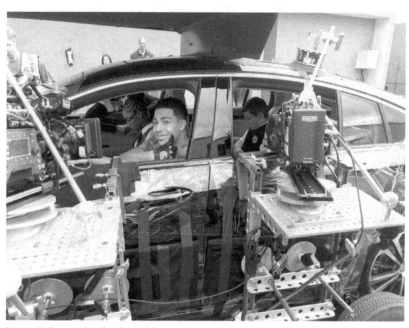

Marcus Scribner ready to hit the road for process trailer driving shots on the "Waltz in A Minor" episode of "Black-ish." (Not in frame: two additional cameras mounted on the hood for singles and a 2-shot of Marcus and Marsai Martin in the front seat.) #directorslife

Setting up motorcycle process trailer shots for a stunt sequence in episode 212 of "A Million Little Things." This was my first episode shot out of the country in Vancouver, British Columbia. #directorslife

On a tech scout for episodes 201 and 202 of "Grownish." Assistant director Deon Boyce (checkered Vans) takes notes to share with the crew as cinematographer Mark Doering-Powell (standing behind me) and production designer Kathleen Widomski (hat under right arm) look on. #directorslife

Giving adjustment notes for a two camera dolly move on "Grown-ish." #directorslife

My mobile village view from the back of the tow truck. Notice the actors, Jason Ritter and Sutton Foster, are sitting on the motorcycle via process trailer rig. #directorslife

Dummies for Sutton Foster and Jason Ritter. It's movie magic! #directorslife

Between scenes on the set of "Grey's Anatomy" with James Pickens Jr. and Kelly McCreary. #directorslife

Obligatory wrap photo with Issa Rae on the last day of shooting episode 302 of "Insecure." #directorslife

Getting the Marvel "Eternals" grip from Kumail Nanjiani after wrapping episode 605 of "Silicon Valley." #directorslife

Season 14 wrap photo with Rob McElhenney and Charlie Day after completing a four episode block of "It's Always Sunny in Philadelphia." #directorslife

On the set of "Mixed-ish" with Mykal-Michelle Harris and Ethan William Childress. #directorslife

On the set of "Atypical" with Robia Rashid, Mary Rohlich, Theresa Mulligan Rosenthal, and Jen Regan. #directorslife

On Cuddeback Lake for the RussFest
opening sequence of "Silicon Valley" with
Chris Diamantopoulos. #directorslife

On the set of "Black-ish" with
Laurence Fishburne. #directorslife

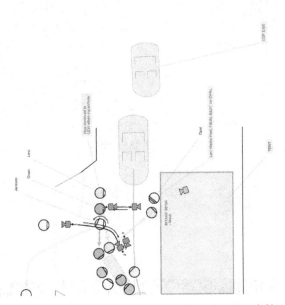

I use the Hollywood Shot Designer app to build shot lists on top of floor plans (provided by production) or diagrams that I create as a reference for a location or set. I made this for a scene of a patient arriving at Grey Sloan Memorial in episode 1706 of "Grey's Anatomy." #directorslife

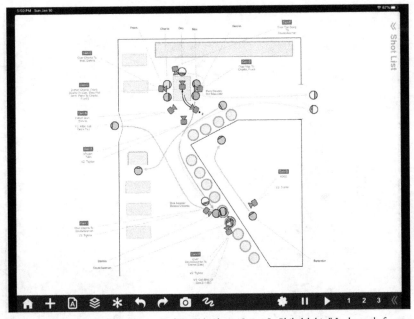

This was my original blocking for a scene from "It's Always Sunny In Philadelphia." It changed after we rehearsed, but you better have a plan before arriving on set. #directorslife

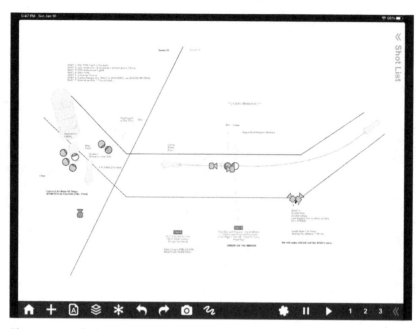

This was my plan for the motorcycle crash in episode 212 of "A Million Little Things." The diagonal line separating Scenes 30 and 31 represents the area of the location I did not want to reveal in either scene in efforts to make the location feel larger in scope on camera. #directorslife

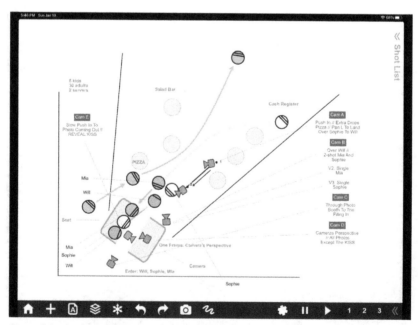

I created this for the tag (final scene before credits) from episode 112 of "Single Parents." We turned a cafeteria on the Fox Lot into a pizzeria with a photo booth (brought in by the art department.) We were very limited in what we could show so the diagonal lines represent my available lines of sight for coverage within the scene. #directorslife

ACT III:
THE RESOLUTION

[2015-Present]

TELEVISION DIRECTOR DEVELOPMENT PROGRAMS

BlackCard premiered at the Los Angeles Film Festival on Friday, June 12th, 2015, as part of the #BlackLifeBlackProtest section. In what would be one of my most exhausting commutes ever, I traveled from New Jersey to Los Angeles and back to New York City in less than 24 hours, as our second screening of the film was just a day later.

▶ **Chapter 11's keyword is: HUMILITY**

My whirlwind Los Angeles excursion offered me the chance to work through the proverbial first screening jitters. Until you've shown your film to a variety of audiences multiple times, it's hard to predict what the response will be — and even then, you can still be off the mark. This particular section of the festival was tailor made for our film, but nevertheless, that didn't mean it would connect. Fortunately, it did, with people laughing at the right times, and you could hear a pin drop during the final moments when the dramatic payoff between the "Leonard" and "Lona" characters unfolded. Dorian and Simone Missick also attended, and we all felt like we had something pretty special on our hands.

I took the redeye back to Newark Liberty International Airport, grabbed a change of clothes and my suit upon arriving home to Jersey City, and then hopped in a waiting Town Car to a midtown

Manhattan hotel for all the festivities related to our next screening as part of the ABFF (American Black Film Festival) HBO Short Film Competition. I'd watched other filmmakers catapult to success from this event, including Ryan Coogler with *Fruitvale* (2013) and *Black Panther* (2018). He had won the competition in 2011 for his short film *Fig*. It was also a bit of a homecoming as almost a decade earlier, I'd screened both *Premium* and *761st* as part of the festival.

BlackCard was one of five finalists in competition — each receiving a $5,000 prize and a licensing deal with HBO. The winning film, as selected by the jury, received $10,000. The ABFF HBO Short Film Competition was designed with the filmmakers in mind — rather than showing all of the films back to back with one Q&A at the end, which could leave audience interaction to potentially be hijacked by interest in a particular film, the organizers structured a moderated Q&A to occur immediately after each film, ensuring all the Directors could be given their due spotlight.

After our screening, a woman injured herself going down the steps of the theater, putting the entire event on pause until the medics arrived at the Times Square AMC Empire 25. This created an unexpected opportunity for additional audience interaction that propelled me on my journey into episodic television (thankfully, she was alright).

I was approached by Brett King, Vice President, Creative Programming, Diversity & Inclusion, at Sony Pictures Entertainment. He was looking for filmmakers for the second year of the Sony Diverse Directors Program and, having enjoyed the film, he strongly suggested that I apply. Kelly Edwards, Vice President of Talent Development at HBO, who was integral to the ABFF HBO Competition in which we were screening, told me Brett was great and, with no lack of clarity, instructed me to get my application in ASAP! I had just a couple of days to cobble together my submission, which included securing recommendations, the stamp of a notary public, and the crafting of the essay of all essays that would communicate my talents, commitment, and readiness to excel, if given a chance.

I'd had my eye on television directing for some time now, particularly after my friend Seith Mann's career had begun to take off. Seith had gone through the Disney/ABC Directing Program (for which I had already applied several times). He'd written me a recommendation for the HBO Access Directing Fellowship in 2014 (for which I did not get past the first round), and always pointed me toward similar opportunities when they arose. His first episodes of television were for *Grey's Anatomy* in 2006, followed by a diverse group of shows including *The Wire*, *Sons of Anarchy*, *Entourage*, *House of Lies*, *Friday Night Lights*, and more recently *Raising Dion*, *Homeland*, and *Blindspotting*. His NYU short film, *Five Deep Breaths*, which put him on the radar of the Disney/ABC program, was incredibly thoughtful, artistically executed, and I was slowly envisioning a world where I could be the next Seith.

Let's pause for a moment to chat about the birth of these diversity programs. In a Director's Guild of America study from 2013–2014, out of 776 total episodic directors, across all platforms, the demographics of who was given the opportunity to sit in the director's chair was as follows:

- 647 (83%) were male
- 129 (17%) were female
- 681 (88%) were Caucasian

- 52 (7%) were Black
- 24 (3%) were Latinx
- 19 (2%) were Asian-American

There was no reason — other than bias, racism, and gender discrimination — for these numbers to be so abysmal. Armed with this information and a clear picture of an industry not reflecting America as it existed, the DGA worked with the studios to create pipelines to make them aware of talent they'd previously been unaware of and in many cases, were outright overlooking. Talent like me.

This resulted in the infrastructure for diverse Directors to learn how television is produced, including the opportunity to meet the executives and creatives responsible for hiring decisions, as well as the chance to shadow working directors to see what they experienced in real time. Some studios were ahead of the curve in setting up programs, as illustrated by Seith's journey, while others did not really take action until forced. Brett King and Kelly Edwards were the stewards of these programs at their respective studios, and I'd soon meet their counterparts at NBC Universal, Disney/ABC, CBS, and more. I'd also see just how differently each program was designed.

Now, back to the Sony Diverse Directors Program. I made it through the interview process with Brett and his team and was selected as one of fifteen Directors for its second year. Having had success with my psychological pivot on *BlackCard* — no more triangulating and <u>simply creating content that I was passionate about</u> — I worked to determine realistic expectations in relation to any television directing program for which I might be selected.

I identified three things that I could guarantee to myself, no matter what happened.

MY THREE GUARANTEES:

1. I'd learn the business and creative aspects of how television is produced (*something I knew nothing about*). . . .
2. I'd meet the people behind the scenes who power the industry (*folks who I did not already know*). . . .
3. I'd take this information back to New Jersey to elevate whatever passion projects I would direct next. . . .

These three things could NOT be taken away from me. I did not have to be selected to shadow on a show, or be given an episode to direct, or secure representation for a television directing program to have been fruitful or successful for me. "My Three Guarantees" were attainable because I would focus all of my attention on making them happen.

This perspective shift had also been informed by Ava DuVernay's, 2015 SXSW Film Festival keynote address, where she spoke about the "desperation coat" filmmakers often don't realize they present when they walk in a room. They are often cloaked in desperation, so thirsty for their project to get made, that it's not only the first thing that people see upon meeting them — it's the only thing. Unfortunately, anything delivered through desperation fails to generate excitement. In turn, it makes the person on the other side of the conversation feel like your project or career would never happen unless they made the decision to answer the call, which makes it appear as if you're selling something that has not found any buyers to date.

This is where we get back to that keyword of "humility." I had accomplished a lot on my own over the past 16 years since graduating from NYU's Tisch School of the Arts. However, the bitterness of my expectations would not serve me on this new journey, nor would any sense of entitlement. I decided that I would treat this entry into television directing as if I literally knew nothing. I didn't try to process what I learned through my prior experiences, and I only applied those lessons if it became clear that they'd be helpful. This was an important energy to bring into this journey, as along the way, I would shadow people with less experience than me and identify opportunities for a Director to excel that I'd ultimately need to keep to myself as a silent observer. Humility is key whenever you step into a new environment, and as I continue to build a career in episodic directing, it's something I still take with me to each new show that I direct.

I carried "My Three Guarantees" into Sony's six-week program, which took place over individual sessions between September and October of 2015 on their Culver City studio lot. We were divided into three groups of five — two groups of Drama Directors and one group of Comedy Directors. In an effort to determine where I saw myself fitting, Brett King asked which group I wanted to be placed in, leading to one of the most important conversations I had at the start of this journey. Well, it didn't begin as much of a conversation, as I rambled on, not quite sure how to answer. While I had often directed comedic projects, my driving force for every film had always been something dramatic, and usually historical. Sensing that my word salad was not doing anything for my cause — perhaps it was the silence? — I asked, "What do you think I should do?" Brett replied, "If you prove you can tell a joke, you have a shot at transitioning to drama."

He was absolutely right. I reconsidered all of the Hollywood history I'd studied since NYU and immediately thought of Jamie Foxx. The comedic giant who starred in "Booty Call" was the same dramatic craftsman that won an Academy Award for *Ray*. On the Director side, Adam McKay was an example of what I plan to do with the rest of my career. The man who brought us the hilarious *Anchorman* transitioned to bringing audiences some of the best dramas on film and television, including *The Big Short*, *Vice*, and *Succession*. I was sold.

Each week, our comedy group had an intimate conversation with a working episodic Director and either an executive or creative collaborator to provide complementary perspectives. We diligently moved through an overview on the business workings of the industry, pre-production, production, post-production, equipment, and more. The

"prize" of the program was an opportunity to shadow on a Sony produced television show.

I'd been keeping in touch with Kelly Edwards at HBO, making sure to update her on my journey and searching for any pearls of wisdom that might help me avoid amateur mistakes along the way. She provided another lesson that I hold dear to this day — *ask for what you want*. She suggested I ask Brett what the path to being one of the five shadowing directors would entail. He replied, of course, that "there is no clear path or guarantee," but I viewed it like the lawyer who blurts out something that the judge instructs the court to strike from the record. You know the jury heard it and it just might continue to resonate in their minds, even though they've been ordered to forget it. At a minimum, I wanted to communicate my passion to Brett for what this opportunity offered, and if I were the only one of the Directors to ask this question, it would surely help to set me apart. I continue to be this straightforward as I move through my career, always working to make sure, before the ask, that I leave a good impression so people can envision me filling the shoes of my request — however big they may be.

Ultimately . . . drumroll . . . I was selected as one of the five Directors to shadow on a Sony production. Although I was in the comedy group, I lived in New Jersey and was placed on an episode of *The Black-list* because it shot in New York. I was excited to be slated to visit my first ever television set.

Another thing I had quickly realized during the Sony program was the value of my experience working with Tony Patrick on *BlackCard*. Episodic television is the writer's medium. Your job as Director is to understand the showrunner and creator's vision for the show, how your episode fits into that vision, and apply your directorial abilities to visualize that kernel of the story while maintaining the show's overall DNA. This does not mean you don't bring your unique talents to it — surely, we've all seen bad episodes of shows we love, so it does matter who sits in that chair and how they do their job — rather, it just means that it's not your feature film where your authority hovers over the entire process. My experience with *BlackCard* was similar. For over a decade, that premise, the world, and the characters continued to resonate with me, so as Tony and I navigated our way to the shooting script, my focus was to maintain the integrity of his original concept.

I brought all of these lessons to the next program I was selected for — the HBO Access Directing Fellowship in June of 2016 — run by Kelly Edwards. Relationships, relationships, relationships. The three selected Directors would direct a digital pilot of a script that had gone through the HBO Access Writing Fellowship the year before. Each pilot would have a $100,000 budget and be tethered to the HBO executive who had guided the writing fellow through development. I'd be working the same muscle I'd developed with Tony, as each Director would be collaborating with the writer to cut their scripts down from half hour episodes to twelve-minute pilots.

I directed *Lady Bouncer* from a script by Sarah McChesney. One of the stars was Christina Elmore, who continued her relationship with the HBO family four years later as "Condola" in *Insecure* Seasons 3 and 4. The cast was rounded out with Blair Beeken (*Dead to Me*), Jon Huertas (*This Is Us*), Lisa Vidal (*Being Mary Jane*), Deray Davis (*Snow-fall*), Susan Slome (*Silicon Valley*), and Justin Welborn (*Justified*). My cinematographer was Kira Kelly, who went on to shoot the *13th* and *Queen Sugar* for Ava DuVernay, as well as an episode of *Insecure*.

It was an amazing process and provided me with an invaluable lesson about coverage. The days were over-scheduled, as we had to capture the entirety of our shows in three days — no matter what. *Lady Bouncer* opened with a chase/stunt sequence that took much more time than budgeted, but I felt like I had to get what I needed, so that the first thing viewers saw would be well executed and compelling. I figured I could make adjustments in the coverage for my later scenes, though I discovered there's a limit to such decisions within the world of television directing.

There was an office scene between Blair Beeken, Christina Elmore, and Lisa Vidal, for which I never shot an over-the-shoulder in the reverse direction of the master shot, saving time so we could make the day. I made the creative decision to cover Blair and Christina with clean singles on their side of the desk, separating them emotionally from Lisa's character. Well, when I delivered my cut, everyone wanted to see the matching over-the-shoulder shots of Blair and Christina, and when I replied that I hadn't gotten that coverage, it became an issue. The takeaway was clear — avoid blocking scenes, based on time, in a way that won't allow me to capture matching coverage. Had it been my film, no one would have questioned it, but again, TV is the writer's medium and networks expect options so they can sculpt a scene the way *they* see fit in the edit. When you're a new Director, this may be viewed as inexperience instead of mastery of craft, and I knew I would have to improve my blocking and camera set-ups moving forward to avoid this pitfall whenever I secured that coveted first episode. This was an incredible lesson to learn when the stakes weren't as high as they'd become in the future.

HOW TO DESIGN YOUR BLOCKING AND COVERAGE FOR TELEVISION

Once you book your first episode of television, your next task will be to actually direct it! These are the questions I ask myself for each and every scene (after having completed all of the necessary prep work driven by the needs of the script):

Which direction provides the most depth for my Master Shot?

Your Master Shot will capture the entire scene and needs to not only hold the movements of all characters — it must also be visually interesting. Depth is the first step to ensure an attractive composition for your frame. If you can, choose depth first.

Which character has the most important entrance?

Your Master Shot should ideally be angled toward receiving the entrances and exits of your characters. If you have multiples of those, identify which entrance or exit *most* impacts the scene and the overall storytelling. This is a pretty hard and fast rule for broadcast television and basic cable, but on premium cable and streaming platforms, where there's more time and money for nuanced storytelling, you may have a creative reason for going against this instinct.

Which angle provides a view of the largest number of characters?

Some scenes are so large — either in featured cast or scripted action — that answering the above questions may not yield the best coverage. In these instances, you're ultimately governed by getting as much as you can in your Master Shot, knowing that your additional coverage will "put eyes on" the important beats of the scene. That said, this concept (like any rule or guide) needs to be ignored at times. In my *Silicon Valley* episode, entitled "Tethics," one of the opening scenes featured the "Russ Hannemann" character showing a video presentation to four members of the Pied Piper team. Rather than designing a Master Shot focusing on the four Pied Piper members, I placed the camera behind them, shooting over their four backs toward "Russ." It was more important to put the audience in the position of Team Pied Piper, receiving this crazy pitch, than to angle on the largest number of characters.

What blocking, if any, helps to communicate the subtext of the scene?

While the blocking will ultimately be a collaborative effort between you, the talent, and sometimes the camera department, the first iteration of the actions each character will take (in addition to what's scripted) will come from you. What door or hallway will they enter from? Will they remain standing the entire scene? Move to the island in the kitchen? Make a sandwich? Get out of bed and pace? Who sits next to whom in the big dinner scene?

Whatever you choose should be strategic and serve the following purposes:

1. It should give the actors business connecting to the emotions of the scene. . . .
2. It should keep the scene dynamic and visually interesting. . . .
3. It should easily fold into the rest of your coverage for the scene. . . .

The dirty little secret of TV directing is that if you're really smart about your blocking and your Master Shot, you will be able to add your unique voice and vision to the episode. Once you fall into your 50/50 shots, over-the-shoulders, closeups, etc., the show will essentially begin to shoot itself.

How can I keep this blocking positioned in a style where it can be captured with the fewest additional camera angles?

Understanding the 180-degree line is important. Have your characters move all you want, but understand that if they pivot and move downstage, upstage, or cross the invisible line, you may be committing yourself to additional shots. Coverage, in television, means every shot you have on one character is "matched" on the other side with the other character, and I can't tell you how many times I've seen Directors fail to make their day because they over-complicated their blocking.

Another dirty little secret of TV directing is that if you have your characters take the marks previously held by other characters in the scene, it will feel much more dynamic and visually interesting without having had to move the camera.

How does the show tend to shoot scenes like this?

You'll actually have answered this question before any of the above. In your prep, you will have watched enough episodes of the show to know exactly what the style is so you can work within that framework. I know on *Grey's Anatomy*, Debbie Allen likes a "functioning master" which is basically a Master Shot that starts wide enough to establish the set or location, then develops into coverage, allowing the camera to move and the scene to be shot with a little more speed. On *Black-ish*, I know that Kenya Barris likes the 2-shot for much of the comedy and, when possible, to avoid having characters moving while delivering a joke. On *Insecure*, Issa Rae typically does not want the camera moving unless the actors are moving. All of these different stylistic guidelines are guide rails as you design your blocking and coverage for every scene.

How important is this scene to the episode?

Is this a montage piece? Is it the culmination of a multiple episode story arc? Is it setting up a storyline that will be explored further down the line? Being able to weigh the importance of a scene will help you decide how much time and how many resources you want to devote. When I directed the Season 17 mid-season finale for *Grey's Anatomy*, there were some scenes that I shot as a "one-r," while others that I spent significant time on (while still making my day), because I knew they had tremendous weight not only for the characters, but for the audience.

Of course, there are many more decisions that come into play, but these questions center me, allowing me to focus on a perspective from which to approach the scene and furthermore, design the episode.

After HBO Access, I was selected for NBC Universal's directing program. This program took place in August of 2016 and was managed at the time by Karen Horne, Senior Vice President, Programming Talent Development & Inclusion. It offered a shadowing opportunity for a select number of the Directors, though I was not chosen. Everyone, however, participated in a one-day boot camp, composed of many of the topics I'd begun learning about during the Sony sessions. We met amazing executives and creatives, including Jaffar Mahmood, who had previously been a fellow in the program and was beginning to find success in the industry directing half hour, single camera comedies. He was another example of a living, breathing Director that made the leap from program to getting paid!

A bit of kismet occurred when Linda Mendoza (*Ugly Betty*, *Scrubs*, *Brooklyn Nine-Nine*, *Wanda Sykes: Not Normal* and more), a talented Director of both single and multi-camera comedies, as well as live events, shared her journey with us. She mentioned that she was booked for an upcoming episode of *Black-ish*, and since I had a standing invitation to shadow on the show (more on that in Chapter 13), I asked if she would be okay with me observing her. She was forthcoming and genuine and I felt she'd be the perfect person from whom I could learn about the craft. Linda agreed and I took that information back to my agent and manager (yes, I'd finally gotten one — more on that in the next chapter!) who took it back to ABC.

My fourth and final directing program began in September of 2016 and would last for two broadcast seasons, concluding in August of 2018. I was finally selected for the Disney/ABC Directing Fellowship, following in the 2006 footsteps of my friend, Seith Mann. This program, spearheaded at the time by Janine Jones-Clark, Executive Director, Creative Talent Development & Inclusion and Emerlynn Lampitoc, Manager, Creative Talent Development & Inclusion was unique, not only because of the duration and opportunity to shadow on multiple shows, but the fact that each fellow would be given two mentors from whom to seek advice. There was an executive mentor (someone from the network or studio to help you understand the business) and a DGA mentor (a working Director who could speak to the specifics of your potential creative journey).

My executive mentor was Sydnee Rimes, Vice President of Current Programming at ABC Studios. My DGA mentor was Ken Whittingham (*Parks & Recreation, 30 Rock, The Office, Grace & Frankie, Atypical, Modern Family*, and more). Under closer scrutiny, it appeared to me that these mentors perfectly aligned with my career goals of getting a start in episodic directing via half hour, single camera comedy. I asked Janine Jones-Clark if this was the case and she smiled. The answer was "Yes."

During my time in the Disney/ABC Directing Fellowship, I shadowed on *Black-ish* and *Grey's Anatomy*, booking episodes on both shows. I even met my lovely, future wife on the set of *Grey's Anatomy* while observing Nzingha Stewart, another NYU alum who had participated in the 2014–2016 program. She was another living, breathing example that I could make this happen.

In 2020, the DGA announced that for the first time, the industry was nearing parity in the diversity of hiring. I'm hopeful about the prospects of how the industry continues to respond to the #BlackLivesMatter movement, as well as the content sure to come from the diverse creators and showrunners getting their long overdue shot at telling stories that reflect America as it truly exists.

I gained a great deal of knowledge over the course of these four programs, nurturing many relationships that continue to this day. My hope is that Directors following in my path will find an industry fully aware of the value we bring to all storytelling and an executive suite that doesn't need to be coerced into acknowledging diversity. Heightening inclusion behind the desk must also happen.

▶ CHAPTER 11 KEYWORD: HUMILITY

What you've achieved in one arena often means nothing in another.

As you step into new spaces as a Director, it's important to remain humble and return to the Keywords that powered you through *Act I: The Set-Up* and *Act II: The Confrontation*.

Your colleagues will respect your *Curiosity, Discipline, Flexibility, Honesty, Sacrifice, Reputation, Repetition, Resilience, Pivot,* and *Expectations*.

RESOURCES

- **SELF HELP:**
Worksheet 8 — What You Know vs. What You Don't Know (Page tbd)

- **INSPIRATION:**
Podcast
Let's Shoot! with Pete Chatmon, Episode 19
Anu Valia on Discovering Comedy to Break Into the Industry
Available on Apple Podcasts, Spotify, and all Podcast Platforms

WORKSHEET 8:
WHAT YOU KNOW VS. WHAT YOU DON'T KNOW

I can't tell you how many Directors I've seen feign a mastery of craft because they're governed by the fear of looking like they *don't* know what they're doing. The people who *do* know, however, will see that you're posturing, and your inevitable missteps will only damage your reputation and, potentially, the project you're directing.

You have probably heard people praise others for "knowing what they don't know" — well, now's the time for you to claim your ignorance!

Take a look at the categories I've added below to get you started. I encourage you to add as many as you can to the list, even if it requires creating a spreadsheet of your own. Place an "X" in the appropriate column for each category, then get to turning all of your "What I Don't Know" columns into "What I Know" columns as soon as possible. Hit Google, read a book, ask a friend, etc.

And, moving forward, be honest when confronted with new frontiers. You must never stop learning.

	WHAT I KNOW	WHAT I DON'T KNOW
What is a tone meeting?		
What does a Chief Lighting Tech do?		
When should I get a publicist?		
What is the latest DGA Rate Card?		
What do my reps do every day?		
Green-screen vs. Blue-screen?		
Do I have to provide a shot list?		
How do I deal with difficult people?		
What are the best apps for Directors?		
What is a Producing Director?		
How do I deliver notes to actors?		
What are French hours?		
Rear projection vs. process trailer?		
What should I carry with me on set?		
When are Directors typically hired?		
TBD: Keep the list going!		

BRANDING

SECURING REPRESENTATION

You're probably expecting this to be a much longer chapter, but it's not. One "event" led to securing representation, but this moment would not have been possible without the journey you've read over the prior TBD pages.

▶ **Chapter 12's keyword is: BRANDING**

Remember how I mentioned being selected as one of five Directors to shadow coming out of Sony's 2015 Diverse Directors Program? Well, on November 5, 2015, at 10:53 a.m., Sony shared a press release via Deadline.com announcing Alberto Belli, Kate Barker-Froylan, Ellie Kanner, Solvan Naim, and myself as the recipients. I had no idea this had happened until I was alerted to ten voicemail messages on my production company's Google voice number (on which I never received any calls).

I immediately logged in to find all of the messages were from managers interested in meeting me to discuss potential representation. After everything I've outlined in this book — the entirety of my journey from 1999 until 2015 — it was an online announcement saying I was selected to watch *another* Director helm an episode of television that helped to close the deal.

I signed with Stephen Marks of Dialed-In Entertainment.

As far as the industry had been concerned, for those 16 years, my body of work was so varied, my "brand" so "unclear," that until I got into a program and *re-branded myself specifically as a half hour, single camera comedy Director* — they didn't know what to do with me. Being a Black Director of the type of content I was driven to create only added to the "confusion."

Here was the trickle-down impact of effective branding:

1. Branding myself helped Sony identify me as a Director they might successfully develop. . . .
2. Sony's press release provided a stamp of approval to the industry that they, as a production company, viewed me as an emerging Director to consider and perhaps other production companies and networks should, too. . . .
3. With new value as a Director (read: I might potentially get hired sometime soon), it was now easier for a manager or agent to see opportunity in me and for everyone to potentially make money. . . .

The rest would be up to me, because once you get "in the room" you're on your own. Moving forward, branding myself as a half hour, single camera comedy Director to as many people as possible would become, much like fundraising, becoming NYU faculty, and building a production company had been — my new awareness campaign.

I'll leave this chapter with two of the comments posted on that life-changing Deadline announcement. They communicate just how challenging it can be for a Director of color, a woman, or any other non-white male to break into this industry. Consider that it is not unlikely that these opinions came from someone in a position of power, and when that power is yielded, the impact of that power is *never* anonymous. It affects a very specific demographic of highly accomplished people who have been overlooked for far too long.

Anonymous:
"Politically correct nonsense. It's 2015. Compete on your merits, not your race or gender."

Anonymous:
"It's more correct to work your way up to director than be awarded a handout."

Wow.

▸ CHAPTER 12 KEYWORD: BRANDING

This keyword is applicable to any leg of your journey, but I have placed it here because of its importance in my transition to episodic television Director.

Stepping into a new arena can be daunting, but you do have one advantage — if people don't know you, then you can define yourself before they get a chance to mislabel you.

Define, protect, and broadcast your brand far and wide.

RESOURCES

■ *INSPIRATION:*
Podcast
Let's Shoot! with Pete Chatmon, Episode 22
Matthew A. Cherry on His Journey From the NFL to the Academy Award
Available on Apple Podcasts, Spotify, and all Podcast Platforms

Deadline Article with Anonymous Comments
https://deadline.com/2015/11/sony-pictures-tv-2nd-annual-diverse-directors-program-participants-announced-1201609259/

CHAPTER 13

SERENDIPITY

THE ROAD TO MY FIRST EPISODE

Every aspiring Director wants to know how they will secure their first episode. Unfortunately, I can't just say, "Make two feature films over a nine year period, you see, then six years later, my friend, make a short film that HBO will, of course, license, then, young whippersnapper, shadow on ten different shows. . .," etc., etc., etc. In the years since I've started directing television, however, I have come up with a handful of metaphors to explain a journey that may appear to be without a roadmap.

▶ **CHAPTER 13'S KEYWORD is: SERENDIPITY**

The roadmap, in my opinion, is to follow certain guiding principles as you build the awareness campaign around your target goal. Having a very specific target is a must. For me, as I've mentioned throughout this book, it was to direct half hour single camera comedies. Everyone that I would meet until the day I booked my first episode would know that this was my goal in no uncertain terms.

Now, back to the most relevant metaphor to booking your first episode:

You're basically a yacht without a dock (that's right, a yacht, because you offer luxury.)

Your mission is to leave a wake of positivity behind your yacht for as long as you're out there circling in the open water, waiting for a slip to dock your boat (the slip is your first episode). You're letting everyone in sight know you're looking to dock your boat. You're letting people hop on deck, have a look around (these are your meetings), and walk away with a positive experience that they take back to their friends on all the other yachts (those are the industry gatekeepers that you're trying to meet). You want them to say, "That Director out there patiently waiting to dock is really cool. And, the boat's luxurious!"

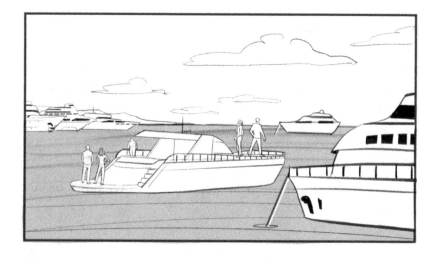

At some point in time, that no one can predict, someone is going to assist you in docking your yacht, getting out of the open water, and putting your feet on solid ground.

This will be how you get your first job.

Before I was scheduled to shadow on Sony's *The Blacklist*, Kelly Edwards at HBO reached out to me with an offer to shadow on Season 3 of *Silicon Valley*. Obviously, I jumped at the chance and headed out to Los Angeles for two weeks in November 2015. To make sure I didn't embarrass either one of us, Kelly introduced me to Todd Holland, a prolific Director/Producer (*Malcolm in the Middle, Shameless, The Real O'Neals, Black-ish*) who previously conducted a workshop for Directors in the DGA about the shadowing experience. He made sure I understood the environment I'd be stepping into when I arrived on set. One thing that I appreciated was Todd's take on how to view the overall experience. "You're an Observing Director. <u>Not</u> a shadow." The "shadowing" of it all speaks to the level of invisibility you are trying to maintain while being directly in the mix, but when conversing with folks and introducing yourself, saying you're a "shadow" diminishes your value and professionalism (that's where the yacht and luxury come back in).

After about thirty instructional minutes on the phone with Todd, I was ready. I drove to Sony's Culver City studio lot and met Jim Kleverweis, my contact for the show who was also the unit production manager. I was ready to observe, take notes, ask the occasional question if the timing was right, see and not be seen, and still look like I had the confidence to direct the show while simultaneously fading into the background. It's a dance! Most importantly, I made sure to be a friendly, engaged presence on set and to absolutely avoid being a walking resume. No one would be looking to hear my elevator pitch on my awesomeness while spreading cream cheese on a bagel.

The Director I was observing was Charlie McDowell (*Dear White People, On Becoming a God in Central Florida*, and the 2014 film, *The*

One I Love). He was assigned a two episode block, meaning all of the scenes from both episodes would be shot at the same time, creating a schedule that might hop from one episode to the next as you moved through a single day's shoot.

I loved every bit of the experience. The mechanics of television production were being slowly demystified, and I was certain I had the skills to be an episodic Director. It was clear to me that Emotional Intelligence is the Director's superpower — knowing how to read the room and navigate personalities en route to achieving your vision — and this was something I'd already been nurturing with my branded content work dealing with clients and agencies. Not to mention my experiences teaching at NYU Film School.

I also met a lot of great folks and built new relationships, particularly with the crew members in stationary or sedentary positions because we both had no place to go! The sound mixer, Ben Patrick was an NYU alumnus and shared great intel with me about the show and how it worked. Dempsey Tillman, digital video assist, was one of the few Black folks on the crew, so we immediately bonded and he was able to share additional insights with me. In video village, I developed a relationship with Adam Countee, a writer hailing from Wayne, NJ, just minutes from where I grew up in South Orange. All of these relationships would come back to help me in the years to come, just like the folks who take a look at your yacht before going back to their own. When I directed the "Tethics" episode of *Silicon Valley* in Season 6, it was amazing to return to the show and collaborate with the folks who had been so welcoming to me four years earlier.

Before heading back to New Jersey, I emailed Todd Holland to let him know about my experience, and thank him for all of his advice. He had helped me avoid potential landmines and enhanced the context through which I viewed my on-set experiences. I told him I'd keep in touch and looked forward to watching the next episodes of *The Real O'Neals*, as well as anything else he'd be directing.

In December 2015, I shadowed on *The Blacklist*. Thankful for having gotten one shadowing experience under my belt, I took what I'd learned in Culver City, California, to Chelsea Piers in New York City to watch Producing Director Michael Watkins tackle his episode. My major takeaway from him was to read the script over and over and over and over again. Read it at your desk. At a coffee shop. In the morning. At night. Why? Because each reading will yield a different takeaway, and ultimately the architecture and DNA of the story will get in your blood.

The Blacklist experience was different from *Silicon Valley* — not only because of the distinctions between comedy and drama, half hour and hour, premium cable and broadcast — but because the writer's room for the show was in Los Angeles, while production took place in New York. This meant a great deal of bi-coastal negotiations over the script, particularly regarding locations. New York City is not the easiest place to shoot, and some of the scripted scenarios would prove prohibitive in making the day. Observing Watkins and the production team navigate these challenges was very informative. It was also a pleasure to watch Hisham Tawfiq work as "Dembe." He'd played "The Commissioner" in my short *BlackCard* and it was inspiring to see him in his element on a network television production.

I met a few more good folks on the "yachts" that were docked on that set. Hollis Meminger was a camera operator (and now a cinematographer) who I've stayed in touch with, and years later, I would have a conversation with Michael Watkins about potentially directing a movie that his schedule would not allow him to do. The "positive wake."

When the episode concluded, I reached out to Brett King and the executives at Sony and told them how well everything had gone, thanking them for the opportunity. It had been expressed to me that I'd be unlikely to land a show like *The Blacklist* as my first episode, but we'd have a different conversation in February of 2018.

2016 arrived without much fanfare, but I was focused. I traveled back to Los Angeles in February to meet with my new manager, Stephen

Marks of Dialed-In Entertainment. We had a two-pronged strategy for my one-week trip. First, I would begin having "general meetings," which are basically an opportunity for me to introduce myself to people in the industry; and second, we would meet with potential agents. The most important general meeting was with Sydnee Rimes, VP of Current Programming at ABC Studios (later my executive mentor while in the Disney/ABC Program) and Michael Petok, executive producer on *Black-ish*. This meeting put me on their radar, and I was able to leave with a standing commitment to observe a Director on the show at some point down the line. This was what I cashed in on when I met Linda Mendoza during the NBC Universal Directing Program boot camp in August of 2016.

HOW TO DESIGN A GOOD MEETING

There's only one kind of meeting in Hollywood and that's the meeting where you sell yourself. This can take the form of a "general" (a meeting introducing you to the other person) or a project specific meeting (to potentially hire you to helm an episode of television or a feature film). It can take place in an office, at a restaurant, at a party, over Zoom, or anywhere else that people might connect — *planned or unplanned*.

No matter the designation or location of the meeting, the two most important components to prepare for a good meeting are to:

1. *Know yourself*; and
2. *Know about the person you're talking to*

It's simple, but you'd be surprised how many Directors fail to do this.

Knowing yourself means being clear about what you want from the industry and what you want as a result of your meeting. It means designing your elevator pitch like a thesis to support you getting what you want.

When I was targeting a transition into episodic television directing, I was very specific about wanting to direct half hour, single camera comedies. I did not talk about one-hour dramas, I did not mention multi-camera comedies, and I never uttered the words "reality TV." I had a singular focus. As I worked on my personal bio, I carved out anything in my work experience that did *not* support the idea of me being prepared, or at least on a trajectory, to direct half hour single camera comedies. Highlighting an experience, even if it felt "impressive" but didn't scream "you should hire me for this job I've never done before" would have done me no good.

If your resume is thin, or perhaps heavy with work experience that doesn't seem to correlate with the job you're seeking, then perhaps you might be able to extract something you learned from your prior experience that would be useful in the directorial space you're transitioning into. In my case, having produced, directed, shot, and edited over 1,000 pieces of Branded Content, I had learned how to work with advertising and marketing executives, honor the visual language of a storied brand, and still manage to add something unique to the final product. This creative tightrope is the superpower of the episodic television Director, and communicating that I not only understood that, but had been developing that muscle, assisted the people I had meetings with in seeing me on a trajectory toward the half hour single camera comedies I was interested in directing.

Knowing about the person you're talking to means knowing their:

- Personal bio (*where they grew up, what college they attended, what organizations they belong to. . . .*)

- Career trajectory (*the various jobs they've had in the industry. . . .*)

- Responsibilities of their current position (*you can't know what you want as a result of this meeting if you don't have clarity on what they are empowered to do. . . .*)

I can't tell you how many people I discover are from New Jersey when I go on these fact-finding expeditions (aka Google). Or, how many people have worked with someone else I know (thanks to IMDbPro indicating which projects and people you share in common). Or, what they most want the industry to be aware of (via personal websites and social media accounts). These easily determined tidbits provide useful information to hopefully warm up the exchange and propel me toward building a rapport with the other person. If you've been building your personal network, you also have the ability to ask around in search of what other people you know may say off the record about the person you're scheduled to meet. This off the record intel, should, of course, *remain* off the record if you want to maintain these relationships.

Careful combination of the components above will provide you with the tools to have more result-oriented meetings as you navigate your personal Director's Journey.

The agency meetings were an education in trusting my gut. When considering your team (agent, manager, lawyer, publicist, etc.), it's important to remember the Five Pillars of this partnership:

1. Your reps work for you (*they don't get paid if you don't work. . . .*)
2. Your reps need to be able to get you "in the room" (*the rest is up to you once you're in there. . . .*)
3. Your reps need to have the same "positive wake" behind them that you do, so you can benefit from their years of experience and relationships. . . .
4. Your reps need to vouch for you, fight for you, advocate for you, champion you (*you get the point*). . . .
5. You need to trust that your reps *can* and *will* do all of the above. . . .

The glue holding all of the above together is that all-important key-word: honesty. Unfortunately, this industry has its fair share of bullshit artists and it's important that you have a team that not only keeps it real with you, whether good or bad, but has the necessary radar to spot the bullshit from their position, too. If you're lucky, the partnership with your reps can yield not only creative success, but lasting friendships. All of my reps attended my wedding in 2019.

Stephen and I met with several agencies, but I ultimately decided to go with a smaller firm where I felt the Five Pillars above would be better realized. I didn't want to get lost in the mix with an agent representing an entire roster of Directors more likely to get the jobs than me. I asked each agency to pitch their vision for me en route to directing half hour single camera comedies. What could they do that I hadn't thought of? How would they collaborate with Stephen? My gut told me to go with the most passionate agents I had met, Bradley Glenn and Michael Kolodny from Kaplan Stahler. I was building my team.

Before packing my bags and heading home, I observed a half-day of shooting for a live taping of *Undateable*, directed by Phill Lewis. This gave me another opportunity to see how multi-camera episodes are shot, which I had gotten a glimpse of on the set of *Dr. Ken* while in the Sony Diverse Directors Program.

I set a return trip to Los Angeles for April 2016. I put together a list of all the half hour, single camera comedies that I was interested in

directing across basic cable, premium cable, broadcast, and streaming (see Resources at the end of the Chapter). I had big swings for shows like *Insecure* and *Silicon Valley* that I hoped I would get to direct — knowing premium cable is highly coveted — as well as shows that I watched and enjoyed and figured I could do a good job in the Director's chair. I threw in a few one-hour dramas, too, so my team would see how my tastes extended in that direction (which I ultimately wanted to add to my resume down the line).

I shared the list with Stephen and Bradley, and they began setting up meetings with all of the people connected to the shows. These people — our folks on those yachts already docked — were the triangle of stakeholders who would be involved in hiring potential episodic Directors. They included:

- **The Creator, Showrunner:** *the person who created the show and/or was responsible for guiding the show over the course of a season, overseeing storylines and everything else that goes into getting the show on screen, week after week....* (In the case of *Atypical*, this would be Robia Rashid.)

- **The Production Company / Studio:** *this is the company that bought the idea for the show from the creator. They spent money developing the idea before taking it out for pitches....* (In the case of *Atypical*, this would be Sony Pictures Entertainment.)

- **The Network:** *this is the channel or platform on which the show airs. They purchased the pitch from the production company who needed this final piece of the puzzle to get the show in front of viewers....* (In the case of *Atypical*, this would be Netflix.)

In some cases, the production company and network might be under the same larger organization, for instance with ABC Studios and ABC Networks, but no matter the case, there are different people within those different departments who will need to get to know you. And, in all cases, none of these parties is interested in having to go to war over their selection of a potential Director. TV is the writer's medium so each of these stakeholders is more interested in going to bat over storylines, character arcs, seasonal themes, etc., than who will call action and cut.

If I'd learned anything by now, I had become fluent in the currency of people, politics, and passion, and I was ready to put what I'd learned to the test. Stephen and Bradley set up twenty meetings over the week in April that I'd be in Los Angeles. That broke down into four meetings per day, typically at 10 a.m., 12:30 p.m., 2 p.m., and 4 p.m. — perfectly spaced out across the sprawling city to allow for notoriously bad traffic and a well-designed playlist.

I prepared for these meetings by working on my personal pitch, specifically refining my bio to communicate how what I'd already done along my journey uniquely positioned me to transition into episodic television directing. I researched every person that I'd be meeting with so I could find shared interests, relationships, or any opportunity to turn a cold room into a warm one by building rapport with the person (or people) on the other side of the table. While these meetings may have been scheduled as "generals," I had a very specific target regarding conversation and what shows I wanted them to know I really loved and hoped to one day direct.

Jaffar Mahmood, one of the directors I'd met moving through the various directing programs, had shown us his spreadsheet for keeping track of all the people he met when he got his start. Never one to let good advice pass me by, I built my own replica in Google Docs and started inputting information. I kept track of everyone's name, title, place of employment, shows they oversaw, the particular show that I was angling to get on their radar about, and any action item(s) to follow up on after the meeting.

HOW TO KEEP TRACK OF YOUR NETWORK

In this industry, you will meet a *lot* of people on your journey. Folks who will one day collaborate with you, folks who will one day hire you, and — as you move through your career — folks who you may one day hire. You never know when these moments will come, and better yet, you never know which people will fall into what category. That's why it's important to keep track of your network (including following the movements of the larger industry via the trades and industry websites).

When Director Jaffar Mahmood (*Young Sheldon, Unbreakable Kimmy Schmidt, Brooklyn Nine-Nine*) visited my class of Directors in the Disney/ABC Directing Program, he described a spreadsheet he'd developed to manage his relationships. He was just beginning the transition from directing programs into working professionally, and I figured if it worked for him, then I'd see if it would work for me!

Here's the breakdown, with a few tweaks on implementation that I've added over my journey:

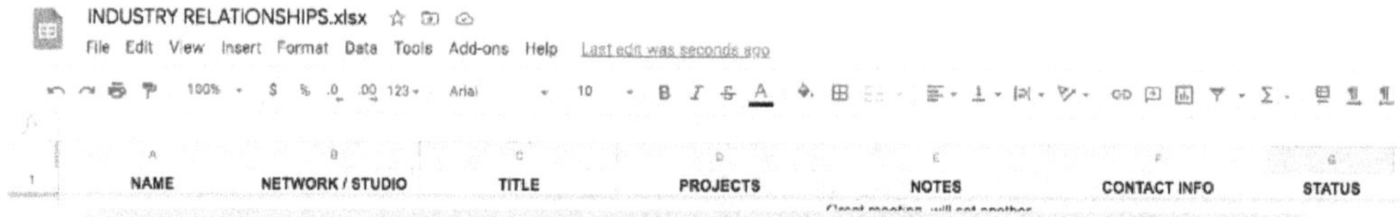
INDUSTRY RELATIONSHIPS.xlsx
File Edit View Insert Format Data Tools Add-ons Help
Last edit was seconds ago
NAME
NETWORK / STUDIO
TITLE
PROJECTS
NOTES
CONTACT INFO
STATUS

All of the fields are self-explanatory, but I'll provide a little more info on a few areas.

Network/Studio refers to their place of employment. In the event it's a craftsperson, like a fellow Director, Writer, Cinematographer etc., this field would be left blank.

Title refers to their position at the production company, network or studio where they work. This would be where I list the specific talents of any craftsperson (Director, Writer, Cinematographer, etc.)

Projects refers to any shows, films, books, or other properties that the company or individual has worked on.

Notes refers to anything strategic I might be able to do on my end, outside of the meeting, like "Reach out to Person X to tap their shoulder about me" or "Send a congratulatory gift for the premiere of their pilot." You get the point.

Status refers to anything I am awaiting an answer on, or any next steps that I need to take. It might be "email sent on June 1, awaiting response" or "currently reading my script."

Once I'd created this spreadsheet, I added every person who I met into the grid. Whether it was a general meeting set up by my agent or manager, an email introduction from a friend, or a chance meeting at a party — if I met you, you made the list!

I followed the trades to stay up-to-date on industry moves, revising my spreadsheet accordingly as people bounced around to different companies. Every Friday, I would reach out to people to either congratulate them on their latest successes, or update them on whatever project milestone I'd hit that supported the topics of our initial meeting. As my list grew, I began to break it into fourths, allowing me to devote my attention to 25% of the entries each Friday (completing a full list review over the course of the month). *It's important to add, if there was nothing to say or announce, I never forced it. There's no need to clog up people's already overburdened inboxes with your own personal version of spam.*

Currently, my spreadsheet is approaching 400 people, but more importantly, nurturing my network has turned many of these "entries" into real friends based on real relationships. Never forget, success in this business is based on working with people and being a thoughtful human being — not a transactional industry leech.

Two particular meetings stand out. My very first meeting of the week was at Fox21 with Gloria Fan and Kira Innes. It was quickly evident that I'd never get an episode of one of their shows as my first — they produced *The Americans* and *Homeland* amongst other projects — but I promised to let my yacht metaphor be my guide and leave a positive wake. I would not tune out because it seemed that my goals were no longer in reach within the room. I talked about my journey, what made me tick creatively, and sought to learn more about both of them. We had a great conversation for the standard thirty or forty minutes, at which point I asked, "Is there anything you think I should be doing that I'm *not* doing as I work to land my first episode of television?"

Gloria thought for a few moments before offering, "Ask your agent to introduce you to all the Producing Directors that he represents." I raised my eyebrows in disbelief. This was brilliant, and it was right in front of me! The art of collaboration at work. And, if I had tuned out once it seemed like my goals were out of reach in this room, I never would have gotten this gem of advice. I left Fox21 and immediately emailed Bradley with this request.

The list he sent me included maybe ten or twelve different Producing Directors, mostly on shows that shot out of the country. One name, however, stood out — Debbie Allen. Debbie was the Producing Director on *Grey's Anatomy*, the show where my buddy Seith Mann had gotten his start, so I knew they could be open to new talent. Bradley passed Debbie a link to *BlackCard* and six months later, when I'd be one of three Directors in the Disney/ABC program sitting in her office

with an interest in shadowing on the show, I had the warmest introduction of the trio because she'd watched my film, was aware of me, and we shared the same agent.

The other meeting that stood out was with Kristin Martini, Vice President of Television at John Wells Productions. At the time, their offices were on the Warner Bros. lot and I had gotten turned around in search of their building. A kind gentleman asked if I needed directions and pointed me in the right direction. Moments after he walked away, I realized it was John Wells himself. He was a super nice guy, which put me at ease for the meeting, as the energy at any enterprise typically trickles down from the leadership.

Kristin and I also got to know each other over the standard thirty or forty minutes and a nice bottle of water. I'd made it a point to turn this general meeting into a focused conversation about *Shameless*. I'd watched every episode twice, made notes about the themes explored and style of shooting, editing, etc. When our time concluded, Kristin told me that while it may be a long shot, they'd add me to their list of Directors to consider down the line. As far as I was concerned, this was almost as good as booking an episode! My theory about the yacht and my "positive wake" was being reinforced again and again. In the summer of 2018, my schedule would be too busy to direct on *Shameless*, but this meeting, and all of my subsequent outreach to Kristin, and later Erin Jontow, Executive Vice President of Television, was paramount in propelling events toward that conversation.

Let's chat for a second about the dirty word somewhere in the back of your mind — "networking." When I hear that word, I immediately envision the person you meet at an event who barely listens to your name, surely couldn't repeat it just moments later, and is already looking over your shoulder for someone more worth their time and presence.

I prefer to spend my time *nurturing*, not "networking." You've noticed repeatedly that I maintained contact with people along my journey in an organic fashion. It doesn't have to be weird, and it can certainly be

genuine. I'm known for often saying in workshops and on my podcast, "literally, just be a person." A thank you goes a long way. A congratulations on a new project or Deadline announcement feels amazing to someone who's worked on something for years, waiting for this moment to arrive. A quick update on your projects or career path that doesn't require a response will never feel like a burden. You can also be helpful — what about sending over a clipping from a newspaper article related to something the other person mentioned during your lunch?

This is what real people do. It's how you nurture any relationship and at the end of the day, in my opinion, it's driven by a desire to simply see other people win. I want everyone out here fighting their respective creative battles to get some points on the scoreboard, and if I can help with a nudge, some applause, an introduction, or even my creative services, then I'm here to do it. And, I think, because of this real human interaction, this may set me apart from the next person looking to build a purely transactional relationship.

In June 2016, my first official job opportunity via my newly acquired representation was to direct *American Koko*, a webseries for ABC Digital and Viola Davis' JuVee Productions. Written by and starring Diarra Kilpatrick, the show follows Akosua Millard, codenamed "Koko," as she investigates and solves sticky racial situations in a post-racial

America as a member of the E.A.R. Agency (Everybody's A Little Bit Racist). I was put on Diarra's radar by Simone Missick, star of my short *BlackCard*, who grew up with her in Detroit. After several interviews, I was hired for the show, which consisted of two six-episode seasons, to be block-shot over fifteen days. The shoot for *American Koko* would be in December of 2016.

The Disney/ABC Directing Program kicked off in September of 2016, and the coordinators informed me that I would, in fact, get to shadow Linda Mendoza on Episode 312 of *Black-ish*. The shoot took place in late October/early November. This was the most welcoming set I'd visited yet. It didn't hurt that when Kenya Barris came down to watch a rehearsal, we shared a pound and a hug, which may have placed an extra stamp of approval on my presence. The cast was great, I had conversations (when approached) with Anthony Anderson, Tracee Ellis Ross, and Jenifer Lewis; and the crew was super open and friendly.

By this time, I'd developed my shadowing formula, which was quite simple. I treated each episode as if I'd been hired to direct it myself, ensuring I treated the experience with the proper professionalism. Sitting in video village all day does not translate to what it feels like to direct an episode. Only when you place yourself in the midst of all the decision-making and politics you'll have to navigate, can you even begin to feel what it's like to sit in the Director's chair (without the responsibility). To that end, I'd request the floor plans from the art department, load them into my Hollywood Shot Designer app on my iPad, and block out the movements of the actors and cameras. While shooting, I'd have two hand drawn columns on my script — one with stick drawings of my shots and one with stick drawings of what the hired Director was doing. This was a great exercise in grasping how to place two cameras at once, whether shooting directionally or cross-shooting. Additionally, looking at these choices side-by-side helped me understand how to accomplish more in fewer shots. Occasionally, as time went on, I found that what I was doing was just as efficient, but in my style. There was no magic to the job, just process. All of this was affirming.

At some point during my time in video village, almost without fail, someone — usually a writer or producer — would ask what I had on my iPad, offering an opening to move out of the "shadow," so to speak. "This is how I laid out the blocking and cameras for the next scene. If you have a second, does it seem like I'm in the right ballpark?" More often than not, I would be because I'd studied the show and worked to understand the visual language. If not, I showed adaptability as well as the ability to take a note, thinking quickly on my feet to offer another solution from their critique. This interaction was designed to be another ripple in my "positive wake" with the hope that it might run up the ladder if/when other folks checked in to see how the "shadow" was doing down there on set.

All of this was helpful in developing the process I would eventually apply to my first episode. But it was also physical, visual evidence that I wanted out in the world when I inevitably made it known to the triangle of stakeholders that I wanted to direct an episode of their show.

2017 arrived with less fanfare than 2016 — especially with the results of the presidential election. On a rainy inauguration day, I had my first in-person meeting with Todd Holland. Though we'd corresponded via email since November 2015, I'd never had a general with him and we'd never met face to face. I updated him on all that had transpired since my last emails, including directing *American Koko* and my *Black-ish* shadowing experience, and of course, promised to keep him in the loop. Later that afternoon, while grabbing a coffee with my friend Tamara Bass (writer and co-director of 2019's *If Not Now, When?*), I checked my email to find myself blind copied on a message that Todd had sent to Kenya Barris.

He said that if his show *The Real O'Neals* were coming back for a fourth season, I'd be a Director he'd give a shot, and in turn, he thought Kenya should, too. I was floored. Todd didn't know that I knew Kenya, but this email sent on my behalf, without my request, surely added toward the dominos falling in my direction for an episode of *Black-ish*.

In February of 2017, I shadowed on *Grey's Anatomy*. The Director was Nzingha Stewart, an alumna of the Disney/ABC Program in 2014–2016. We had mutual acquaintances from NYU, and I'd admired her body of work in the music video space, so I was excited to watch a young Black woman navigate the realities of episodic television.

There were many lessons and life experiences to be taken away from this episode. Most importantly, I somehow managed to meet my future wife, Kelly McCreary, while observing Nzingha.

Kelly plays "Maggie Pierce" on the show, and was completing a huge episode arc where her mother, played by LaTanya Richardson, dies from cancer complications that she'd hidden from her daughter. It was impressive to watch Kelly work, flawlessly navigating the comedy and drama that comes with any ShondaLand production. (In the second edition of this book, perhaps I'll share how the observing Director ended up dating a series regular.)

HOW TO MANAGE YOUR EMOTIONS ON SET

The era of the arrogant, yelling, dictator-like Director is over — and I'm thankful for it. There's no need to create from a place of fear. And, in television, a Writer's medium, this just doesn't fly, anyway.

To manage your emotions on set, my advice is to . . . drumroll . . . prep, prep, prep, and then prep some more so you can be prepared for anything. That will provide you with the necessary sense of calm confidence to gain the respect of your cast and crew.

Additionally, it's important to recognize that there are some relationships that are simply ripe for potential confrontation — based on the job description alone. As Director, you will inevitably want more time and more toys to achieve the scene that you envision, but the Producers will need you to get things done as quickly and cheaply as possible. You may also want more takes in a particular scene, but your Actors may be used to offering only three or four takes in their coverage. Knowing these inevitabilities, why yell, scream, and get bent out of shape? Everyone is doing their job.

Keep your cool, and I guarantee you'll be able to create even cooler things on set than you would have if you lost it.

The other lesson came under the watchful eye of Producing Director Debbie Allen. Unlike most shows, when you shadow on *Grey's Anatomy*, Debbie is going to see what you're about, to determine if you have what it takes to sit in that Director's chair. Sharp questions could be thrown at you while grabbing a coffee, she could magically appear in video village and ask you what the next set-up should be, or she might watch from afar with you never being the wiser of being surveilled.

Grey's Anatomy was the first one-hour drama that I shadowed, and with a show in its thirteenth season (at the time), I wanted to watch as many prior episodes as possible to get the creative DNA in my blood. I like to see what may have changed over those thirteen years as far as shooting or writing styles, follow all the character arcs, and find my particular thematic entry point into the world, so I can maintain the integrity of the show, while bringing something unique to the table. I implemented my usual strategy of blocking out the actors and camera moves, but with perhaps too much time dedicated to watching episodes, multiple draft revisions, a 60+ page script, and a general sense of being overwhelmed as I moved through the final days of prep — I decided to take a little shortcut. I looked at the preliminary schedule for Day One, made sure I had my blocking plans and shot lists for all scheduled scenes, and figured I'd be able to make more informed decisions for the handful of remaining scenes after watching a day of Nzingha directing.

When I arrived on set for the first day of production, Debbie approached, wanting me to run her through my plan for the entire day. I grabbed the nearby sides and my jaw dropped. The schedule had been changed. The first scene up was now the scene *after* where I had stopped my work. We walked over to the set, my heart racing, where I proceeded to bullshit my way through "my plan." Debbie stopped me, gave me her cell phone number, and told me to call her "when I was prepared." That stung. I spent, literally, the next ten minutes trying to determine the master shot for this simple, two-hander of a scene. I'd lost all confidence until finally I just said, "Fuck it . . . it's gonna be what it's gonna be . . . trust your gut."

I brought Debbie back to the set and ran through my coverage. Everything was challenged, prompting me to either defend my ideas or adapt to her feedback. It became a nice dance of on-the-spot, creative brainstorming and it seemed she appreciated my vision, but better yet, my temperament. I made a promise to myself to not respond defensively, even though as a "shadow," one could argue I was not necessarily required to have all of these answers. But, if I wanted to get in that Director's chair, it was *indeed* my job, and I knew Debbie was operating under the same principle. I redeemed myself a bit and we proceeded to go through my prepared plan for the rest of the day. To my relief, this flowed much, much smoother.

Forty-five minutes later, we sat on a gurney on the emergency room set at which point Debbie said, "I hope you don't think I'm being too hard on you. I think you're talented." I told her that I appreciated the teachable moment and mentioned that many of my shadowing experiences included higher-ups finding creative ways to avoid acknowledging me as opposed to investing in my growth.

Next, I thought long and hard about how to exit this moment. What would be my dismount from a routine that started off so poorly? I did not want to be defensive, but I felt compelled to communicate that I knew what was expected of me as a Director. I told Debbie, "I know there's no difference between a reason and an excuse, but I understand that if I were hired to direct an episode, anything can change at a moment's notice and it would be my responsibility to arrive on Day One prepared to shoot any scene from the entire episode." Debbie raised an eyebrow and smiled before walking away.

February 2017 also brought my first interview for an episode of television as I had a meeting to potentially direct in a Season 2 slot of *Insecure*. I had met Issa Rae on my *Double Down Film Show* podcast in 2011 and seen her a few times over the years while doing client work at Essence Music Festival in New Orleans. The other folks in the room included showrunner Prentice Penny, who spoke to my group of directors during HBO Access in 2016; and Jim Kleverweis, my point of contact when I shadowed on *Silicon Valley* in November 2015, now a co-executive producer on *Insecure*. The "positive wake," y'all. It's real.

I did not book an episode, as there was some hesitation to hire a first-time episodic Director after some prior experiences (often the main challenge in getting that first episode), but a few weeks later, my team reached out and informed me that HBO was considering shooting *Due North*, a show-within-the-show for Season 2, and wanted to know if I was interested in directing. It wasn't definite, as they had to decide what kind of money they'd allocate to it, but if it did move forward, I'd be their guy.

In March of 2017, I shadowed Millicent Shelton (*30 Rock*, *Hunters*, *Luke Cage*) on *Ballers*. Kelly Edwards had reached out to me again to see if I'd be interested and of course, the answer was yes! There was some conversation within my team as to whether or not I was at risk of becoming the "guy who shadows but can't book an episode," but I was driven by the principles of that "positive wake" and continued to feel that if I can get in these rooms, I will increase my chances.

So, I persisted.

Meetings and meetings and meetings continued through all of the events in the above timeline. With each episode and each meeting, I'd return to my Google Doc spreadsheet and update it with all of my new contacts. I had well over 150 entries at this point. Every Friday, I'd review the spreadsheet and see if anyone in my contacts had anything in the news that I could ping them about, or a new project that I could watch. If I had any updates, I'd let them know what I'd been up to as well as how I was moving along on the journey to directing my first episode of a half hour single camera comedy.

Things were feeling pretty good. I did not know what the exact path would be, but I really felt like the wake behind my yacht was what I'd envisioned. In early April 2017, I met up with Kenya Barris at Palihouse West Hollywood, and cutting right to the chase, he told me they were going to give me an episode of *Black-ish* in Season 4.

"FINALLY!!! SHIT!!! YES!!!"

At least, that's how I felt inside. I could have jumped in the air, but I probably said something more like, "Thanks brother, I won't let you guys down and appreciate the faith you're putting in me."

I couldn't help but think about the serendipitous moment that led to it all. If I'd never met Kenya at Fatburger on Santa Monica Boulevard in 2002, would I have gotten this job? Would he have been aware of the two feature films, multiple shorts, and other aspects of the journey that didn't make a blip on the radar of many of the other stakeholders I'd met along the way?

I left that meeting with Kenya and finally docked my yacht. As I walked back to my rental car, the solid ground of La Cienega Boulevard had never felt so beautiful.

I traveled to Atlanta for the remainder of April to shadow Janice Cooke (*How to Get Away With Murder, Instinct, Charmed*) on a Season 2 episode of *Greenleaf*. This would be my second opportunity to observe a Director on a one-hour drama, coordinated outside of the Disney/ABC program via my agent, Bradley, who had a relationship with the Lionsgate executive, Kerri Hendry, Vice President, Current Programming, who covered the show. She had started her career as his assistant. Again, the "positive wake!"

With Episode 412 of *Black-ish* slated to shoot in late October/early November, I packed up my things in May of 2017, and moved from Jersey City, New Jersey, to just outside of Santa Monica, California.

HBO proceeded with *Due North* for Season 2 of *Insecure* and I directed that project on May 31st. It featured Regina Hall, Scott Foley, and Michael Jai White. I may not have booked a Season 2 episode, but this "show-within-a-show" was the job that got me into the DGA and was an incredibly fun experience. My three DGA endorsements for membership came from Todd Holland (who first talked to me about observing directors on *Silicon Valley* in 2015), Ken Whittingham (my mentor via the Disney/ABC Program starting in 2016), and Millicent Shelton (whom I had shadowed on *Ballers* just two months earlier).

On June 1, 2017, I woke up bright and early to hop on a plane from LAX to Cabo to celebrate my 40th birthday. I was a mixture of proud, relieved, elated, and anxious about the road ahead.

Kelly, whom I was getting more and more serious with, would come join me for the last few days of my trip.

Perhaps, I was gonna need a bigger boat.

EPISODIC SHOWS OF INTEREST (Working Draft) ← | → 2

AMC

STARZ

BET

AMAZON

NBC

ABC

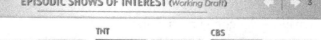
EPISODIC SHOWS OF INTEREST (Working Draft) ← | → 3

NETFLIX

TNT

CBS

FX

FOX

USA

COMEDY CENTRAL

OTHER?

▶ **Chapter 13 Keyword: SERENDIPITY**

Along the journey, you'll try everything you can think of, leaving room for the universe to reward you in unexpected ways.

You can never predict the value of a moment, project, or relationship, so be sure to leave a "positive wake" behind you.

Over a long enough timeline, serendipity will reveal itself.

RESOURCES

■ *INSPIRATION:*
Podcast
Let's Shoot! with Pete Chatmon, Episode 10
Ten Commandments for Episodic Directors
Available on Apple Podcasts, Spotify, and all Podcast Platforms

Blog Posts
- *Black-ish Shadowing* — https://petechatmon.com/disneyabc-program-announces-directors-for-2016-18-seasons/
- *Grey's Anatomy Shadowing* — https://petechatmon.com/disney-abc-program-greys-anatomy-shadowing/
- *Blackish x Walmart Interstitials I Directed* — https://petechatmon.com/black-ish-x-walmart-interstitials/

REFLECTIONS AND NEXT STEPS

Things got rolling rather quickly after booking that first episode of *Black-ish* — primarily because of the relationships I'd built en route to my now 400-entry spreadsheet. And, the fact that I was perhaps more ready than most to hop in that Director's chair. I was becoming an overnight success at 40 years old!

> ▸ **CHAPTER 14's KEYWORD is: BALANCE**

The first episode of television I'd actually direct, however, would be *Grown-ish*. Once the Yara Shahidi vehicle was given the green light for Season 1, I was assigned an episode that landed a few weeks ahead of my *Black-ish* episode. The stamp of approval from Kenya Barris and Sydnee Rimes had everything to do with this.

The next six months unfolded as follows:

- *Grown-ish*, Episode 105 (Sep. 2017)
- *Black-ish*, Episode 412 (Oct./Nov. 2017)
- *Grown-ish*, Episode 112 (Nov. 2017 — *the highly coveted return invite to direct a show!*)
- *Greenleaf*, Episode 306 (Feb./Mar. 2018 — *my first one hour drama*)
- *Atypical*, Episode 208 (Mar. 2018)
- *Insecure*, Episode 302 (Apr. 2018)

I can't pass up a final opportunity to comment on "my positive wake" metaphor.

When my *Black-ish* episode aired in February 2018, I updated Brett King, who in turn, rounded up the executive team at Sony for a meeting with me. While they weren't the place that would take a chance on me for that ever-elusive first episode, they remained supportive, and with the co-sign of ABC and an aired episode under my belt, the Sony folks set me up to meet with Robia Rashid, creator, and Mary Rohlich, executive producer, of *Atypical*. This would be the first episode of television that I booked without having shadowed another Director on the show. It was also the first show that I directed with a non-Black cast, removing a ridiculous stigma that often gets placed on Directors who book shows with a majority Black cast. Some executives seem to wonder, "Can they direct a show with white actors?" It's crazy the thinking that creates the need for this to even be a question.

SELF HELP:
THE ADJUSTMENT

ARRIVAL

It's easy to think that the journey is complete because we've reached our goals, but everything in life continues to evolve. That's why the most compelling hero's journeys have sequels. New trials arrive to test us, yet time and time again, we step up to the challenge and persevere.

Industries never stop moving, but successful Directors never stop adapting, learning, and creating.

Four years later, I'm approaching 50 episodes of television under my belt on many of my favorite shows. I started in half hour single camera comedies and with each season I'm adding more one-hour dramas to the resume. Every January, I share a "Career Goals" vision board with my reps, so we can keep track of what's been accomplished so far, but more importantly, recalibrate for my new creative targets (see Resources).

I've directed almost every show that I shadowed along this journey, have been invited back for additional episodes on most, and have become a trusted collaborator to creators, showrunners, and producing directors alike.

I continue to be supported by the friends I made at the beginning of this episodic television journey. The full circle aspect of it all is befitting a classical hero's journey, hence the three parts to this book. In May 2019, while in Bali on my honeymoon with Kelly, I couldn't help but marvel at the fact I was on a shaky signal FaceTime call with Mike Judge and Amy Solomon about potentially directing an episode of *Silicon Valley*. The third person on that call? Executive Producer, Jim Kleverweis — the man who was my first ever point of contact on anything TV related, way back in November 2015 when I shadowed on Season 3 of the show. As he told Mike about working with me on *Due North* and *Insecure*, it became obvious that he was going to bat for me to get the job. Amazing.

I've since added Commercial Director to my resume, securing representation through the agency and production company Superlative, in Culver City. How'd that come about? One of the filmmakers whose work I screened at my "Short Shorts" event almost eight years ago in New York City was now an executive at the company and reached out to see if I had interest in doing a national Spectrum commercial. Again — amazing.

What's next?

It's all about finding the **balance** that I've identified as this chapter's keyword. I've worked incredibly hard, learned how to work smarter over time, and now I'm working to find that delicate work/life/love balance for even higher levels of happiness.

Creatively, I'm working to get back to the feature films that started it all. For an industry that has only come to know me as an episodic television Director, you can bet I'll be employing the principles I've shared with you in this book as I pivot and redefine myself yet again. The "Wednesday Morning" project I directed in October 2020 is my most recent example, showcasing what I can do as a writer with Candice Sanchez McFarlane and a Director in the emerging space of narrative podcasts.

I'm also pitching episodic television shows. I've learned a lot working with some of the best in the game, and look forward to getting my voice out there to make an impact and empower my community with entertainment that educates. Hopefully, something that I create will spark the same fire in another storyteller that *Do the Right Thing* lit within me.

I hope that this book will do its part in pushing you toward your directorial voice and mastery of craft. My podcast, *Let's Shoot! with Pete Chatmon* will continue serving up conversations that operate on the three levels around which I've designed this book to power your journey — *How-To, Self Help, and Inspiration*.

At the end of the day, however, the most important driver of your success will be your unshakeable belief in yourself, your abilities, and your potential. You deserve everything that you desire, but without your belief, the journey will be without an engine.

I can't wait to see how all of you Directors achieve your dreams and change the world.

Action!

▶ **CHAPTER 14 KEYWORD: BALANCE**

Once you achieve balance, you're on solid ground to harness all of your skills as a Director. No project, challenge, or target is out of reach. You will know what's expected of you and be able to make choices that keep you happy in all aspects of your life. You will be able to live in your truth and create some of the best artistic work of your life.

I can't wait to see what you do!

RESOURCES

■ *INSPIRATION:*
Podcast
Let's Shoot! with Pete Chatmon, Episode 26, Carl Seaton on Getting Comfortable with Nervousness
Available on Apple Podcasts, Spotify, and all Podcast Platforms

Blog Posts
■ *Pete Chatmon Directs Episode of Grownish* — https://petechatmon.com/pete-chatmon-directs-episode-of-grown-ish/
■ *Pete Chatmon Directs Episode of Blackish* — https://petechatmon.com/pete-chatmon-directs-episode-of-black-ish/
■ *Pete Chatmon Directs Episode of Greenleaf* — https://petechatmon.com/pete-chatmon-directs-greenleaf-season-3-episode/
■ *Pete Chatmon Directs Episode of Atypical* — https://petechatmon.com/pete-chatmon-directs-atypical-season-2-episode/
■ *Pete Chatmon Directs Episode of Insecure* — https://petechatmon.com/pete-chatmon-directs-insecure-season-3-episode/

Career Goals
2019 Vision

WHAT ABOUT US?
Produce this Limited Series, targeting a Fall 2019 shoot...

Episodic Directing Assignments
The Year In Review

2018 brought (12) episodic assignments for a total of (17) episodes since September 2017 (*details below*). In 2019, I want to branch out to Broadcast Networks (NBC, FOX, CBS), direct (3-5) 1-hour dramas, the number of Premium Cable & Streaming Service episodes, and for Pilots & Producing Director positions. Most importantly, I want produce and direct my limited series **WHAT ABOUT US?**

15	**2**	
1/2 HOUR COMEDIES	1 HOUR DRAMAS	NETWO
(6) Grownish, (3) Blackish, (2) Last OG, Insecure, Single Parents, Atypical, Mythic Quest	Grey's Anatomy, Greenleaf	ABC, HBO Apple, Free OW

Career Goals
2020 Vision

WHAT ABOUT US?
Continue pursuit of Securing SHOWRUNNER and PRODUCTION COMPANY for this Limited Series...

Episodic Directing Assignments
The Year In Review > The Year Ahead

...eptember 2017 (*Incl. ...r strategy of landing ...hour Premium Cable ...on Limited Series of

9	
NETWORKS	
...ple, Netflix, ABC, ...X, TBS, FreeForm, ...OWN	

CONTENT CREATOR
[1] CREATE & WRITE (1-2) ADDITIONAL SHOWS to pitch to Production Companies and Networks, [2] PRODUCE WEBSERIES to assist in establishing creator credibility and track record, [3] WRITE FEATURE SCRIPT ...

PUBLIC RELATIONS
Design a P.R. COMPONENT to increase my visibility as a director (starting with "Here We Go" PODCAST)...

Career Goals
2021 Vision

TheDirector
The Year In Review >> The Year Ahead

In 2020 we landed 10 episodic assignments for a total of 37 episodes since September 2017 (*Incl. episodes booked into May 2021*). We also secured our first Producing Director/Executive Producer position for *The Education of Matt Barnes* (Showtime) and released the narrative podcast **Wednesday Morning.** >> **2021 Goals:** [1] land episodes at the remaining Broadcast Networks (NBC & FOX)... [2] direct (3-5) 1-hr Premium Cable or Streaming Dramas, Incl. action/superhero... [3] pursue more Pilots & PD positions on Limited Series... [4] develop profile as a feature Director.

Additional goals incl. writing, directing and producing original content are on the right.

THE GUILD
Increase involvement and seek leadership positions in the AFRICAN AMERICAN STEERING COMMITTEE...

WEDNESDAY MORNING

CONTENT
[1] CREATE (1-2) SHOWS to pitch... [2] Price $FREE 99 to NARRATIVE PODCAST SERIES... [3] Write FEATURE SCRIPT on Fathers & Sons ...

27	**10**	**10**
1/2 HR COMEDIES (13 SHOWS)	1 HR DRAMAS (6 SHOWS)	NETWORKS
(5) Grownish, (5) Blackish, (4) It's Always Sunny In Philadelphia, (3) Mythic Quest, (2) Last OG, Silicon Valley, Insecure, Dickinson, The Unicorn, Miserdish, Single Parents, Atypical	(3) Grey's Anatomy, (2) All Rise, (2) You, A Million Little Things, Station 13, Greenleaf	HBO, Apple, Netflix, ABC, CBS, FX, TBS, FreeForm, OWN, Showtime

PR
Increase visibility as Director with [1] PODCAST, [2] BOOK [coming Jan. 2022] and [3] SOCIAL MEDIA (daily).

THE DIRECTOR'S CUT: ACT III

HUMILITY.
BALANCE.
SERENDIPITY.
BALANCE.

I needed to harness and master the principles of these keywords in The last five years of my journey have been moving at what feels like warp speed. With all of the lessons learned in The Set-up and The Confrontation, *The Resolution* has been powered by my ability to make good decisions quickly and to pivot the moment I notice I need to adjust.

I'm a Director in every medium — television, film, and commercials — and I'm also beginning to branch out, as far as the industry is concerned, as a writer and producer. The future is as exciting as it was in 1993 when I first picked up that Super 8mm film camera.

Humility helped me find mentors and cheerleaders. . . .
Branding let the world know who I was and
what I offered creatively. . . .
Serendipity revealed itself at just the right moment. . . .
Balance will propel me forward to more success
in my future endeavors. . . .

Refer back to Chapters 11–14 in Act III for specific *How-To, Self-Help,* and *Inspirational* tools to propel you along your path as a Director.

2015-PRESENT

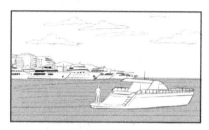
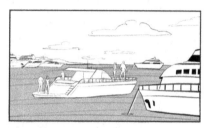

ACT III: THE RESOLUTION

- Pete secures representation with Bradley Glenn of Kaplan Stahler Associates
- *BlackCard* premieres on HBO
- Pete begins having general meetings with production companies, networks, studios, and showrunners with a focus on directing half-hour, single camera comedies
- Pete is selected for the HBO Access Directing Fellowship and directs the $100,000 digital pilot, *Lady Bouncer*
- Pete is selected for the Disney/ABC Directing Program
- Pete is selected to shadow on ABC's *Black-ish*
- Pete directs the two season, 12 episode digital series *American Koko* for ABC Digital and Viola Davis' JuVee Productions

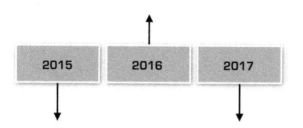

| 2015 | 2016 | 2017 |

- *BlackCard* premieres in competition at the ABFF HBO Firm Festival, winning a $5,000 prize
- Pete is selected as a second year fellow in Sony Pictures Entertainment's Diverse Directors Program
- Pete is selected to shadow on Sony's *The Blacklist*
- Pete secures managerial representation with Stephen Marks of Dialed-In Entertainment
- Pete is selected to shadow on HBO's *Silicon Valley*

- Pete is selected to shadow on ABC's *Grey's Anatomy*
- Pete interviews for a season two episode of HBO's *Insecure*, reconnecting with Issa Rae whom he interviewed in 2011 on his *Double Down Film Show* Podcast
- He is not hired for the episode, but offered an opportunity to potentially direct the "show-within-the-show"
- Pete is selected to shadow on HBO's *Ballers*
- Pete is selected to shadow on OWN's *Greenleaf*
- Pete books his first episode of network television after a meeting with Kenya Barris, whom he first met in 2002 while on a fundraising trip for *Premium*

- HBO hires Pete to direct *Due North*, the show-within-the-show for *Insecure* season two, starring Regina Hall, Scott Foley, and Michael Jai White
- In May, Pete relocates from Jersey City, New Jersey to Los Angeles, California
- Pete joins the Director's Guild of America
- In October, Pete directs Episode 412 of *Black-ish*

The Director's Cut

- Present: Pete becomes one of the most sought after episodic directors in half-hour, single camera comedies with episodes on shows including *Black-ish*, *Silicon Valley*, *Insecure*, *Mythic Quest*, *Mixed-ish*, *It's Always Sunny in Philadelphia*, *Grown-ish*, *The Last O.G.*, *Single Parents*, and *Atypical*
- Pete adds one hour dramas to his resume on shows like *A Million Little Things*, *Grey's Anatomy*, *Station 19*, *Greenleaf*, and *All Rise*
- Pete directs national commercials, securing representation via a filmmaker he met almost a decade earlier at his *Short Shorts* monthly film event on the Lower East Side of Manhattan
- Pete launches a new podcast during the pandemic, *Let's Shoot! With Pete Chatmon*, quickly making its mark on Apple Podcasts and allowing Pete to share his love for storytelling with new audiences
- Pete is developing multiple episodic television ideas to pitch to networks and writing a new screenplay for his return to feature filmmaking
- Pete completes the manuscript for *How To Succeed As A Creative Professional* (aka *Transitions*), taking his 27 year journey and repurposing it as a blueprint for how to pursue one's creative endeavors and make money

↑

2018 - Present

HOW I DID IT

DIRECTORS REFLECT ON THEIR JOURNEY TO THE DIRECTOR'S CHAIR

Matthew A. Cherry

Romany Malco

Seith Mann

Rob McElhenney

Molly McGlynn

Keith Powell

Millicent Shelton

Michael Spiller

Nzingha Stewart

Anu Valia

MATTHEW A. CHERRY

Matthew A. Cherry is a Director, best known for his work on *Hair Love*, *The Last Fall*, and *Black-ish*. Born in Chicago, it wasn't until he retired from the NFL in 2007 that he began his journey as a Director. Matthew has transitioned from production assistant, to helming music videos, to winning the Oscar for his animated short. Matthew continues to direct episodic television and feature films, as well as produce content through his overall deal with Warner Bros.

Below are excerpts from Episode 22 of the *Let's Shoot! With Pete Chatmon* podcast:
Matthew A. Cherry on His Journey From the NFL to the Academy Award

Q: How did being an athlete benefit you when it came to directing?

A: I played in the NFL for three years, and then my first year after retiring, I was on set as a production assistant. Talk about a wakeup call, you go from getting served to being the server. Teamwork is obviously a big thing, knowing that it's not just about you, not just about your position. I think that was probably the most humbling of it all. When you direct, you're basically directing traffic. It's more like a coach as opposed to a player, where you have to answer every single question. Why is the shirt red? Why is the car blue? Why are the walls this color? Everything relies on you. As a wide receiver, I could run a perfect route, and the quarterback could get sacked because the linemen messed up on their blocking, and now I don't get a pass. It's the same thing with filmmaking. You can have the perfect take, give the actor the perfect direction and they're killing it, but the shot's out of focus and now you've got to go again.

Q: How did *Hair Love* come together?

A: I think this was 2014 or 2015. I'm watching the Oscars and paying close attention. I was like "Wait, sound mixing gets an Oscar, gives a speech? Documentary short, gets an Oscar, gives a speech? Looks like it's the same Oscar that Best Picture gets, the same Oscar that Original Screenplay gets." I promise you — and this is no lie — I called my manager, Monica, and I was like "Monica, I think I have an Oscar-winning short film idea." That idea was *Hair Love*.

That same year I put a tweet out, being bold, saying I have this Oscar-worthy short film idea and I'm looking for a 3D animator. At the time we were trying to do it in 3D and it was kind of crickets — nobody really responded. (*After about three to four months*) I blindly reached out to Vashti Harrison (*who had posted an image she had drawn, with hair more realistic than Matthew had ever seen*). I was like, "I've got this project I'm working on. It's called *Hair Love*. I'm about to do this Kickstarter in a month and you know, we need characters. Can we connect?" Today, she's a New York Times bestseller, but this is like six months before her first book comes out.

I described the dad: the gentle giant, the locks. The little girl about six, seven years old with big hair — she loves it. When I got the first image of Zuri (*the daughter*) I tweeted it out saying "project soon to come" and the shit did like 50,000 likes. It was the artwork, and I just knew this project was going to be something.

I was getting a lot of signs to rethink the idea. I would repost a lot of videos of dads doing their daughters' hair, and every time I'd repost it was the same thing, 25,000 to 30,000 likes. Then, I would post moms with their daughter or the son and those posts would get 10,000 . . . 15,000 . . . 20,000 likes. So, a light bulb went off. It was like, all right people, I know dads that do this shit all day, every day, but for whatever reason, people are looking at this as a unique thing. They're not used to seeing Black men in this image, and I was like, all right, if we can harness the heartfelt-ness and this love in this kind of general concept and put a cool story behind it — this could be a monster.

Q: What was the hardest thing to learn when you transitioned into directing episodic television?

A: I think Hollywood is a very passive-aggressive industry. A lot of times people may have an issue or want to say something, but they don't. Then, you find out later and you're like, "Man, I didn't know it was an issue."

The thing I'm so grateful for is the fact that it took so long (*to get here.*) What ends up happening is every project, big or small, short film, web series, music video, you're going to come across an issue, you're going to be tested live in the field, like, okay, I have five setups and only an hour left to shoot — what do you do? I have a difficult actor who has an issue with a crewmember — what do you do? You're basically getting live tested in every single scenario, so that by the time you are put in this game in a real way, it's like, all right, boom! This is just like the situation I dealt with on a little web series, fifteen years ago. That's easy. I think it was delayed for me because I needed all of those lessons.

Q: Do you have a favorite moment or scene of which you're most proud?

A: Probably from the first episode I directed, *The Last OG.* There's a scene where Tiffany Haddish and Tracy Morgan are giving their son, "Shahzad," the "police talk" and there's a lot of comedy, but also a lot of realness and drama in there. It was one of those scenes where if you land it, you understand what the show is and what the episode is all about. To come out of that victorious, and with a really solid scene — it was one of those things where you go home at the end of that night, and you're like, "I think I could do this for real."

Q: How has the process for *Young Love* (the new HBO Max animated series based on *Hair Love*) been?

A: It's tricky, man. It's tricky because I love directing, and there's nothing I'd rather do. So being in the writer's room is a totally different process. It's very much being in the weeds and figuring out every single element of the show. I think the more I go through it, the more I'm kind of like, there are a couple of specific examples where I want to be involved at this level. Other than that, I just want to direct.

The cool thing with TV directing, and I knew this even back when I was PA-ing, was you'll see these dudes having forty to fifty year careers. You're always at work and I think that's the thing. No matter how popping or slow my own development stuff gets, there's always that to come back to. That's something I'm really looking forward to.

Q: If you had the keys to the castle and could change anything about the business or about being a Director — what would it be?

A: More days. Just more time man . . . more time to do it right. There are so many parts of TV directing where the clock can be motivating, but there are also parts of the clock that can be very limiting. Sometimes, you're basically trying to fit into this already established puzzle, and in some instances a little bit more time would be freeing in terms of putting your own flavor on it.

ROMANY MALCO

Romany Malco is an Actor, Writer, and Director who began his journey as an artist at the age of 7 when he started rapping. Best known for his performances in *40 Year Old Virgin*, *Think Like a Man*, *A Million Little Things*, and *Weeds*, in 2018 Romany wrote, produced, directed and starred in his debut feature *Tijuana Jackson: Purpose Over Prison*.

Below are excerpts from Episode 08 of the *Let's Shoot! With Pete Chatmon* podcast:
Romany Malco on *The Million Little Things He's Learned and Tijuana Jackson*.

Q: What is the best note you've given an actor when directing them?

A: When we did our first table scene (in *Tijuana Jackson: Purpose Over Prison*), Tami Roman, Alkoya Brunson, Baadja-Lyne, and myself ran it. It was early in the shoot. Everyone was, for lack of a better term, just kind of shucking and jiving and I just stopped. I was like, "Listen, you all. I need to believe these characters. I don't wanna believe that you acted this scene great. I wanna believe that you take these problems home. This isn't really a film. It's supposed to feel like a documentary. We're making a mockumentary. I know that it says that it's funny, but the funny is in the irony. The funny is not in us trying to nail one-liners."

Well, that cast flipped the script. The next take people were crying. I just remember the whole crew looking at me after the first take with all the over-the-top, broad comedy, knowing that they were probably thinking the same thing I was thinking. But that following take after the notes were given? Oh, my god.

Q: If you had the keys to the castle and could change anything about the business, whether it's specific to acting or any of the other hats that you wear, what might that be?

A: It would be the messaging. How people are portrayed. We're planting these seeds into people, early in life, to dehumanize communities — people of color and women. Sometimes even emasculating men. One of the reasons I am a storyteller is because I realized that media is a very powerful tool and, unfortunately, for most people in the United States of America, it is their higher education. I want to use it responsibly and I want to use it for good.

Q: Being a multi-hyphenate, do you ever find it challenging to focus on just one role?

A: I grew up in the hood where dudes could play basketball on a pro-level and were brilliant. That dude could sleep through a whole class and get straight A's. That same dude was also an amazing football player . . . but the problem was, that dude ended up not really going anywhere. The reason was because he was so good at so many things that the minute something got challenging, he switched to the next.

I've kind of suffered from that, where I succeeded in all these different things to a degree, but in every one of those things I've hit that glass ceiling. Then, I'll easily just float to the next thing, no problem. Experience some mediocre success there and hit the glass ceiling.

Acting was the first time I said, "Oh, I'm completely conscious of the fact that I'm hitting a glass ceiling, and clearly I'm the common denominator. These are my own limitations." No matter what I do, I'm gonna carry these limitations with me. So, I'm going to stick this out this time, and it has seemed to pay off.

One of those limitations was the fact that I needed to do everything myself. I didn't know how to incorporate a team into the fold. As a result, I limited my abilities. I think that part of the reason I needed to do everything myself was because I needed to be in control. There was a fear that by not being in control, I would somehow end up failed or hurt. So, getting over that fear definitely helps.

Q: What three traits do you think someone needs to make it in this industry?

A: One of the biggest mistakes people make in this business is that they underestimate how much work it will take. When they start facing the psychological challenges they get discouraged and quit. No. That's actually par for the course. So, one would be don't underestimate how much hard work it takes.

Two, would be you really need to learn your craft. Hone in on your craft. You need to study, go to class and learn. Actors are always training and taking acting classes . . . they might be terrible the first six months of acting class. Then one day they go up there and nail a scene, they're building a confidence they can't build anywhere else. So, now they have a confidence in the cold read and the cold read can get them the job. You have to give yourself the opportunity to exercise that muscle.

The third thing is patience. It's gonna take a minute. The bottom line of this is the film industry is an *industry*. You have to make money. You have to show that you can monetize the content, period. It's messed up to say that, but when it really boils down to it, if you're trying to make the bucks, you gotta show that you can aid in the monetization of content.

SEITH MANN

Seith Mann is a Director best known for his work on *Homeland*, *Friday Night Lights*, *#FreeRayShawn*, and *Blindspotting*. Originally from Washington D.C., Seith discovered his love for storytelling after watching Spike Lee's *She's Gotta Have It* and *Do the Right Thing*. He graduated from Morehouse College and NYU's Tisch School of the Arts, where he produced his award-winning short film *Five Deep Breaths*.

Below are excerpts from Episode 14 of the *Let's Shoot! With Pete Chatmon* podcast:
Seith Mann Being A Complete Filmmaker and How Timing Led To "The Wire"

Q: What are three traits that you think an emerging Director needs to make it in episodic television?

A: Patience, passion, and a facility with people.

Q: When did you realize you wanted to become a Director?

A: I accidentally graduated from Morehouse a semester early, so at this point in what should have been my second semester of my senior year,

I was back at home. I visited NYU and while I was there, I mentioned to a brother, who happened to have been a Morehouse alum, that I was interested in film, and he was like, "You know, we have the best film department in the world. You should meet our dean." So, I met Sheril Antonio and Susan Carnival. They told me all about the film school and everything like that, and I was like, "Yeah, that sounds cool." But, I wasn't really sure I wanted to do that. I hadn't really declared that I wanted to be a Director yet, even though I was doing all this stuff that I now recognize are the steps.

They were like, "Well, you know, we also have a Sight & Sound course. It's a six-week boot camp. It gives you an idea of what film school would be like, if you wanna do that." I was like, "Okay, cool." So, then I went home. I'm talking to my mom and I'm telling her about this trip. I tell her about the film school and she's like, "Oh, that sounds cool. What do you think of that?" I was like, "I don't know about film school." I told her about the Sight & Sound thing, and she's like, "Well, what do you think about that?" And, I was like, "Yeah, yeah. It's a lot of money, I don't have it." You know, I was living at home but I insisted on paying rent because I was one of them – "I'm a grown 22-year-old." I'm a man, so I've got to pay my rent if I'm gonna live here. My parents tolerated me and took my money.

I said, "It's too expensive. I can't afford that," right? And, she's like, "I'll help you with it," and I was like, "Well, no, I can't ask for your help. You know, I'm a man. I'm independent." She's like, "I'll help you with it. I have some savings, I'll help you with it." I'm like, "No," she's like, "Yeah, no, I'll help you. I think you should do it." . . . This goes on, and on, and on, to the point where it gets uncomfortable, her asking me what it is I wanna do, and me saying, "I don't know."

Finally, I say, "You know what? I wanna be a Director."

It was a moment. It was an eruption. It was that thing that I had been scared to say. That was my mom's point. She was like, "All right. When I was your age, I wanted to be an actress, but I was scared. I was scared to say it, and I'm not, and I've never been an actress. So, my job with you is to make you say what it is you wanna do. Now that you've said it, you have to do everything in your power to do it, so I'm gonna help you."

When I got to that Sight & Sound class, it was like the first time in my academic life where I just loved the material. I loved everything. I would just devour it. I was passionate about what I was learning. I was like, okay, so if this is what film school is, then I need to go. After that six-week boot camp, I turned around and applied to NYU and I got in, and that's how I ended up in film school.

Q: How did you get the opportunity to shadow on *The Wire*?

A: There was a producer on *The Wire* named Bob Colesberry, who saw my film (*Five Deep Breaths*) and set up a coffee with me. We met for maybe fifteen minutes. We had coffee somewhere in Manhattan, he asked me some questions, talked about the film a little bit and was like, "'Listen, would you be interested in shadowing on *The Wire* when we start production back up?" I was like, "Absolutely." And, then he left.

On my way out, his next appointment was a Director named Eddie Bianchi, and he introduced us, he said, "Eddie, this is Seith Mann, he's a Director." I remember noting that he had called me a Director. He didn't call me a student filmmaker, he called me a Director.

About a month later, Bob Colesberry passed away, unexpectedly, and I heard about it. I'd just met him for coffee, I didn't have a number, I didn't know anyone that knew him, so I didn't even know who to really express condolences to. I was like, "Damn."

I assumed that would be the end of that story, but about month later, Nina Noble, who was a line producer on *The Wire* reached out to me and said, "You know, Bob was a big fan of yours, and out of respect for his memory, we'd love to have you come shadow on the show. We have an apartment ready for you in Baltimore that's normally for the editor, but they're not there for the first episode. Eddie Bianchi has already agreed to let you shadow him, so if you can get down here. . . ." She told me there was a memorial for Bob the night before they started production, if

I wanted to come to that. So, I went to that, and it was strange, because people kept introducing themselves to me, like, "Hey, you're Seith." And I'm like, "What the . . . is going on?" You know what I mean?

So, what I would find out over the course of shadowing was that Bob had taken my short back to Baltimore or wherever, and literally made every executive producer on the show sit down and watch my short, and told them he wanted me to direct. I found this out from David Simon, who introduced himself to me on set the first day with, "Hey, I'm Dave Simon. I'm the showrunner." I remember him saying that because I didn't know what a showrunner was at that time. He was like, "Bob's secret plan was for you to direct an episode this season. We're still finding our way without Bob, so I doubt that's gonna happen. But we wanted you to come and to learn everything you could." Then, he was out the door and I was like, "Wow."

So, Bob Colesberry literally ushered me in to *The Wire* from beyond the grave.

Q: How did you land a second episodic opportunity?

A: They always say it's hard to get your first episode in television, and harder to get your second, right? So, I was very fortunate. I shadowed on *The Wire*, then I got into ABC's director training program and moved to LA to do that. I ended up shadowing Adam Davidson and Peter Horton on *Grey's Anatomy*. Peter, who's the Producer Director ended up championing me to get my first episode of *Grey's Anatomy*.

Then simultaneously, *The Wire*, which I don't know if you remember this, but *The Wire* was on the bubble after their third season. They didn't know if they were gonna come back. There was a whole website, savethewire. com and all that. So, I didn't even know if they were gonna be a show, let alone if I was gonna get an episode. Then they got their fourth season order and Nina called me up and was like, you know, "What's up?"

So, suddenly I had the opportunity to direct two shows before I directed my first show.

Q: Describe a moment where you were most proud of your direction. . . .

A: It was a scene between a husband and a wife. The woman is confronting her man about a lot of things, but ultimately ends up confronting him about a certain infidelity.

We rehearsed that scene for a while, and I kept changing the blocking, and I kept asking the actress not to start the scripted dialogue until something happened. Then in the process of rehearsing it, it was like, something happened. It was magical and it was powerful, and I was like, "Oh, this is the scene." It was the whole thing that needed to happen before we could start the scripted dialogue, for the scripted dialogue to work. The scripted dialogue was fine, it wasn't one of those things where it was like, the dialogue wasn't there, but it was the context that preceded it that needed to actually be discovered in that space, in that scene, for the scene to work.

We discovered it. At a certain point, thirty minutes into the rehearsal and it's still not "that thing," and you don't know what "that thing" is, but you know that there's something more that you should be getting out of the scene. You can feel the breath and the eyes (from the producers) but it's like, I know something is missing — and then you find it.

I thought to myself, "I'm a Director today."

Q: What's changed for you as a Director?

A: I'm not a starving artist anymore. That's changed. I think I know a lot more. I just have a lot more experience, in terms of filmmaking experience, in terms of working with actors experience. I have a lot more knowledge of what I'm doing. I've literally lost count of how many episodes of television I've directed and I've now EP-ed three different shows, one of which I'm very proud to say just got three Emmy nominations.

I'm still striving as a filmmaker. There are still stories I wanna tell that I haven't told yet. I just feel like I actually know what I'm doing, whereas in 2003, it was all sort of raw talent, not necessarily wisdom.

ROB MCELHENNEY

Rob McElhenney is an Actor, Writer, Producer and Director. After years of hard work with no luck, Rob decided to take matters into his own hands and in 2005 created *It's Always Sunny in Philadelphia*, establishing himself as an actor and opening the door to becoming a Director. In 2020, he teamed up again with Charlie Day to create *Mythic Quest*. He has several new episodic series in development.

Below are excerpts from Episode 06 of the *Let's Shoot! With Pete Chatmon* podcast:

Rob McElhenney on How Desperation Created It's Always Sunny in Philadelphia

Q: What are you looking for as a Producer/Creator when you get a Director's cut in post?

A: One thing that really, really saves your life, and you feel such a tremendous amount of joy and gratitude for, is when you get a Director's cut that is 30% to 40% of what you're looking for in the episode. I say that with all honesty.

Charlie and I have been working on *Sunny* for fifteen years. If Charlie alone worked on a cut, it would be about 75% of what I was looking for, right? That's because he can't get into my head. If I worked on a cut, it would be the same thing. We couldn't be any more aligned in what we're trying to do with the show, it's just that you can't get into someone else's head. So, you get it as close as possible. What I've found is 30% to 40% is a game-changer, because you're now taking weeks off of that part of the process.

Part of the fun of all this is collaborating with other people, having them challenge me on what my preconceived notions are, not only about my work, but about the world and my worldview, and then eventually coming to some consensus on what this show is. Then you put it out to the world and it's done. Even when I look back on it now, I'll see finished episodes from Season 4 of *Sunny* and wish I could go back in the editing room to fix it. That's the way it goes.

Q: Are there any tips that you have for Directors when they're trying to fine-tune?

A: Everybody is different. So, I can only speak to what I personally would rather see from the cuts (*the editors will do a cut and then the Directors will do a cut*). Generally, what we'll see is the Director's cut. But, then sometimes we'll say, "Oh, okay. Can I see the editor's cut version of this?"

I wanna see an episode that works. You might have a great, really well executed scene, but it falls flat. The reason it falls flat has nothing to do with the scene, it has to do with four previous scenes that slowed everything down and fucked you for the rest of the episode. That's just a judgment call. So, I'd rather see a cut that a Director says, "I believe this works . . . and you know that joke, Rob, that you delivered as 'Ian' in scene three? I cut that shit and I cut the entire scene."

That's a dicey situation, right? But you and I work well enough together, and hopefully I communicate this well enough to all the Directors that that'll never offend me. That won't upset me. I'm not gonna hold that against somebody. I'll go, "Great. That was your take on it. And you're fired or you're not."

Q: What is the hardest part about production, to you?

A: Writing is the hardest part. Its the most enraging and terrifying because you're just walking into an empty whiteboard and you have to fill that whiteboard. But, when it's working, and you are feeling like you're in the zone, and you crack through whatever that problem is you're having or that story issue, it's such a powerful feeling because you are creating something from nothing and that just feels so good.

The thing about acting that's fun is that you're sharing an emotional experience with other emotion-forward people. That can still be comedic, right? When you're vibing with somebody on a comedic level, it's still an emotional and very personal relationship that you're having. I find that, especially on a comedy, there's less pressure and you're just there to kind of have fun. It's ultimately the job of the Writers, Producers, and the Directors — to allow the space for Actors to enjoy themselves and have fun, and that's why actors get coddled as much as they do.

Q: Any advice for new Directors looking to challenge a show that already has a "set" way of shooting?

A: Any Director that comes into the *Sunny* experience, I'm just very conscious of the fact that people are walking into a show that has been up and running for fourteen years, in your case. It's a very difficult thing, because we have a way that things work and yet we still want to bring in people that have ideas and, yet, there are things we know just won't work and we don't wanna stifle people's creativity, but we also have to keep things moving. We love our families and we love to go home to them.

With *Mythic Quest*, that was great to have everybody there for that first season and specifically you, because you were bringing something to a brand new show. We kind of had the template because David Gordon Green shot the pilot, but you're always kind of finding your footing.

I remember very specifically there was a scene we shot, and you were showing me some camera move. You were explaining it to me and I was like, "Pete, it's gonna take forever. I don't know. It's 7:30 a.m. I gotta shoot. Let's just move." Then you were like, "Just come watch the rehearsal." I came and watched the rehearsal and I was like, "Solved. Yeah, that's it. Got it."

I'm so grateful for that. You hire talented people, you want them to come in and challenge what you think the show is, to make it better. That's the gig. Otherwise, why bring a Director in? Right? So, I'm always fascinated with how you and Directors like you are able to kind of jump in and navigate those waters.

What also helps is just coming in and being somebody that people want to spend time with. You're dealing with people who love what they do and are passionate about what they do, and everybody feels as though what they do is the most important part of the process — which they should. That's part of the deal. Then, on top of that, it's just tricky to navigate creative discussions, especially if you're dealing with difficult subject matter. So, it really comes down to, "Do I want to engage with this person? And, am I engaging with his or her ego right now, or am I engaging with their creative brain?" That's what I want. I want their brain and their heart to be fighting with me, you know, collaborating . . . challenging me — but I don't want their ego, or my ego, for that matter, to be challenging each other because that doesn't get shit.

MOLLY MCGLYNN

Molly McGlynn is a Director, best known for her work on *Mary Goes Round* and *Bless This Mess*, where she also served as Producing Director. Born and raised in Montreal, Molly got her start with the short films *I Am Not A Weird Person* and *How To Buy A Baby*. Additional episodic television credits include *Speechless*, *Grown-ish*, and *Little Dog*.

Below are excerpts from Episode 15 of the *Let's Shoot! With Pete Chatmon* podcast:
Molly McGlynn on Rejection Being How You Become A Filmmaker

Q: How do you navigate during a period of rejection?

A: Rejection is how you become a filmmaker. I think people like us, I feel like to persevere through those valleys, there's self-belief and then there's maybe a little bit of delusion. You're just sort of deluded into thinking it'll work out, and I don't think, in that context, its a negative thing.

Q: What pushed you to make your first short film?

A: The thing that pushed me to make my first short, which is called *I am Not a Weird Person*, is my roommate (Marni Van Dyk) and I lived in Toronto over a convenience store where we'd smoke cigarettes on the fire escape and watch the raccoons. I was talking about wanting to direct, and she was a comedian and writer and she wrote a script. She said, "Why don't you direct it?" and I said, "I can't do that." She said, "Well, if you wanna be a Director, you're gonna have to direct at some point." I said, "Okay, when are we doing this?" She pulled out her calendar, picked a date, I think it was like a month out. I was like, "How are we shooting this? We have no money. Who's producing this?" and she said, "We are."

So then, a week into it, I was like, "Ah, something came up that weekend, I can't," and she's like, "No. Cancel whatever you're doing, you're directing this thing." We made a very lo-fi Indiegogo video and raised a couple grand. Off we went. I really credit Marni as the reason why I'm a Director today, because I needed the kick off the ledge. She's Dutch, she loves to just get things done, she's very pragmatic.

It was pretty chaotic. Marni wrote it, she was starring in it, it involved a cat, we didn't know she was allergic to cats, she's covered in hives, we don't know what we're doing. You know, the whole thing. She stayed up till 4 in the morning making craft for everybody, and I remember she slept in a parking garage because the equipment was in the van — it was bananatown. Once I did that, it really activated the addiction part of my brain. I was just like, "Oh god, I can't stop doing it now."

Q: What are some things you've learned about writing and directing your own content?

A: I would say, just because you wrote something, doesn't mean you can't do the directing prep. It doesn't mean that you intuitively know how to direct a scene. You still have to craft each scene as if it were given to you like someone else wrote it. I think that was a big takeaway. I was so lucky to work with Aya Cash who is an amazing actor, who is super respectful and knows how much work goes into the material, but would still suggest things. You have to work with actors, if you're lucky, that want to make your work better as well. For a character film like *Mary Goes Round*, Aya is the whole thing. So, if something doesn't feel right to her on the page, trust your actor to know that. Like, on Day 16, they get the vibe. If they wouldn't say this line, they're not gonna say this line.

The other thing is just the longevity. It's just relentless. I don't think I had any clue how taxing it would be, both physically, emotionally, mentally, financially. Just every fiber in your body is devoted to this, and it doesn't end when you wrap. The editing process, it's both heart-breaking and exhilarating. It's a wild ride. Then, you picture wrap it and, for me, interestingly, a film becomes a film in the sound mix. When you're hearing it in a proper theater, there's this like dimension-ality to it where it's like, "Oh, it's a film."

Q: Whats the difference in note giving to an actor on something youve written versus something where youve been invited to direct, like a television show?

A: When you've written the material, you are the author. You came with the intent, you know the intent. So, when you give a note, you are the author. That's not to say that your note is the right note, but there is just some trust that you understand the material.

I think the only way to give a good note to an actor when it's not your own material (*on a television show*) is to fucking know that script. Read it as much as you can, be as familiar as you can. That being said, ask the Writer. If something's not clear or you don't understand, they're there to help you, they also want a good episode.

Q: How do you handle situations when you are told to give a note that you emphatically disagree with?

A: You have about fifteen seconds to walk from video village to that actor to think of a really clever justification. There's sort of a clever-ness on your feet that, hopefully, is to your advantage. Do not say, "So and so wants you to try this." Don't. You're the middleman, if you get shot, fine, but don't bring the Producer down with you. Pose it as a question. You know, "I think the last two takes you did this so well. This is out of left field, what about this?" Then, if they don't wanna do the note, I would try to have a conversation where you get a third take of something so that, when you go back to village, there's some change. Sometimes the producers can't quite articulate the note. If you get some shift, it might have satisfied the note.

Q: How has the industry changed, and what do you think still needs to be addressed for women in the Director's chair?

A: There was sort of this predatory thing of like, "We need women Directors now," and I can see it happening with, "We need people of color Directors." Which is great, people want to change numbers, but it's like, "How are we actually supporting those people in this environment? How are we absorbing failure? What happens if my second feature sucks . . . do I have a third?"

I often feel like a lot of white men can make many mistakes in a film and they continue to direct, or they do a crappy episode and they keep going. I will say, this is a gross, gross generalization, but women directors I find come super prepared — binders, clipboards, whatever, their PDFs — because it's almost like they are walking in expecting to be challenged on some of the decisions they've made. I'm not saying that men don't prep, that is not the case, but I presume also people of color on set feel the same way. You're walking in where you're like, "I'm gonna prove that I know what I'm doing because it's predominantly a white-male space."

I'm somewhat bubbly, I'm outgoing, but early on I had to make it clear that, yes, I am this but don't get it twisted, "I know what I'm talking about." There is a precision that needs to happen in order to make a day. There's a lot of money at stake and I understand the mechanisms of that. In terms of set culture and what constitutes leadership or communication styles, we need to be more open-minded. However, you have to be a leader, and leadership looks like many things. You have to have good communication skills and you need to be a leader, whatever that looks like to you.

I think the events of this past year have brought up a lot of conversations, and I think everybody's learning, myself included. It's been eye-opening. But ultimately, I do feel really optimistic for where things are going and the types of people who are gonna be working. You know, things are bleak right now but let's see what kind of work we're looking at in five years. I think its gonna be really cool.

KEITH POWELL

Keith Powell is an Actor, Writer, and Director best known for his onscreen work on *30 Rock*, *Connecting*, and *This Is Us*. Behind the camera, he has lensed episodes of *Dickinson*, *Single Drunk Female* and *Superstore*. Originally from Philadelphia, Keith knew at an early age that he had no choice but to become a storyteller. He started a theatre company in Delaware in his 20s, has written feature films for the likes of HBO, and has produced and directed a short film of his own every year for the past eleven years.

Below are excerpts from Episode 08 of the *Let's Shoot! With Pete Chatmon* podcast:
Keith Powell on *The Moment Oprah Saved His Job*

Q: How did your childhood inform your art and your voice?

A: I grew up with four women in my house and all of them wanted to always remind me that they were strong Black women. That was drilled into my head from day one. I believe that it's kind of helped me as a storyteller be a little bit more sensitive in my storytelling, understanding nuances that, you know, growing up in a house with testosterone might not have noticed.

My family was really, really passionate about education and history. I became a storyteller because I wanted to talk about Black history. My family, my great grandfather, my grandmother's father, was the first Black principal in Delaware. He got his Master's degree at Columbia, and education became a major component in his life because his grandfather was a man named Harmon Unthank.

The Unthanks were given reparations. They were given forty acres in North Carolina. Actually, they were given more than forty acres. Harmon Unthank became a major civil rights leader. His children became educated, and one of his children was a prominent doctor, one of his children was a prominent architect in Portland, Oregon. There's a park named after the Unthanks because of that. So, holding onto that kind of history was so important to us that I had no choice but to kind of be a storyteller and tell stories.

Q: Being a multi-hyphenate, what do you identify as?

A: I see myself as a storyteller. I'm not a Director, I'm not an Actor, I'm not a Writer, I'm a Storyteller. There are stories that require me to direct it, there are stories that require me to write it, and there are stories that require me to be the vessel through which actors and directors need to tell the story, and that's me as an actor. It's never about what I can get a job in, it's never about what drives me today, it's always about what story am I telling and am I telling this story in the best way, using whatever particular skill that I have to help tell the story?

I went to NYU for theater directing. I got my degree in theater directing. While I was at NYU, I started getting hired as an actor in commercials. When I graduated from NYU, my grandmother, who was one of my parents, got cancer, and so I left New York City to go to Delaware to take care of her in the last two years of her life. While I was there, I was bored, and I was drinking a lot. On a night that I was bored and drinking, I saw that in Downtown Wilmington, Delaware, there was a brand-new theater that was sitting empty. So, I scheduled a meeting with the executive director of the building. It was a nonprofit, and said, "What the hell are you doing in that theater?" He's like, "We just built it. We don't know yet." I said, "Well, I'd like to put a theater company in there." I was, you know, 24 years old, so I thought I could do anything.

For the time that I was taking care of my grandmother, she passed away during this time, but for about a year, they gave me an office in that building for free. I spent that year raising a couple hundred thousand dollars to do a first season. We did one play in that first season. I didn't direct it. I just produced it, and it was a play starring the actress, Lynn Redgrave. She won Oscars and Tonys, and she was a huge theater star who came and did my play when I was 24. That really was my graduate school. I learned so much from Lynn. There wasn't a day that went by that she didn't call me a fucking genius and a fucking idiot, often and in the sentence. Lynn Redgrave was my education. Watching her work was every bit of graduate school that I could ever have hoped for.

What Lynn taught me and what has stayed with me as an artist is that, first of all, actors are not interpretive artists, they're creative artists, and you're always putting yourself into your art. It's never about doing what other people have asked you to do, or doing what other people have required you to do, or are saying they require you to do. It's answering whatever little voice inside of you that is congruent with the work. That was a fucking powerful lesson to learn at 24, do you know? It's how Lynn embodied her entire artistic life. Every role that Lynn has ever played is a little bit of Lynn. It's her finding her way into it. That's what started guiding me as a storyteller.

Q: How would you describe the role of the Director?

A: In television, the writer is King. So, that begs the question, "Why the hell is the Director there?" I believe that the Director is there to help tell the story that the writer has created in its purest, most emotional way possible, right? It becomes a living, breathing thing.

Television is such a machine, and I think that there's beauty in the machine, frankly. But because television is such a machine, it's very important, especially as a Director, to find the humanity in it, because that's ultimately what the writers are looking for, right? The writers are searching for the thing that's human, the story that's human, and that connects. It's the Director's job to honor that and to make it human. This is the conversation that I have with so many people and executives in television, where I feel like we're all trying to — in comedies — we're trying to find the pathos and in dramas, we're trying to find the levity. That's how we get to human. A Director absolutely is the person that should be the instrument in that process.

Q: What's the best direction you've given an actor?

A: I was directing Keith David and Jasmine Guy in this play. Jasmine was having a particularly hard time memorizing one particular paragraph in a speech she had to give. Every time we got to it in rehearsal, she'd fumble and it would be really rough and she had to really fight for it. Then finally, she was getting so frustrated, she came to me and she said, "Keith, there's this line in this monologue that trips me up, this sentence, that trips me up. Can I just cut it? If I cut it, I'll know this monologue like that. It's that one line that trips me up."

I said, "No." What I said to her was, "Jasmine, I want you to go away tonight and figure out why the playwright put that line, that one sentence into the play, and come back to me and explain why that one sentence is there. If you can't figure out why, then we"ll cut it. But I have a feeling that that sentence is in there for a reason." She said, "Okay, fine." She went away, and she came back and she said, "Oh, my God, I know this whole thing now." It's like, "Well, what happened?" She said, "Well, first of all, I learned the line wrong. So I learned this particular sentence where it's like a 'you' instead of a 'me,'" or whatever it was like a little word, a little article. She goes, "And, it's interesting, because that one sentence now tells me about the entire character that I had been overlooking."

I did nothing, but just say, "You can cut it. You can cut it if you can tell me why." But it was a lesson to me as an Actor, and a lesson to me as a Director, and it was a lesson to me as a Writer, that everything is there for a reason, and you can't just, like, willy-nilly go past it. You have to explore it and you have to figure out why it's there. It's one of those things where a good Director will stop and go, "Why is this line here?" Then a good Director should be able to offer an alternative, a way to . . . You can't just say, "Fix it." You have to be able to offer a path forward, but you've got to know why it's there.

Q: What should people binge for directing?

A: *Breaking Bad*, *The Sopranos* and *The Silence of the Lambs* are master classes in directing.

Q: What three traits do you think someone needs to make it in this industry?

A: Fortitude, an open mind, and passion.

MILLICENT SHELTON

Millicent Shelton is an Emmy Award-winning Director, best known for her episodic work on *30 Rock*, *The Flash*, *Hunters*, *Insecure* and *Run The World*, for which she directed the pilot. She also directed the feature films *Ride* and the upcoming *End Of The Road*. Born in St. Louis, Missouri, Millicent's first job was working as a PA on the sets of *Do the Right Thing* and *The Cosby Show*. From there, she moved up the ranks in the camera department before directing music videos, which led to her big break in narrative storytelling.

Below are excerpts from Episode 16 of the *Let's Shoot! With Pete Chatmon* podcast:
Millicent Shelton on Applying Education and Life Skills to the Craft of Directing

Q: How did you get your first gig?

A: I had graduated from Princeton, and my sister went to Yale with Spike Lee's brother, David. This is when Spike was just sort of starting out. My sister said, "You know, David's brother is doing a movie, why don't you give him a cover letter and resume to see if you can get on his movie?" So, I gave David the letter, and then I didn't hear anything.

I went back to St. Louis and the first week I was back, I was like, "You know, Im gonna call Spike and see if he got the letter." I called up and I said, "Hi, this is Millicent Shelton for Spike Lee." They put him on the phone, and I'll never forget it . . . I was upstairs in my house, he got on the phone, and I was like, "I'm a starving student and I, you know, need a job" and he said, "You know, I need to interview you. When are you supposed to be back in New York?" At the end of that interview (*a few weeks later*), he said to me, "Okay, I'll hire you as an intern." At that point, I had been offered a job in DC that was paying like $300 a week so I said, "How much are you paying?" He goes, "It's an internship. It's free." I was like, "Um, No. I have a job in DC that's gonna pay me $300 a week." Spike said, "If you take that job, it's going to be the biggest mistake of your life. How soon can you be back here?" I was like, "I don't know, like three weeks," and he said, "You have two days."

So, I went home and told my parents, "I'm gonna go back to New York to work on this guy Spike's movie." I literally left with two bags of all my stuff and I had no money. I slept on my other sister's floor who lived close to 40 Acres (*production offices*). I slept on her floor and got paid no money. I worked with Ruth Carter (*Costume Designer*). I did such a good job that they bumped me up to a PA, and so I got paid I think it was like 100 bucks a week.

I ended up getting paid because I worked so hard. I was like there's no way that I can take any other job. I thought I could work for *Do the Right Thing* during the day and then work and do something else, but because I worked so hard, and I was so good, when I did go to them and say I needed money, they were like, "You're valuable." That's a lesson to everybody. It's important to get your foot in the door, and then, it's important to show your ability, because the thing about this industry is if you work hard and you're smart, people see it.

Q: What are two or three things that you learned from directing music videos that you've applied to TV?

A: I learned to manage money, production, and crew. As a young woman, when I walked on set, everybody thought I was one of the dancers, so at one point, I cut off all my hair, and then they thought I was a little boy. To learn how to manage a primarily male crew, I had to find my strength. When I ended up finding my strength and my power, I realized that my appearance had nothing to do with my ability as a Director.

It helped me learn to manage artists. There are all sorts of personalities. I had to disarm people and take their guns. I remember Heavy D was like, "I've heard things about you," because I used to stand at the doorway and not let people in. My AD was Big Mike, he was huge, 6'6", and Mike would be like, "I ain't doing that shit." So I would stand there, and I'd be like, "You're not coming on my set unless you drop that gun." They'd be like, "Is she for real?" And, I'd be standing there, and everybody would be like, "Yeah, man, serious as a heart attack." You're not getting on my set with that gun. No one's getting on my set, you have to stay off my set or drop the gun. I don't care.

Q: How did you make the pivot to drama?

A: We made a concerted effort to push, to break me into drama. At first, it was one-hour dramatic comedies. So, I get the one-hour in my belt. Then, it was pushing for straight drama. It was a real effort, because it was hard. I can't tell you how many meetings I had. When people said, "You do comedy." I was like, "No, storytelling is storytelling. If I understand the arc of a character, I understand the heart of where the comedy is, I can understand where the heart of a dramatic beat is." I can tell that story. Then I got a couple of episodes and did really well. Then people started believing that I could do both. After that, I got my feet in drama, so I was securely doing drama and securely doing comedy. Then I was like, "Okay, now I wanna do action."

The first action show I got was *The Flash*, and to this day, I still don't know exactly why they gave it to me. I have a feeling it was David Nutter (*who directed the pilot*), but he will not take credit for it. I met with a lot of action Directors for advice and listened to what they said. I remember my *Flash* episode was really long. It came out to be 12 days on the first board (*schedule*) and I was like, "Oh, my God, how are we gonna do this?"

The visual effects people had their board, and stunts had their own pre-viz. Special effects had theirs, and so I brought everybody together in this little office and locked the door and said, "We're gonna beat out every sequence together. So, we're all on the same page." We had the storyboard artists there and we went through everything. It was this crazy meeting, but it was the best thing I ever did. We were all on the same wavelength and we put out a really great episode. I got other episodes of *The Flash* and from there, I moved on.

Q: How did you make the transition to pilots, which is like the coveted destination for a lot of Directors?

A: I got a pilot soon after the Emmy nomination (for *30 Rock*.) I'm actually looking at the poster right now, which is crazy. It was *Awkward* for MTV, that became a series. It went on for like five seasons. I didn't work on the show after the pilot and to be honest, I did not have a good relationship with the showrunner at all. When I got the script, I loved it, I knew I could shoot it. I knew I could make it in a manner that was going to get the show picked up, and she was very into, "I want to be by your side and know everything that you do." I was like, "Well, I sit on set." It was this crazy power struggle that did not have to be what it was, and I'm the type of Director, I like to be free. I'm an Aquarian. I love to be free.

I didn't get offered another pilot for a while, and finally, it pissed me off. I was like, "You know, I should be directing more pilots." So, I had to open my eyes. I think for a while I just put my head in the mud and stayed in episodic directing because, you know, I could fill up a slate with episodes and not have to really go out there. Then, just recently, I started deciding that, "No, I want to go back into the originality of what we had with music videos, but incorporate the storytelling." And, then I started actively saying, "I want to direct pilots" and the Starz pilot (*Run the World*) just kind of fell into my lap.

Q: How did you seek out leadership positions in the DGA?

A: When I directed *Ride*, I did it for Dimension Films, and I was a music video director. They came to me and begged me to do it non-union. I didn't know anything about the guild, and they said they were going to give me everything that a DGA director would get, and it was in my contract. Then the Weinsteins wrote me off, and they didn't pay me.

My lawyer negotiated and negotiated with them, and called me and said, "Yeah, they're not gonna pay you the money that was written in the contract." They said, "Yes, we acknowledge it's in the contract, but no, we're not going to pay her this. She can take us to court, but if she does, we'll bankrupt her." My lawyer advised me just take what you have and walk away.

I remember being so heartbroken and talking to Paris Barclay (*director and former president of the DGA*) and he said, "You know, you should have gone union" because he had done a show for Dimension and they tried the same thing, and the guild had attacked Dimension because the DGA has power. They stood up for him and he got paid. From that moment on, I have been in the Directors Guild and very loyal to it.

I felt because they went on to protect me in later projects, that I owed them. I still do. It's my guild and they protected me, and I feel like I have to be there to help lift them up and then protect the future of other filmmakers like me.

Q: What three traits do you think are a requirement for someone to make it in this industry?

A: Perseverance, thick skin, and confidence. I think you have to believe in yourself, and you have to trust your gut, because there are so many voices that come in at you, so many voices that want to make you doubt what's in your spirit and in your soul.

At a certain point, you have to say, "I'm gonna live and die by my own sword." I'm gonna trust my gut and if I die by the sword, then I can say it's because I did it myself, not because I listened to some idiot who is afraid or had some other opinion.

MICHAEL SPILLER

Michael Spiller is a Director, best known for his episodic work on *Modern Family*, *The Mindy Project*, *Scrubs*, *Black-ish* and *The Mighty Ducks*. Born and raised in Brooklyn, New York, he picked up a camera to begin documenting his childhood, ultimately leading to him becoming a Director of Photography for music videos, commercials, documentaries, and television shows. After establishing himself as the DP on *Sex and the City*, he transitioned into the Director's chair with a Season 2 episode of the show.

Below are excerpts from Episode 08 of the *Let's Shoot! With Pete Chatmon* podcast:
Michael Spiller on Checking Your Ego At The Door

Q: What led you to wanting to get involved with cameras and film?

A: When I was five, I moved to Brooklyn and grew up around the corner from Spike Lee. There were actually a lot of filmmakers who were coming out of the three-block radius where I grew up, and that move was very key to my becoming a filmmaker, I think. First of all, the neighborhood itself was larger than life. It was predominantly Italian and, you know, mob-based — a lot of mob in the neighborhood.

I like to say that my childhood was like the first twenty minutes of *Goodfellas*. And, it could have gone either way. But it was interesting, because I was both an observer and a participant. After many years of being an outsider, getting my ass kicked because my hair was long and my parents were hippies, and I wasn't 100% Italian, I discovered that I could actually pass. So, I sort of adopted the persona of a kid in the streets, and started running errands for the guys in the social club. My Brooklyn accent got really, really strong. I learned how to speak Sicilian in the local grocery store where I worked. I was part of this whole exciting community, but then I'd go home and I would step back, and I was like, "Okay, I'm a straight A student" and my parents didn't really know the degree of things I was doing. So, I had one foot in the world as a participant, and then also I could observe it and tell the stories to, you know, my friends and kids at school.

Q: Do you find that your experience as a DP is helpful in communicating what's happening on camera to Writers, Producers, and Actors?

A: My experience not only as a cinematographer, but the years leading up to that and working in different capacities on the crew — grip department, electric department, and the camera department — I've loaded, focused . . . I've operated, I've key gripped, I've gaffed . . . so I have a lot of experience and a lot of respect for the people who do those jobs on set.

When I first was making my transition from shooting to directing, I think I was more comfortable on the camera side of it. There are definitely times where I probably had my hands in that person's job description a little too much. And, there's certainly some people who I worked with who were just threatened by the fact that I was probably as good a cinematographer as they were, maybe better, I don't know.

But there are certain tricks as a DP that if you don't wanna talk to a Director, there's ways that you can sort of smooth talk, right. "Just go back to the monitors, you know, I'll call you when I'm ready for you." And, you know, people couldn't do that with me because I knew all those tricks. But it made it easier to communicate my ideas. I'd heard them so many times and I spoke that language, and I understood the tech side and the gear. I think my respect was palpable to the crew and you don't always get that on a TV show when guest Directors come in. Some Directors really don't bother to get to know the crew at all — which is a huge mistake.

Q: How would you describe the job of the Director?

A: It's a different job description (*episodic television directing*) than if you're shooting a commercial or shooting a feature. My job is to bring to life a script that I've been given that I didn't get to choose. There's a pre-existing world that I need to fit into and simultaneously expand. So, it has to be part of a continuum. It's part of a larger story and you wanna bring something to it. You want to elevate it. You wanna get your thumbprint on it. Finding yourself in the story is one of the best ways to do that. That's part of the beauty of this job. I'm always learning. I haven't mastered this yet. I'm always learning how to do this job better. Every ingredient is a contributing factor to how you're able to do your job. Every crew person, every cast member, every Writer, and the particulars and details of the story are going to impact how you do your job. You can never know all of that and that's what's exciting.

Q: Describe a "good fit" when hiring a new Director.

A: A Producing Director is someone who may direct the lion's share of the episodes, but is also responsible for hiring. Some of these descriptions will vary job-to-job. The ones I've done I've been responsible for finding new talent, bringing Directors to be considered for a show I think they'd be a good fit. A good fit has a lot of components to it. One of the most important, of course, is personality and your ability to step into an unfamiliar situation and get along with people, get the job done, bring something to it, and elevate it.

When an agent is submitting someone that you don't know, you look at their resume, you call a couple of people they've worked with, get the feedback, and watch their episode. Sometimes it's hard to tell a "good fit" or not by looking at an episode of an existing TV show, because no one lets a Director fail. They may be a complete asshole . . . they may not have done their homework . . . they may be unprepared . . . they may be rude or dismissive to the cast or the crew . . . but still, because everyone is so invested in the success of that show, understandably, the episode will turn out okay.

We could take a few more creative risks in terms of the people who might not have that strong of a resume on paper, so I'm often meeting with people or sitting down with people who have only done a couple of shows, or they've done a totally no-budget indie feature, but they've got a voice. I'm looking for people who traditionally have had a harder time cracking this nut of getting into this profession, you know, women, people of color — it's just been much harder. It's not been a level playing field. So, I certainly search out for people that weren't already on the studio or network's list of typical choices.

Q: What three character traits do you think have been most important for you in navigating this journey as a Director?

A: I think my ability to get along with other people. I can adapt myself to situations and not "lose my cool."

I love solving problems. I love building things. I love being like, "Here's this problem, how are we gonna solve this?" I love being surprised by what other people will bring to the table. Directors who come up with a shot on their very first episode on a show I've been doing for five years and I've never thought of that shot. It's like, damn, but also like yes, good, I love it.

Third quality — I've had like three qualities in every one of these answers — but I'm generally an optimist. I have a sense that things are gonna be okay. I trust that things are gonna be okay and it's only a movie.

NZINGHA STEWART

Nzingha Stewart is a Director, best known for her episodic work on *Little Fires Everywhere*, *Black Monday*, and the upcoming *From Scratch*, for which she served as Producing Director. She alsodirected the feature film Tall Girl. Originally from Brooklyn, Stewart was raised in Atlanta, Georgia but returned to New York to attend NYU. She began her career directing music videos for local artists, which led to her collaborations with industry icons including Erykah Badu, 50 Cent, Jay-Z and Missy Elliott. After writing screenplays, directing features, and completing the Disney/ABC Directing Program, Stewart transitioned to episodic television where she has recently branched into directing pilots and executive producing.

Below are excerpts from Episode 23 of the *Let's Shoot! With Pete Chatmon* podcast: ***Nzingha Stewart on Having a Strong Vision***

Q: Where did you grow up and what led you to the world of music videos?

A: I was born in Brooklyn and lived there until about nine. Then, high school was Atlanta, and I moved back to New York for NYU and got into music videos. I wasn't in Tisch, I was in school for philosophy and Black Studies, but you still got the student discount on film and had access to equipment. I started doing music videos for people who earned money through questionable means and I put together my first reel through those pharmaceutically-funded music videos. I was also writing treatments for other Directors and a couple of the Directors that I wrote treatments for forwarded my reel to a rep, and that's what started to really get me work.

I loved music videos. You could be experimental. You could create beauty for beauty's sake. I love musicians. I love being around them, working with them, talking to them. But, the industry began to change. When I got into it, there were like 30 labels and by the time I was done, there were like three labels. The budgets were slashed. I don't even know how kids who do music videos now even live — they must have a bunch of roommates. It all started changing at a time when I was starting to mature and wanting to take what I learned about style and creating beautiful images into a narrative format.

Q: How did you transition into television directing?

A: It was really difficult. I got into a fellowship program based on music videos but then it became an obstacle trying to shadow (*other Directors.*) I decided to start writing things. I wrote one thing . . . then I wrote another thing (*With This Ring*) that got turned into a Lifetime movie, which got people's attention. I finally got to shadow and then people that I shadowed really liked the Lifetime movie. They wanted another one in a similar vein, so I directed another movie (*Love By The 10th Date*) and then, after having done those two films, I started to get work. It was like, "she can do two feature-length films" and then it just hit that one point where it was off to the races.

Q: What's the main difference between being a Guest Director and a Producing Director?

A: The big difference in the beginning is, as a Guest Director, you come into somebody's home and are going to cook for them. You want to make the best meal, you want to ask, what are your favorite foods? What do you want to avoid? That's kind of your job and you do the best with the ingredients they have in their house. You can't bring in another cinematographer — you're cooking with what they have in the house.

When you're a Producing Director (*from the beginning of a series*), you are the architect of the house. You're stocking the fridge, but you're also building the house. Every department head is somebody you have hired or approved. You're watching reels and you're going through resumes, you're interviewing people. You're making sure you have the right team around you to hold that house up.

Q: If you had the keys to the castle and could change anything about the business or being a Director – what would that be?

A: So much of our prep is so other departments can have their questions answered and I feel like the work would be better, and the work would be more fulfilling, if there were just a couple of days carved into the schedule where you can do proper script analysis. Where you can properly live with the script, let it sink into your subconscious, and then start shot listing and answering questions.

Q: What three traits do you think someone needs to make it in this industry?

A: A thick skin. I say that because you just can't take things personally. If you don't get a gig, who knows why? It doesn't matter — it wasn't for you. If an actor had a fight with their wife this morning, and comes in and screams at you, it's not even my business, you know. I think in the beginning, I was like, "I hope people like me. I hope the show runner likes me." Then, I started to adopt an attitude of, that's none of my business, that's manipulating to try to get them to like me. They get to feel however they want about me. Then, people love you because there's no pressure, it's just easy. I'm just here to do the best I can for your show. So, I would say that ability to not take things personally.

Vision. What's not on the page that I can bring to this episode?

Maximizing your physical health. I don't know how to put that into one word. I think it's so important to take care of your physical health in a job like this, where you can run yourself down.

ANU VALIA

Anu Valia is a Director, best known for her work on *She Hulk*, *Generation*, and *Shrill*. Born in Indiana, Anu fell in love with art at an early age, with a focus on diversifying representation in media. Her short film, *Lucia, Before And After* won the 2017 Sundance Film Festival Short Film Jury Award, introducing her to the industry. Additional television directing credits include *Mixed-ish*, *First Wives Club*, *Love, Victor*, *AP Bio*, and *Never Have I Ever*.

Below are excerpts from Episode 19 of the *Let's Shoot! With Pete Chatmon* podcast:
Anu Valia on Discovering Comedy To Break Into The Industry

Q: How did your upbringing help you to become a Director?

A: Both of my parents are from India. When we were kids, my dad would show us movies that touched him in his early 30s and he was like, "You children, at 10, maybe you'll connect to *Seventh Seal* in the same way I connected to *Seventh Seal*." I grew up with a thought that there was no difference between an art film and a commercial film. It was just "art is cinema" and art can touch you. We would watch Indian films, we would watch European films, we'd watch films from China and Japan. I spent a lot of time being confused. I thought that was a natural space to be and that plot wasn't really important.

Q: Describe the early years of your journey into directing.

A: I was taking photos and shooting movies on VHS cameras, and they were bad. I was so frustrated that my craft wasn't as good as I wanted it to be. I was directing plays in middle school, but then when I was 15, I wanted to be an actor. My mom said I couldn't be an actor, which is a whole thing we'll unpack at some point, so then I went to my dad and told him I really wanted to go to New York Film Academy. They had a one-week summer program, and I couldn't believe it. You could go to Los Angeles and you could shoot on 16-millimeter film. I went and I was like, "This is it . . . there's no going back," you know?

I had a movie I'd written (*after graduating NYU*) that I wanted to make, but I wasn't writing films that took place in one house, so I couldn't get my films made. I started my first production job working at CollegeHumor because in New York it was easier to get web jobs and I didn't know how to get into television or films. I stayed there for a couple of years, and then became a coordinator and then a producer, and then I was an actor for them. I think they needed a brown person so I got to be on camera, but through that I started working with comedians — which was not something I really had prioritized or thought about.

Q: Were there any other significant steps before you made your short film, *Lucia, Before and After*?

A: I left CollegeHumor and I basically was like, "Okay. I wanna be directing now. I want people to think of me as a Director." For a while, I was producing for money and just directing friends' stuff for free, producing sketches for free, and trying to make my own short films. I wrote *Lucia, Before and After*, which is a short film that follows a woman traveling 300 miles to get an abortion, and finds out when she gets there that she has to wait 24 hours because there's a 24 hour consent period before you can get the procedure done. She didn't know that so she spends a day just kind of wandering around.

I remember finding out it had gone to Sundance right after Trump got elected. It was such a dark time, which made me think about our intentions, like why do we make our art? Is it for others? Is it for us? It's a question that I think we are always thinking about. Anyway, it went to Sundance, and one of the judges was Patton Oswald who is a comedian and actor. I did not know he was also a film nerd. I remember seeing him watching the movies and I was like, "Oh, that's interesting. My movie's not funny. It's probably not gonna win. . . ." And it won the jury prize for U.S. narrative shorts.

Cut to February 2020, I was directing *A.P. Bio*, which Patton Oswald is on, I was like, "You probably don't remember, but you and the other judges really changed the trajectory of my life and I am so grateful I get to now work with you." He was very sweet about it, and he said he remembered, but who knows.

Q: What was the transition like into television?

A: After Sundance, my managers were like, "You know, you should meet with a couple of people." I ended up signing with UTA (*United Talent Agency*), but it was hard to get a job because people were like, "You made a short. Why does that mean you can do anything else?"

When you're a first timer or really new to TV directing, I think they're hiring you because you can add something. You're not adding experience. What you have to add is a new way of thinking. Also, be honest about what you don't know and learn quickly. As soon as you make a mistake, learn so you can pivot. You don't wanna get intimidated or too in your head, because it's not about you — it really is about making a good episode of television.

You really have to be like water. You have to listen and learn because each show is very different. It shouldn't feel like "This person's trying to like do their own thing," it should feel like you are expanding the show itself, which is not about ego. It's about, "Oh, this would make the audience more into the scene or the blocking's quite interesting." It's juggling a lot of things at once. They choose Directors because they want these Directors to put their own interesting spin on things.

Q: What would you tell your younger self right now?

A: I think I would tell her to watch all the movies you can, go to plays, be in your community art space. At NYU, I didn't participate as much as I should have. I wish I had taken more craft classes. I didn't take the camera classes or the lighting classes.

I would tell the younger version of myself, "Fill the coffers up with books." You cant be an artist unless you've got things to say. I think there are things I didn't take advantage of enough, because I was too focused on "I gotta make my things" and I wasn't being a part of my community, listening to other people's stories. That to me makes you a much more valuable person and makes you a better and more valuable artist.

ABOUT THE AUTHOR

With a deft ability to balance both half-hour single camera comedies and one-hour dramas, Pete Chatmon has directed episodes of HBOMax's *The Flight Attendant, Insecure, Silicon Valley,* and *Love Life,* Netflix's *You* and *Atypical,* ABC's *Grey's Anatomy, Black-ish, A Million Little Things, Station 19, Mixed-ish* and *Single Parents,* CBS's *AllRise* and *The Unicorn,* Starz' *Blindspotting,* FX's *It's Always Sunny in Philadelphia,* FreeForm's *Grown-ish,* TBS's *TheLast OG,* OWN's *Greenleaf,* and the Apple TV+ series *Mythic Quest.* He is also in development on *The Education ofMatt Barnes* with Showtime, for which he will direct the pilot and serve as executive producer.

His debut feature as writer/director, *Premium,* starred Dorian Missick, Zoe Saldana, and Hill Harper, and premieredon Showtime after a limited theatrical run. Chatmon also wrote, produced, and directed *761st,* a documentary on the first Black tank battalion in WWII, narrated by Andre Braugher. He received the Tribeca Film Institute "AllAccess" Program's Creative Promise Narrative Award for the heist screenplay, *$FREE.99.* Through The Director, his Digital Studio, he has directed, shot, and edited content for advertising agencies and Fortune 500 brands.Chatmon's career began in 2001 with the Sundance selection of his NYU thesis film, *3D,* starring Kerry Washington. His most recent short film, *BlackCard,* premiered on HBO, and his narrative podcast, *Wednesday Morning,* engaged voters around the 2020 election. He is developing several episodic concepts and feature films while booking episodes for the upcoming cable, broadcast, and streaming seasons. His podcast, *Let's Shoot! with Pete Chatmon* is available on YouTube, iTunes, and all podcast platforms. Follow him on Instagram @petechatmon and @letsshootwithpetechatmon

MICHAEL WIESE PRODUCTIONS

IN A DARK TIME, a light bringer came along, leading the curious and the frustrated to clarity and empowerment. It took the well-guarded secrets out of the hands of the few and made them available to all. It spread a spirit of openness and creative freedom, and built a storehouse of knowledge dedicated to the betterment of the arts.

The essence of Michael Wiese Productions (MWP) is empowering people who have the burning desire to express themselves creatively. We help them realize their dreams by putting the tools in their hands. We demystify the sometimes secretive worlds of screenwriting, directing, acting, producing, film financing, and other media crafts.

By doing so, we hope to bring forth a realization of 'conscious media,' which we define as being positively charged, emphasizing hope, and affirming positive values like trust, cooperation, self-empowerment, freedom, and love. Grounded in the deep roots of myth, it aims to be healing both for those who make the art and those who encounter it. It hopes to be transformative for people, opening doors to new possibilities and pulling back veils to reveal hidden worlds.

MWP has built a storehouse of knowledge unequaled in the world, for no other publisher has so many titles on the media arts. Please visit www.mwp.com, where you will find many free resources and a 25% discount on our books. Sign up and become part of the wider creative community!

MICHAEL WIESE, Co-Publisher
GERALDINE OVERTON, Co-Publisher

CPSIA information can be obtained
at www.ICGtesting.com
Printed in the USA
JSHW020928021221
20870JS00004B/4